Highly
Favored
of the Lord

Volume 1

Michael Stroud

PRAISE FROM AROUND THE COUNTRY FOR

"HIGHLY FAVORED OF THE LORD"

"Brother Stroud's insights into the Gospel of Jesus Christ have impacted us far more deeply than either my husband or I expected! Our understanding of doctrine has deepened to a level of understanding that has blessed us in a multitude of ways. His knowledge of the scriptures and his ability to create a cohesive line of thinking as he references them has opened our minds to the truths therein."

- Alicia Blickfeldt, author *They Told Me I Would Die*

"Understanding gospel truths just got easier! Listening to these podcasts is like looking through a child's kaleidoscope and seeing the dots connect and create beautiful designs with intricate patterns. Just as a new design appears with the turn of the kaleidoscope, I've experienced many awe-inspiring and mind-blowing learning opportunities. Truly life changing!"

- Ivy Keawe Kapolei, HI, LDS Institute & Sunday School Teacher

"For years I have immersed myself in the scriptures, poured over written works pertaining to gospel topics, revealed in the Spirit. It wasn't until I found Brother Stroud that I was introduced to the meat of the gospel and doctrines of Christ. He has taught me not only to hunger and thirst after righteousness but how to partake of the divine fruits of the gospel. He is truly a Master Teacher, sharing his love for the Lord and personal desires to assist the sons and daughters of God in their pursuit to become *the pure in heart*. He has helped me better understand my relationship with the Savior and the power through obedience to His commandments. Mike Stroud is an ensign of hope, faith, and light in a darkening world. I will be ever grateful for his willingness to nurture my testimony through his counsel and teaching. He has helped me recognize true discipleship, the power of agency, the gift of covenants, blessings of the Second Comforter. Thank you, Brother Stroud! This book is a must have in every gospel library."

- Lory Van Valkenburg

"Mike Stroud is a master teacher. His gospel-centered lessons have touched my most inner spirit. His lesson on "The Second Comforter" has helped me take a closer look at my life and encouraged me to reach up to higher heights. After listening to Mike, I am better able to study the scriptures and apply them to my life. I highly recommend Mike Stroud and his gospel-centered lessons."

- Bonnie Barney

"When I was introduced to Bro. Stroud's information, I listened with a hunger like never before. His work is so inspired, so genuine, so clear and plain to understand. I am grateful for each lesson. As I listened to each podcast and reviewed the information in the scriptures, it opened my eyes even more to what the scriptures were actually saying.

I have used his lessons to give talks in Sacrament meetings, teach Sunday school classes, and personal study. I have shared the information with everyone who will listen.

He is a gifted, inspired teacher of church doctrine-- opening the scriptures to those who are seeking to draw closer to our Father in Heaven."

- Charlotte Flemming

"I was recently introduced to Mike Stroud's podcasts and have listened to all of his thoughts and teachings. I love that he relies on the scriptures and words of the prophets to guide us to a new level of understanding. My mind has been opened to a greater level of spirituality. My spirit has awakened inside. I have been brought to ponder greater and deeper. My understanding has been enlarged. My desire to return to my Father and inherit all that He has has been ignited with full force.

I know great blessings are waiting if I but reach out for them . . . and now I know how. I misspoke, I have listened to all of Mike's thoughts and teachings multiple times, once isn't enough to take it all in, each time you will learn more and more and be compelled to study further. I must sit with scriptures and notebook to read and record all of the marvelous insights I have learned as the Spirit continues teaching me. Thank you is not enough."

- Alethea Galke

"Reading this book has brought me a greater desire to earnestly study and ponder the scriptures.

The book invites the reader to contemplate the greater portion of the word. It is the author's intent to bring us closer in deepening our personal relationship with our Lord and Savior, Jesus Christ."

 - *Rosemarie*

"Through Mike Stroud's work, I received a call-out from dim spiritual mediocrity. Now I feel great enthusiasm for studying and living the gospel. Thank you, Brother Stroud!"

 - *Anna Brown*

"I remember the one and only time I met Mike Stroud. He and my husband were both employed by the church as Seminary and Institute teachers. Our teaching areas had recently been combined and it was our annual meeting. Mike was retiring and I remembered as I watched the presentation about his career thinking, 'Wow, it really would have been a blessing to know and be taught by Mike.'

Fast forward several years and finding myself increasingly interested in being a better student of the gospel, and someone mentioned podcasts by Mike Stroud. Because I knew who he was, I listened to his class on the atonement and was deeply moved by his trials and how he overcame them. I felt I could trust his knowledge enough to listen to more. Doing so has blessed my life tremendously. I continue to be impressed by his study and the sharing of his insights, and the Spirit that attends what he shares."

 - *Dawn Norton*

"About a month or so before I learned about Mike Stroud's Podcasts, I was struggling spiritually because I felt like I had hit a roadblock in my spiritual growth and studies. I was praying to Heavenly Father to help me get beyond this roadblock and take the next step up in my spiritual progress. I was not sure what I needed to do. It was shortly after this that I was on the 'No Fear Preps' site and learned about these amazing podcasts by Mike Stroud.

I began to listen to them and could not get enough. I would listen to them once and then listen again taking notes and searching the scriptures. *As is says in*

Mosiah 5:1-3, I am having a mighty change of heart. I have no more disposition to do evil, but to do good continually. The messages in these podcasts have lifted me to a higher level of spiritual preparedness I have never felt before.

My view of myself as a daughter of a loving Heavenly Father has expanded beyond measure. My love for Jesus Christ and the Holy Ghost is tremendous. I look forward each Sunday to see what amazing spiritual topic Mike Stroud will share with us. These podcasts have truly been an answer to my prayers. Mike Stroud is an amazing son of God sent to help so many of us understand the Gospel with clarity and strength. Words cannot express my gratitude for him and his sweet wife for sharing their insights, knowledge, and testimonies. May they be blessed for their great service to us."

  - Brenda Stephenson

"Mike Stroud's grasp and teaching of gospel principles are both sublime and exhilarating. Prepare to deepen your understanding and experience many "Ah-ha" moments as you draw closer to God by learning more fully of His gospel plan for us in mortality and through the eternities."

  - Dr. Kyle Christensen, author *Herbal First Aid and Health Care: Medicine for a New Millennium.*

"Mike Stroud is my hero. His Insights have taken my understanding of the Gospel to a new level. He gives me great hope and I love his way of using scriptures to teach us. He is the eternal optimist. I cherish these lectures and what they have done for me. It amazes me how many trials he has faced and overcome. You will love this book."

  - Vickie Hacking

"Working on this project has become one of the most important projects I will ever work on. Mike has a talent for teaching, but more than that he has a relationship with the Savior that we all hunger for and he is willing to teach us."

  - Shelle McDermott

DEDICATION

To my beloved Margie, who continually inspires me
to be the best that I can be.

Highly
Favored
of the Lord

1 Nephi 1

CONTENTS

Links to listen to the audio podcasts correlating with the chapters in this book.

Introduction: Accessing the Atonement
https://www.podomatic.com/podcasts/mstroud/episodes/2016-09-19T12_32_15-07_00
001 The Holy Spirit
http://mstroud.podomatic.com/entry/2016-02-16T16_47_15-08_00
002 The Telestial World
http://mstroud.podomatic.com/entry/2016-02-16T17_57_00-08_00
003 Adversity
http://mstroud.podomatic.com/entry/2016-02-21T19_32_03-08_00
004 Mighty Prayer and Personal Revelation
http://mstroud.podomatic.com/entry/2016-02-28T19_48_49-08_00
005 Angels and Precious Promises
http://mstroud.podomatic.com/entry/2016-03-06T19_55_22-08_00
006 Accusations and Advocacy
http://mstroud.podomatic.com/entry/2016-03-15T07_45_41-07_00
007 Tokens and Signs
http://mstroud.podomatic.com/entry/2016-03-20T21_55_55-07_00
008 Baptism of Fire and the Holy Ghost
http://mstroud.podomatic.com/entry/2016-03-23T12_22_29-07_00
009 Claim the Blessing
http://mstroud.podomatic.com/entry/2016-03-27T20_51_01-07_00
010 Channels of Light & Truth
http://mstroud.podomatic.com/entry/2016-04-03T21_23_17-07_00
011 Being Made Perfect in Christ
http://mstroud.podomatic.com/entry/2016-04-10T23_29_40-07_00
012 The Second Comforter
http://mstroud.podomatic.com/entry/2016-04-17T21_49_22-07_00

ACKNOWLEDGMENTS

Thank you to Shelle McDermott for her help in encouraging, organizing, and bringing this all to fruition. Nothing would have happened without her.

Editors
Phillis Ann Postak
Elizabeth Postak

Transcribers
Pat Crisp
Melissa Stromberg
Robert Briscoe

https://www.podomatic.com/podcasts/mstroud

Introduction

Accessing the Power of the Atonement of Jesus Christ

(A talk given by Mike Stroud in 2005 to a group of assembled Church Education
System (CES) men and women during a regional inservice.)

I'm nervous. I don't get nervous, but I'm nervous. This is my last year in CES. I'll retire after this coming year, and I'm grateful for the opportunity to talk to you just a little bit today. But what I want to talk to you about makes me a little disconcerted. I'm not going to talk to you about theology. You all know the theology of the Atonement. And we've read two of the greatest talks you could ever read on that very thing. So, as Ashley gave me this assignment and we talked a little bit about what he wanted me to do, we decided that theology was not the way we wanted to go. Two years ago we had, in this group, a presentation on *The Horse Whisperer*. The theme was on submission and what a great example of seeing a horse broken by that trainer. It is something we can all remember, can't we Ron? Those of us who've got horses and work with them really appreciated watching that. And then we came back afterward and broke off into groups. We were given a packet by our leaders that had numerous quotes by Elder Maxwell and some of the brethren on that topic of submission. We were told to break off into those groups and look at those quotes and read them, and then come back, like we've done today, and talk about that theme. The thing that I was impressed with then, and I saw again today, is that we understand that we all need to submit. And those quotes just reminded us that, through submission, the door for accessing the power of the Atonement opens. The problem was (I'm going to only speak for me, and I see the same thing today, as an observation) that we're told how to do it; we're told that we need to do it, we understand the theology, but we don't know *how* to do it. And so, the question becomes, how do we do that? I remember and can still see our little group back there under the pinion and the juniper trees, saying, "Yes, I know I need to do this, but *how* do you do it?" And we went around in circles for that 45 minutes and basically came away understanding the need for it but not knowing *how* to do it.

And so, in our little group today, we talked about the need to have this **enabling power**. We defined it, and we talked about how great it was that we have a definition of grace and that it *was* a great revelation! Brother Sam said that when the *Bible* dictionary came out, that was a great revelation on grace. And now, we have this great talk by Elder Bednar on grace and yet, how do you access that power and that grace? On the blue worksheet is written, "How do we access the grace and power of the Atonement in our lives?" I'd like to throw in another word there, and this is the part I'd like to chat with you about today. It is: How do we *consistently* access the Savior's atoning power in our lives so that it becomes a consistent force for upward movement and change of our heart, instead of a sporadic thing that comes as a result of circumstances and situations? I'm speaking of my life because all my life my progress in the Church has been, at best, sporadic and inconsistent. I've been a great "silver bullet shooter" and a "flash in the pan." I think back on my career now, as I'm finishing up my time at CES, and I have some regrets. All through my experience as a CES professional, there has been a spirit of arrogance and an unwillingness to learn from my peers. And those old timers who have known me over the years, like Bob Wold back there, Ron Searle and Brent Bullock, maybe you've observed that there's always been Brother Stroud kind of sitting off in the corner by himself, not really wanting to be a part of what the CES men were doing. Unfortunately, that has been pretty much my history in CES up until last 30 months. I regret that because I've probably lost opportunities. There's an arrogance there, thinking that you've become knowledgeable in the scriptures, that somehow you don't need to have the interaction with the men and women who are in the CES family. And so, more often than not I'd be in meetings physically but not emotionally, intellectually, or spiritually. I'd contribute very little, took a lot, or what I wanted to take, and set the rest off to the side and contributed little to the overall health and well-being and viability of our CES family group.

Now, as I'm here with you today, I want you to know my heart is filled with love for the men and women that are in this area. I have not always been able to say that. It comes because of a change that comes because of the Atonement of Jesus Christ. Some people have said they see a change in me. It's only happenstance that the change takes place about the same time that I married my third wife. And so, I hear things like, "Oh boy, the best thing that's ever happened to Mike Stroud is Margaret Stroud." You've all said that! [audience laughing] The stake president has said it. Bishops have said it. I'll be the first to admit that she is the greatest thing that's happened to me, next to Jesus Christ, but the change in my life isn't really because of Margaret. The change is Jesus Christ. Isn't that interesting? Let me share with you some observations. The closer you get to the Savior, the more relaxed you are in using His name. I find it very easy to speak the name Jesus Christ freely and openly. I've never been able to do that before. As a teacher, I've been able to use the name of Christ and Jesus in my teaching and in my classes, but never before have I felt the freedom to use His name, that I do now. What's brought this about? This is the part I feel a little concerned about, but I decided I'm going to go ahead and go with it anyway because I think you all love me. And there is a danger in doing this with CES men, because if there are any of you out there who are like I was, then this could be a stone of offense for you. And I apologize in advance if what I say is a stumbling block. I don't mean it to be. I feel that the only way I can share my feelings with you on accessing the power of the Atonement of Jesus Christ is by sharing with you some very private experiences. And I'm going to do that today.

In 1985, my wife was killed in an automobile accident, and that accident caused my whole family to pretty much "be blown to smithereens." My daughter, Heidi, who called her mother to come pick her up from high school, blamed herself for her mother's death. "Oh, if only I had not called her that day, she would never have been there, and those two boys wouldn't have come across

15

that lane and killed her." She left me with nine kids. I remember that we pulled up at the intersection of Lindsay and Southern, and it was like a battle zone. There were three helicopters, two in the air and one on the ground. I had been called on a cell phone and told she'd been in an accident. She was in a great big three-quarter ton suburban, and I thought, "Oh my gosh! I hope she hasn't hurt somebody!" In fact, I bought that vehicle as a protection in case of an accident. So, my thought was, "I hope that she hasn't hurt somebody." I had no idea that it would be the opposite. The closer we got to it, I could see that it was a battle zone, and some of you who were around then, remember this. I got up there, and the police had it quartered off, and there were emergency vehicles all over the place. As I got closer to it, my anxiety level went up and as I pulled up through the police line, my mother, who was there, came through the crowd and she simply said, "Brace yourself." I went over and found her, and she had our little 18-month-old son in the car with her at that time, and so, I was immediately looking around to find out where that little boy was. I knew the first thing Janet would want to know was, "How is that little boy?" I found out that he had been picked up by the car behind her that got hit. The person left the scene of the accident with our 18-month-old son and took him to Desert Samaritan Hospital. He broke all the laws and all the rules. It's a good thing that he did because that kept him from some trauma injury. Anyway, I got up there, and the boys were screaming in the vehicle: three boys and they were cutting them out. My wife was in the middle of the road, and I had a chance to sit there and hold her in my arms while they were cutting these three boys out. She was unconscious but still alive. There were several acts of kindness that took place in there that had life-changing experiences. But basically, she passed away from that.

Now, I want to jump forward and just say that within six months... you'd think that would be a life-changing experience, wouldn't you? You would think that it would really alter your life, but within six months, I was pretty much the same person doing the same things that I had done before the accident. I remarried, and our family jumped up to twelve. I entered into a marriage that for a good portion of those 17 years was, at best, rocky. There were all kinds of issues involved—blended families and kids who…well, lots of death. I took my sister's children in because both of their parents died. So, everybody in my family had lost both their parents and some of my kids had lost their two parents and one step-parent. And so, we had all these issues, and that spilled over into our marriage. During all of that, I was trying to teach seminary, and I had a marriage that, at times, was not real good. It wasn't my wife. It was just that the situation was difficult in this blended situation. More than once I called my area director and said, "We need to talk." And he'd come, and I'd say, "You need to prepare to replace me in the classroom because I'm not going to be able to come back this year. I can't teach and have the relationship with my family that I have." You [the audience] came in on a little bit of that. A couple of times I contacted trucking firms because I used to be an over-the-road trucker before I was a seminary teacher. I was thinking about getting hired and going back on the road because I didn't think I'd be able to come back in the seminary classroom because of the problems involved in my family. About that time one of our sons died of a prescription drug overdose. At the same time, this one daughter who blamed herself for her mother's death had gone off for 15 years and become a drug addict. And just about anything you can imagine; she had done. We tried one more time to bring her into our home, and that resulted in an argument where I restrained her. She called 911, and Apache County sheriffs came and handcuffed me and took me off to jail. Now, I'm probably the only seminary teacher in the world you'll ever meet that went to jail and is still teaching. I remember that experience, do you?

[Audience comment: "So do I." Laughter]

Brother Olsen, you were just brand-new. Wasn't that your first real challenge? I called him on the phone and said, "I've just come out of jail." And there was this big pause on the other end of the line.

I went the next morning before Judge Sherry Minere. You know Judge Minere, a good member of the church. And she said, "What are you in here for?"

And I said, "I'm in here for… domestic violence is what I was arrested for."

She said, "Brother Stroud," because I knew her, so she said, "tell me the whole story." And so, I told her the whole story. Then she said, "You're in here because you were trying to help your daughter? And you're in jail because of that?"

And I said, "That's kind of the way it is." And so, they arranged to get me out. I remember that night in jail and I remember going into that little cubicle that night and having them shut that door with a little square window that big, in this iron room with iron cots. And I remember thinking, "Here I am, a seminary teacher for the Church of Jesus Christ of Latter-day Saints, and I'm in jail." I remember spending a good portion of that night either sitting on that cot, or on my knees talking to Heavenly Father and saying, "What is going on here? What is happening here?"

Just prior to that, I had an interesting little talk come into my hands, by Hugh Nibley called, *"Work We Must, But the Lunch is Free."* And that's just a talk that means nothing to anybody, but when I read that talk, some little thing in it started me thinking about serving my fellow man. One of the things I'd like to point out to you, brothers and sisters, is this: my experience is that huge life-changing experiences, take place within small, small instances. An accumulation of small things being given to us by the Lord eventually can lead to a mighty change of heart. That's Alma 37:6-7, isn't it? I want to testify to you that that is true. This little talk had an influence on me. And then I looked at the second counselor in the Stake Presidency, who has a reputation for being a service-oriented person, and I looked at him, and I thought, "Boy, I want to be like him!" And so, I started looking for ways to serve my fellow man. And then, after I found ways to serve, I found myself asking, "Why are you doing the good things you're doing?" And I didn't like the answers that came from that. It was one thing to get to the point where you serve, and it's another thing to get to a point where you ask why you're serving. All too often the reason I was serving was so that I could be seen by other people and receive the praise and accolades of people around me. Nonetheless, it's all a part of a process.

Then, in May, two years ago, my wife got sick, and we had a heck of a time. I was thinking of Bryson Jones. He was having a hard time figuring out what was wrong with his sweetheart. For two years they just couldn't find out what was wrong. Nobody seemed to know. Well, that's the way it was with Jenny. We worked on that for months and tried everything. We tried all the

MRIs and everything. We were just giving up. Finally, I was going to leave work for two weeks and go down to Scripps Clinic and had made the commitment that we were not coming back until we could find out what's going on. Remember that? And I had permission to do whatever we needed to do. We went up to Flagstaff, and they did a little exploratory surgery and found out that she had pancreatic cancer and it was into its later stages. If you know anything about pancreatic cancer, you know that it's a vicious "son-of-a-gun." The only good thing about it is that it kills you pretty quick, but it's a hard way to go. Through all of that, we also had one son that overdosed on drugs. They found him three days after he was dead and we had to have a closed-casket funeral. I think that added to the stress of my wife getting cancer and she never recovered from that death.

And then we went through that period of time where I had the chance to bring her into the house and minister to her. My second wife was a very, very private person. It was interesting for me to see how the things that were most important to her were peeled off and shed through the circumstances that were involved. It got to the point where I had to do all of the care in the last stages of that cancer. I gave her all the injections, the suppository pain killers, the anti-nausea medications, and anything else that I was able to administer for my wife, as she just slowly starved to death. You make a decision to starve your spouse; sometimes that's what you have to do. You have to make a decision to stop all food and stop all water and then just make them as comfortable as they can until they pass away. I watched some interesting things happen, and I'll share with you one experience. All of this is adding up to what's going on with me.

Right in the last stages, she asked me the question, "What have I done wrong, Mike? Why won't Heavenly Father let me die? What have I done wrong that he won't let me die?" I had laid my hands on her head and given her a release blessing because I was just sure at certain times that this was going to be something that was going to happen pretty quickly, but she lingered on. Her daughter and her son came and stayed at our house. We had a hospital bed set up right up in the front room so that we could have easy access and we rolled around in shifts trying to take care of her. One day she sat straight up in bed and said, "I need to be washed."

I went over to the bed, sat down right next to her, called her daughter over, and I said, "What did you say?"

And she said, "I need to be washed clean."

I said to Stacy, "I think your mom wants to go in and have a bath."

She shook her head and said, "No." She said, "I need to be washed clean." We pulled our chairs up close, and she was sitting on the edge, just a little skeleton with a big bloated tummy.

Stacy said, "Do you want to shower mom?" And all of a sudden you could watch and you could see her disappear. Her eyes were wide open, but she was gone. She left. She'd just gone.

I went right up into her face, and I said, "Jenny, can you hear me?" And there was just no response. She was looking right at me, but there was nobody there, and I turned to her daughter, and I said, "She's not here."

Her son walked in and said, "What's going on?"

And I said, "Your mom has left us for a minute. I have no idea where she is, but she's not here." After a few minutes, about 5 to 6 minutes, you could see her come back. It was like a vacant stare, and then all of a sudden life came back. And I said, "Can you hear me?"

She said, "Yes."

I said, "Did you go somewhere?"

She said, "Yes," and there was a whole calmness that came about her.

I said, "Where did you go?"

She looked at me, and she focused, and she said this, now here's a message for us all, **"All that counts in life is family."** That's what she said.

And I asked, "Have you seen the Savior?"

She said, "Yes."

"Did He talk to you?"

She said, "Yes."

I said, "What did He say?" And she wouldn't answer. "Can you tell me what He said to you?" She didn't say anything, so I said, "Did He embrace you?"

And she said, "Yes."

"Did you see the prints of the nails in His hands?"

And she said, "Yes, I did."

And within 36 hours she passed away. Now, what happened was, I saw a woman totally change. If she had survived that cancer, whatever happened would have changed her to the degree that she would've not been the same person in any way after that experience. And it was just a short five minutes. Now, brothers and sisters, that can and should happen to every one of us while we're in mortality.

We can't teach above our own level of conversion. We can't do it. Wherever you are in your own spiritual level of conversion: that's the level you can teach at, and no higher with any power. Brother Terry Calton said something one time in one of our meetings, and he doesn't even know what an effect it had. It's one of those little things that had a big effect. Brother Calton said this:

> *The most important thing we can do for our students is to sanctify ourselves.*

Now, he said that at a time in my life when those words sunk deep into my heart, that little statement. I didn't know what this meant, but when he said it the Lord's Spirit carried that into my heart. I knew that if I was going to do any good for my students, for my wife, for my children, or for my 27 grandchildren, and most of all, for myself, it wasn't going to happen unless something called **sanctification** began in my life. When we talk about accessing the blood of Jesus Christ in our lives on a consistent basis, what we're talking about is coming up through a step-by-step level of progression; accessing the Atonement to one degree or another, at all of those different levels, until you arrive at **sanctification**.

My favorite scripture is in the *Book of Mormon*. Let's turn over to Moroni chapter 10. Now, let me show you what I've seen and then I'll share with you just a couple of concluding ideas on that. Verse 32; isn't it interesting that verses 32 and 33, the message of Moroni is an encapsulation of a thousand years of *Book of Mormon* history. If you were the chronicler of the *Book of Mormon* and your assignment was to seal that book up for those in the latter-days, after you and your father compiled and abridged a thousand years of Nephite history; what words would you write to end that record and seal it for future dispensations? What would be your message after everything from Nephi on down? What would be your words? Look how he finishes it. It's a direct challenge to us:

Yea, come unto Christ, and be perfected [not by Him, not through Him, but] ***in*** *him, and deny yourselves of all ungodliness; and if ye shall deny yourselves of all and ungodliness, and love God with all your might, mind and strength, then is his grace sufficient for you, that by his grace ye may be perfect in Christ; and if by the grace of God ye are perfect in Christ, ye can in nowise deny the power of God.*

So, what's the challenge? Come to Christ and what? Become what? **Be perfected**. Now, members of the Church look at that, and they think that that's something that takes place after death and way into eternity. That isn't what Moroni is talking about. He's talking about it happening while we breathe in this life. It's not the same perfection that Jesus Christ had. It's the perfection that each of us can become if we have His divine nature transferred into us. If we have any of His perfected divine nature, in its fullness, as a part of us, through the Atonement of Christ, to that degree, we become perfected **in** Him. Let's see next step that comes after perfection. Look at the sequence:

[33]And again, if ye by the grace of God are perfect in Christ, and deny not his power, ***then*** *are ye* ***sanctified in*** *Christ by the grace of God,*

See, perfection first, **then** sanctification. Perfected means to have those attributes of the perfected Father and the Son transferred into you by the Atonement of Jesus Christ, so that They become **in** you, and you **in** Them; not corporeally but through Their Divine nature. Sanctification means to become holy, to be pure, without spot.

So, I watched her die. And interestingly enough you would think that the accident in the middle of Lindsay and Southern would be something that would change a life, but that really didn't do much to me. It hardened my kids to where they all left the Church. Just one of them now, after 15 years of tattoos and drugs and everything you can imagine; sits in a bishop's office tonight, in Round Valley, and gets her endowment recommend interview. Tonight, after 15 years; coming back.

Well, I met Margie, and that was a story in and of itself. Talk about the grace and mercy of the Lord! The stake president of Snowflake got us together through unrelated circumstances. I took her on our first date on Saturday night. We were in the temple on Wednesday, and I asked her to marry me in three days. She said, "Yes," but by the time we got out to the car she said, "I don't want to see you anymore. You scared me off." So, she accepted the proposal, but within an hour and a half, it was all off. [Audience laughing] Now, I blame that on Snowflake to a great degree. [Audience laughing] But nonetheless, after a while we got together, and it's been a great experience. We had our honeymoon in Hawaii. As we got to the resort at Turtle Bay, we were just taking baggage down to the room, and somebody comes up with a fax. The fax says, "Call home, Scott." Well, can you imagine? I haven't even checked into our honeymoon room, and I've got a fax that says, "Call home." So, we turned around before we even got our luggage to the room, called home and my son says, "I've got some bad news for you. Is Margie with you?"

I said, "Yeah."

He said, "You better get her close. Are you sitting down?"

I said, "Do I need to?"

And he said, "I think you'd better dad."

I said, "What's up?"

He said, "We found Heidi dead this morning."

That was the daughter who blamed herself for her mother's death and had also been walking out on the wild side for about 20 years, since 1985. She had always said, "If only I hadn't made that phone call then we would have never had any of these experiences. It's my fault that dad's second marriage isn't working that well, that the family is blown away, that my brother didn't serve his mission, etc., etc." And so, she carried all of this and died that night. We sat in the room, and I cried, and my new wife held me in her arms. We made a decision as to whether to go back home or to stay on our honeymoon. We figured there was nothing we could do by going home, so we stayed for the week and completed our honeymoon. Then we went home and two days later had a funeral for another daughter.

My experiences are no more severe than what others have had, and many have suffered much, much more. I tell you these things to let you know that in the process of all of this, Heavenly Father brings us to a point where you realize that your way, *your way,* is futile and worthless. Now, I've always been a person who said, "I can do this! Just tell me what needs to be done, I can do it. If it's broke, give it here. I'll fix it." And all of these experiences, one after another, brought me to a point where after all of these years, 25 or 27 years in CES, I finally told myself, "Your way stinks and is at best, sporadic and ultimately futile and worthless!" Now, whatever it takes to get us to that point, then and only then, can the Lord begin to do what He wants to do so that we access the power of the Atonement and have a change of heart.

Go with me to Mosiah 4 for a minute. These are scriptures that have just jumped up off the page for me over the last couple of years. Let's go to verse 5 and then we'll go to verse 11. Just these two verses:

> *For behold, if the knowledge of the goodness of God*
> *at this time has awakened you to a sense of your*
> ***nothingness****, and your worthless and fallen state-*

I'm telling you, whatever it takes for the Lord to bring us to that point is worth all the pain, all the effort, and everything it takes to get us there. Over to verse 11:

> *And again I say unto you as I have said before, that*
> *as ye have come to the knowledge of the glory of*
> *God, or if ye have known of his goodness and have*
> *tasted of his love, and have received a remission of*
> *your sins, which causeth such exceedingly great joy*
> *in your souls, even so, I would that ye should*
> *remember, and always retain in remembrance, the*
> *greatness of God, and your own nothingness.*

Brothers and sisters, the full power of the Atonement of Jesus Christ cannot be accessed as long as we think that we can do **anything** of any spiritual or eternal significance on our own, while in mortality. We can do **nothing**! We have to get to a point where we have to realize that **anything** that takes place in our life that is spiritually significant, ennobling, edifying, and changes the heart, comes only in and through the merits and mercy and grace of Jesus Christ and in no other way. How do we get to that point? That's the key. Adversity and trials, which are a part of life, if we let them, will take us to a point where your heart can be broken. Where Janet's death didn't change me much, Jenny's death broke my heart. Isn't that interesting? My childhood sweetheart, first date, mother of six children, when she passed in a horrendous accident; it really

24

didn't have a great effect on me, not life-changing. But when my second wife died; and we had struggled in our marriage and tried to find happiness and balance in a blended family; when she died, it broke my heart. I remember the **terror,** and that is the right word; I remember the **terror** of thinking about being alone. It absolutely terrorized me after her funeral and then for several months after that. Absolutely the greatest fear of my life was being alone. That again is an experience that takes you to a point where it breaks your heart. All of us, because of our fallen natures, have, to one degree or another, a hardness of our hearts. As long as that stone, that flint, that hardness is there, it becomes an effective barrier to the life-changing, atoning sacrifice that wants to take place. So, the Lord is going to allow us to have experiences that will break our hearts because only once it is pulverized can He then come in and give you a new heart **in** Jesus Christ.

It's interesting that when you have these kinds of experiences, and you feel this mighty change, one of the things that go along with a mighty change of heart, interestingly enough, is the desire to fully and completely submit and consecrate yourself for the first time. I've understood the doctrine of submission. We did a masterful job of teaching it here two years ago. It was wonderful! I understood the doctrine, but I never was given, as a gift, the desire. I want to emphasize this as I sum things up today. I never was given the gift to have the **desire** to submit, until after my heart was broken and the Savior's Atonement began to work a mighty change. **With that mighty change of heart, comes a desire to submit and consecrate.** There's only one place in the scriptures that describes it, and it's back in Mosiah 15:7, where Abinadi is talking to those guys. He says that your will, like the Savior, becomes *"swallowed up in the will of the Father."* Notice that term *swallowed up.*

Two years ago, we gave out a handout with a statement from Brother Maxwell. It was one of those little jewels that when you're *ready*, and you read it, it just means something to you; but before that, it didn't mean much. That little statement was this:

> *The last step in your spiritual progression is consecration and submission of your will to the will of the Father and the Son.*

25

Think about that for a minute, *"The last step in your spiritual progression."* So, we come back to this: How do we access the desire? It all begins with a desire, and if you don't have the desire, nothing long lasting or consistent is going to happen. It's going to be gutted out with knuckled fists, clenched teeth, sheer willpower, and sporadic. So, how do we get to a point where we can have this power in our lives on an every day, every hour, consistent, and a forward-moving basis? And here's the answer: it must be given to us as a **gift** through the Atonement of Jesus Christ.

Here's what I'm learning that I had not known before: Everything that's good that happens to us, in the way of desire, progress, spirituality, knowledge, and whatever else, is a gift through the Atonement of Jesus Christ. It's all given to us, all of it. He wants to give much to us, but we set up barriers and stakes, and keep it from coming into our lives, for whatever reason. All of these things that He has that are foreordained for us and that are rightfully ours, He's ready **right now** to give to us, but we set up the bounds and stakes, and we stop it, for a myriad of reasons. I decided that there's only one thing that Mike Stroud merits and has truly earned in this life, and that is to go to hell. That, I earned. And, without Jesus Christ's atoning blood, that's exactly where I'll go. Anything else on an upward mobility is truly a gift from Him.

So, how do we do this? We access this by asking for it. Isn't that amazing? The most beautiful truths of the gospel are always, *always* the simplest and, once revealed, the most obvious. But until that time, they remain grand secrets and are not seen. We don't get the gifts that will allow us to consistently, versus sporadically, move forward and upward because we don't **ask** for them. The greatest gift manifested among members of the Church is the one gift that's asked for most frequently, and that's the gift of healing. Because we ask for it, we see it. How about we get on our knees and ask Heavenly Father, "Bless me with the gift of humility. Bless me with the gift of meekness. **Endow** me with the gift of charity." And then acknowledge it. Here's another secret: We need to get to point where we say this, "I can't do this by myself." We've got to get to a point where we say that. And then the second part of it is, "Heavenly Father, please help me." [Getting choked up] It's taken me a long time to learn that one. But when your heart is broken, and you're down, and there's no place else to go, then finally,

26

finally, you can look up and say, "I just can't do this by myself, help me!" [Crying] Then it comes. And you find yourself **endowed** with grace and power to do things that you can't do by yourself: to have Him make so much more of you than you could ever do on your own. [Sniffling] Excuse me.

Now, in closing, with this change that comes through the Atonement of Christ, comes the desire to consecrate. And our friends in the Christian world are closer to this, many times than we are. They use terms like, "Give yourself to Jesus Christ." And we back off from that because of the connotation, "doctrinal correctness" that doesn't fit in with our theology. You get to a point where you say, "Take me. I give myself to You, such as it is, not much, but I give myself to You."

I talked to my wife about that and said, "I want to do that."

She said, "Do it!"

I said, "I made a covenant 43 years ago to do that. Maybe all I need to do is activate that covenant!"

She said, "Yeah, that's probably all you need to do is just activate that covenant."

"But, I feel this is so special in my life that I need to do something formally to do that." I had some ideas. So, I went to the temple President of the Snowflake Temple, and I asked him about some ideas, and he gave me some counsel. Most of my ideas were inappropriate. But, that's why I went to him because I really didn't know.

And he simply said this, "Are you ready for that?"

I said, "Yes, I want to. I don't want it *my way* anymore. I don't want to give just part. I want to give **all** of me. I don't ever want to do it 'my way' ever again. I want to do it His way."

And he gave me some counsel. He said, "You've got some horses, don't you?"

I said, "Yeah."

He said, "You live over there in those mountains of Eagar, don't you?"

And I said, "Yes."

"Why don't you just go up there in those mountains somewhere, and spend some time with your Heavenly Father?"

So, I debated back-and-forth on that. I thought maybe that was appropriate. I mean, He had given me tremendous revelations in finding a wife. And I feel the Spirit of the Lord every day I'm in the class. It's not like I don't know He's there. I know He's there. There's not a day that goes by that I don't feel His Spirit. But more often than not, I feel the Spirit in behalf of others, and He blesses me as an instrument. I felt like I'd kind of like to know, "Are You happy with what I'm doing? Is the course I'm pursuing pleasing to You?" And I kind of wanted something just for me.

So, I saddled up one horse and packed up another one. And my wife said, "Where are you going?"

I said, "Up there."

"How long are you going to be gone?"

"I don't know. Maybe not too long, maybe a little while." And so, she gave me a kiss and off into the sunset I rode.

I got up there, and I had two things in mind. Number one: I wanted to formally enter into a covenant with my Savior to submit. SUBMIT. I had the desire. It was given to me by the Spirit of the Holy Ghost, or I could never do it. And the second thing was: I wanted Him to just tell me that I'm OK and that what I'm doing is all right. I wasn't looking for angels; I just needed something for **me**. So, I went up there, and I camped. I hobbled my horses and found a place, and I was all alone in a pretty remote area in Fox Canyon, way up in the White Mountains; nobody anywhere around; a bear and a mountain lion, that's about it! And I entered into a formal covenant with my Heavenly Father, that I was willing to submit my life to His will for the remainder of my life, and with His help, keep His commandments and serve His children; **with His help**, because I can't do this by myself. If I try to do it by myself, at best, it's going to be hit and miss and sporadic, and I don't want that anymore. But with *His* help and *His* strength, I can do this on a consistent basis, to where I'll be blessed by serving my fellow man. I came back after a few days; didn't have any personal revelation and was a little bit discouraged. But, I did do what I went there to do, and that was to enter into a covenant, very private, with my Father.

Now, here's the thought I want to end on. That following year, the Lord poured out His Spirit and knowledge and blessings on me. If I were to take all of my previous life and put all of those things together, it would not be equivalent to the amount that I received in the one year afterward and continue to receive from Him. He is gracious and kind and merciful. [Getting choked up] I feel to sing a song of redeeming grace when I think about Jesus Christ and His Atonement. I know that He lives. I have felt His power and feel it daily in my life. I felt it in our little group as we were talking. I feel it now. [Sniffling] How grateful I am that He is mindful of me, [Crying] who has been so arrogant and self-willed for so many years. And I thank Him for the gift of His Son and testify to you that the changing powers of the Atonement are available **now**, every hour and every day. But, we set up the stakes and the bounds and keep it from happening. It's really quite simple, and the formula is found in the *Book of Mormon*. We all need to ask ourselves a question, brothers and sisters. Have I been born again? Have I received that mighty change in my heart? Have I received the *baptism of fire and the Holy Ghost*? Do you have great views of eternal things? Those are all the blessings that come through the Atonement of Jesus Christ. Do you want to bless your students? My one regret is that only in the last few months have I been teaching, after 27 years, the way I think the Lord Jesus Christ wants me to teach; and that's Atonement-centered and how to access the power. God bless us to do that. Thank you for letting me share that with you. I hope that it hasn't been upsetting or a stumbling block in any way, to anybody. I do not profess to be better in any way than any person in this room. I admire you. I know that you are men and women of tremendous and varied experiences. And that your experiences to you, are every bit as powerful and have life-changing potential as anything I've ever had. I share that with you; only with the hope that maybe it will give you a little key from my experience, on how to help you further and more fully access the power of the Atonement of Jesus Christ in your life. I love Jesus Christ. [Crying] He died for me. I know he lives. God be thanked for the matchless gift of His Divine Son. In the name of Jesus Christ, amen.

Chapter One
Podcast 001 The Holy Spirit

I'd like to go into a review of something that I think is really important. I taught a couple of classes in church this last week, and I'm finding out that this is a doctrine that is not well understood. Today, in our church, the Melchizedek priesthood brethren were asked to administer the sacrament, and I had the opportunity to bless the bread. Another high priest, that's even older than I am, blessed the water. A bunch of elders and high priests passed it. I noticed that there is something in the prayer that we do not understand. For example, it says in *Doctrine and Covenants* 20:77 and 79:

> *That they are willing to take upon them the name of thy Son, and always remember him and keep his commandments which he has given them; that they may have his Spirit to be with them.*
> *[79]That they may always have his Spirit to be with them.*

"They" is meaning us. *"His Spirit"* is **not** the Holy Ghost. **It** is Christ's Spirit.

Let's have a quick review on the Holy Ghost, the Holy Spirit, and how angels and the spirits of *just men made perfect*, fit into this whole scheme of revelation for mortals in a telestial world. What is it we're trying to do? What is it we are seeking when we partake of the sacrament each week? The most frequent covenant that we enter into is a weekly covenant. All other covenants we do just once. The sacrament we do every week. The promised blessing is to have the Spirit of the Lord (and that is Christ, that is the Spirit of Christ) with us as a result of taking upon us His name, always remembering Him and keeping His commandments. So, let's talk just a few minutes and review these two things and how they fit in with each other.

Let's talk about this Spirit of Christ. **It** has many, many names. Here are a few of them: the Spirit of the Lord, the Spirit of Christ, the Light of Christ, the Holy Spirit, the Spirit of Truth, the Light of Truth and others. All these things are referring to this same thing. We're just going to call **It** *The Holy Spirit.* Now, this can get confusing because when we read the scriptures, it is difficult unless we have this doctrinal understanding. It's difficult to understand who it's talking about when it mentions the Holy Spirit. Are we talking about the Light of Christ, which is not a person, or are we talking about the Holy Ghost which is a man? To some, this may not seem like a very important distinction or something to dwell on. But, it is important because this is the mode, the medium, the channel, that Father in Heaven has given us while we are strangers and sojourners in this telestial world so we can receive information from Them to help us complete our journey successfully.

So, I think we should just talk about that: the Spirit of Christ, the Light of Christ, the Holy Spirit, in man, is also referred to as man's conscience. In the animal kingdom, **It** is referred to as instinct. In animals, the things that animals do are done instinctively. They don't need to be taught. They do remarkable things almost immediately after birth. This is all a part of the Light of Christ, the Holy Spirit, the Spirit of Truth, etc., etc. Now, let's go over to section **88** of the *Doctrine and Covenants*. It is probably the one section in the *Doctrine and Covenants* that has the greatest treatise on the Holy Spirit that there is. We want to start at the end of verse 6. Notice the last four words, talking about Christ, and He calls **It** *"the light of truth."* That's another name. You can see up at the bottom of verse 5 it says, *"through Jesus Christ,"* then when verse 6 says "he," it is referring to Jesus Christ:

> **He** *that ascended up on high, as also he descended below all things, in that he comprehend all things, that **he** might be in all and through all things, the light of truth.*

31

Now, that's the same thing that we're promised every Sunday when we receive the sacrament. That is what we're promised. Verse 7:

> *Which truth shineth. This is the light of Christ. As also he is in the sun and the light of the sun, and the power thereof by which it was made.*

So, when you're outside on a June day at noon, and you feel that heat and you see that brightness coming from that planet up in the sky, the greater light to rule the day, which **is a lesser manifestation of the Light of Jesus Christ.** That light, power, and heat come from Him and through Him. The moon, in verse 8; the stars, verse 9; and 88:11:

> *And the light which shineth, which giveth you light, is through him who enlighteneth your eyes, which is the same light that quickeneth your understandings;*

One of the differences between God's children and the lesser creations is that man has this capability to reason; animals do not. Animals function at a lower level. Your ability to reason, as a child of God, comes to you because of the Holy Spirit. That's the reason that you have a mind capable of expansion; you can comprehend things; you can reason; you can think things out. Of all the creations, man is the one that has the greatest ability to do so, and it's because of the Holy Spirit that is in him. You see, it says, *"It giveth you light...It quickeneth your understandings."*
Verse 12:

> *Which light proceedeth forth from the presence of God to fill the immensity of space—*

When we talk about **it** as a spirit, we want to attach arms and legs, a head, body, hands, fingers and toes. We get a little confused there because when we're talking about the Holy Ghost, who is a spirit, we do attach those physical things like a body. But, this doesn't have a body and can be more readily referred to as an **It**, rather than a He. Does that make sense? So, we start to get a feel for this. We can use the word the prophets have used: **It** is a channel. **It's** a channel through which information can flow from God to His children. **It's** a medium. **It** is the agent of God. Whenever God wants to accomplish anything, whether it's a creation, or whether it's giving revelation, or whatever it is, He uses the Holy Spirit as the medium, or channel, or the agent of His works.

Now, this next verse is the probably the greatest of all of them on the Holy Spirit, verse 13. I call it the three **L**'s of the Holy Spirit:

> The **light** which is in all things, which giveth **life** to
> all things, which is the **law** by which all things are
> governed, even the power of God...

"*The **light** which is in all things.*" Now stop and think about that for a minute. Without light, there can be no **life**. So, to have anything that is living, prospering, growing, and increasing, you must have the element of light. "*It is the **light** which is in all things.*" Your first **L** is light. "*[That] which giveth **life** to all things.*" Light and life! See, the two things are married together: light and life. We can't have one without the other. And then there's the third one, which is, "*The **law** by which all things are governed.*" Those three things: light, life, and law are the power of God. So, if you want to know what God's power is, according to this verse, you simply say that the power of God is His Holy Spirit and is made up of at least three things: light, life, and law. Notice that it says that **It**'s the law which **governs** all things.

So, let's take some physical things on this earth. Let's take the law of gravity. The law of gravity is a part of and is in place because of, the Holy Spirit. If there was no Holy Spirit, there could be no physical laws. Any laws in our world or in the universe that take chaos and bring them into order are laws that come into being through the Holy Spirit. Anything that holds anything in order, any law: electromagnetism, electricity, is a part of the Holy Spirit. Interesting that something that we use so much... I mean it is all pervasive. It is ubiquitous. It's everywhere, and yet, if you're to ask people what electricity is, you'd be hard-pressed to get a definition of what it is. We can tell what it does. We can tell how we can generate it. But, to give a definition of what it is, you would be hard-pressed to do it. Electricity is a manifestation of the Holy Spirit. Gravity, magnetism, any of the physical laws, and thermodynamics, all have to do with the Holy Spirit because verse 13 continues and says:

> Which is the law by which all things are governed,
> even the power of God who sitteth upon his throne,
> who is in the bosom of eternity, who is in the midst
> of all things.

Now, let's stop for just a second. Do you have any questions or comments about this thing called the Holy Spirit?

Student 1: I read M. Catherine Thomas' book, and I'll have to go find it exactly, but she said something like, "God couldn't perform work without the Holy Spirit."

Mike: That's exactly right.

Student 1: "That the Holy Spirit could not be used without God." I would have to find out exactly what it says, but they are hand-in-hand. And she did say that Jesus Christ, the Holy Ghost, and God, Elohim, are using this Holy Spirit to perform Their function.

Mike: Very good, I love Catherine Thomas' works. I've read several of them. They are really good. Thank you, [student]. Anybody else you want to comment on that?

Student 2: Is that why the human term *mind over matter*, which allows Man to not really control things, but when they allow their mind and spirit to connect, that they gain power more than in the external...? I can't really find the right words to say it.

Mike: That's alright, I think I understand. Anything of miracles, anything that controls element, and anything that man does that goes above and beyond the common understanding is probably going to be through this channel. Angels work through this. The Holy Ghost works through this. The spirits of *just men made perfect* work through this. So, everything that is godly, whether it is Father in Heaven, Mother in Heaven, Grandfather in Heaven, angels, spirits, anything that is in the employ of the gods uses this channel, this agent, to perform their ministry. So yes, I would not be a bit surprised. Now, if you and I, as mortals, can align ourselves in a godly way, through our obedience and righteousness, then we can also use this channel to do things, just like the gods. I believe that this is the channel through which prayers are answered. I believe this is the channel through which God can hear and answer all prayers. I believe this is the medium through which He is everywhere at once. I believe this is also the power that allows Him to be in the past, present, and future all at once. It is through **this** channel. Now, that science is so far beyond man. It's way beyond us, but if we were to take a scientific course in how the gods performed their ministry, I believe we would find that **this** spirit, the Holy Spirit, is the vehicle through which they accomplish everything they do.

Student 2: Wow! Just a minute. I'm a little confused. When you talk about the Holy Spirit, **It** is not the Holy Ghost?

Mike: No, we are going to talk about the Holy Ghost in a minute, so, two different things. The Holy Spirit is not a man. Let me read to you something here from Brother McConkie. This is in his book *A New Witness for the Articles of Faith,* on page 257 through 259. This is one of the best contemporary definitions of this I've heard:

> *There is a Spirit, the Spirit of the Lord, the Spirit of Christ, the Light of Truth, the Light of Christ, which defies description, and is beyond mortal comprehension. **It** is in us and in all things.*

See? There are four names which all mean the same thing. Now, remember back in section 88, that this is the thing that gives life to *all things.* So if we're alive, which we are, we have life because of this Spirit that is in us. Also, the involuntary things that our physical body does, like breathing, exhaling, inhaling, the movement of the diaphragm, and the beating of the heart; all of these involuntary human physical things are caused by the Holy Spirit.

Student 2: Wow!

Mike: **It**'s a programming that's in you that gives you life. Now, Brother McConkie goes on and says this:

> ***It** is in us, in all things, and is around us and around all things, **it** fills the earth and the heavens and the universe, **it** is everywhere in all immensity, without exception, **it** is an indwelling, immanent, ever present, never absent, spirit.*

Now, that's where we get into trouble when we hear the word spirit, because we are conditioned by Latter-day Saints to think of the word spirit as being a personal being: either a spirit son or daughter of God, or spirit of the Holy Ghost or the spirits of *just men*. See, all of those have personalities. All of those are individual, unique, people. **This** is not! So, to sum it up, you could say, there is nowhere that this Spirit isn't. Anywhere there is life, light, law, and order, that's where the Holy Spirit is, or you would not have those **L**'s. Whether or not the Holy Spirit finds **It**self in outer darkness or whether **It** quickens the sons of perdition, I don't know all of that. The very fact that they live in a place where there is no light, outer darkness, seems to indicate that **that** Spirit is probably not present like **It** is everywhere else.

Continuing with Brother McConkie, he says:

> *It is not an entity, nor a person, nor a personage. It has no agency, does not act independently, and exists not to act, but to be acted upon. As far as we know, it has no substance, it is not material, at least as we measure these things. It is variously described as light and life, law and truth, and power.*

Now, that's a major key. There are two things throughout the whole universe that Lehi talks about, in 2 Nephi 2, *"things that are to act, and things that are acted upon."* The Holy Spirit is only something to be acted upon. **It** does not act independently. **It** doesn't think. **It** has no agency. **It** doesn't make choices. **It** is a vehicle, medium, channel, the agent of God. Continuing on, *"As far as we know, it has no substance; it is not material, at least as we measure these things."* I beg to differ on that because Joseph Smith said:

> *There's no such thing as immaterial matter. Everything is made up of matter. Spirit is made up of matter, but it is more fine, and more refined, and more pure and can only be seen by purer eyes.*

So, I would take a little bit different twist on that than Brother McConkie. He says, *"It has no substance and is not material."* That is not what the Joseph the prophet said, *"Everything is made up of matter. Everything, there is no such thing as immaterial matter."* That's in section 130 of the *Doctrine and Covenants*. Let me finish this quote. Then he goes on and says, *"It is variously described as light and life, law and truth, and power."* Isn't it interesting that in section 88 verse 6, when talking about the Spirit of Truth, it says *"which truth shineth."* Truth shineth! See, we have to change our thinking on that, too. If the truth were to physically manifest **It**self, then **It** would shine. You would see **It** as light and heat. So, truth actually can manifest **It**self in light and heat. Going on he says this:

36

> *It is the Light of Christ; it is the life that is in all
> things; it is the law by which all things are
> governed; it is the truth shining forth in darkness; it
> is the power of God, who sitteth upon his throne. It
> may be that it is also priesthood and faith and
> omnipotence, for these are the power of God.*

Now, that was a very interesting little statement. McConkie comes
out and says that it could be that this thing we're talking about, the
Holy Spirit, could be the very same thing as priesthood, faith, and
the omnipotence of God. Isn't that fascinating? I personally have a
tendency to lean toward the truth of that; faith, priesthood and the
Holy Spirit, all being the same thing; maybe operating in different
ways but the same thing. Then he goes on he says:

> *For these too, are the power of God. It is the
> agency of God's power. It is the means and way
> whereby he comprehends all things so that all
> things are before him, all things are round about
> him, it is the way whereby he is above all things, in
> all things, through all things, and round about all
> things. Because of it, all things are by him and of
> him; even God, forever and ever.*

Any questions or comments about that wonderful quote by Brother
McConkie?

Student 3: I have a question. In that respect then, the Holy Spirit,
which you said **is** truth, then the Holy Spirit also testifies to truth.
Is that like the Holy Ghost or no?

Mike: I'm having a hard time understanding your question. I'm not
quite picking it up. Try that again.

Student: Does the Holy Spirit then, testify of truth?

Mike: Yes.

Student 3: Okay. So, we testify of the truth by both the Holy
Ghost and the Holy Spirit?

Mike: That's a great question. I'm going to say that the Holy Ghost
testifies of truth **through** the Holy Spirit.

Student 1: I believe that. And I want to mention about Catherine
Thomas. You said something about how **It** is acted upon, and
that's what she says. If God will not act upon **It** and use **It**, then it
would be useless. **It** needs to be acted upon.

Mike: That's exactly right.

Student 1: **It** HAS to be acted upon, or something like that.

Mike: Right. <u>Now, that's my opinion</u>. That's what we're going to go with right now. We're going to talk a few minutes about what the relationship is between the Holy Ghost, which is a person, a man, and the Holy Spirit which is **not** a person? So, we want to find out how these two things work.

Let's go over to Moroni 7 for just a minute and look at one other verse so we can find out what the Holy Spirit, the Light of Christ, or the Spirit of Christ is. Let's go to Moroni 7, verse 16. Now, one of the functions of the Holy Spirit, as [student] said, is you can receive truth through this channel. Truth is light. It's interesting that in section 93 of the *Doctrine and Covenants*, that the Lord says this, *"The glory of God is intelligence or in other words light and truth."* We've read that a hundred times, haven't we? *"The glory of God is intelligence or other words light and truth."* Let's pick out the four words: glory, intelligence, light and truth. Now, the way those four words are used in that verse shows that all four words are referring to the same thing. All four words are the same thing. So, if you wanted a definition of intelligence, the definition is the glory of God, light, and truth. If you wanted a definition of truth, then the definition would be intelligence, glory, and light.

Student 1: Can you tell us what scripture that is? We are looking at Moroni 7:16, and that's not it.

Mike: *Doctrine and Covenants*, Section 93:36. *"The glory of God is Intelligence, or, in other words, light and truth."* The point is that these four things, again, are referring to this Holy Spirit because you have the light and truth and God's glory. The glory of God is somehow tied in with Holy Spirit, and that is somehow tied into God's intelligence and man's intelligence. All of these things intertwine somehow, and we need to be asking ourselves the question of how that is. Moroni chapter 7 verse 16, someone like to read that?

Student 1: I can read it:

> *For behold, the Spirit of Christ is given to every man, that he may know good from evil; wherefore, I show unto you the way to judge; for every thing which inviteth to do good, and to persuade to*

believe in Christ, is sent forth by the power and gift of Christ; wherefore ye may know with a perfect knowledge it is of God.

Mike: What are we to learn about the Spirit of Christ? *"The Spirit of Christ is given to every man."* That's not the Holy Ghost. It's the Spirit of Christ. So, every person who comes into this telestial world, and every child that the Gods send away to school (because that's what these telestial worlds are, and there are millions of them out there) are in the school houses of the children of the Gods. They are sent away from their heavenly home, just like parents send their kids off to school on the first day of school. The school bus picks them up and hauls them away. This is what the telestial worlds are: they are one-room school houses just like the old pioneer days. You have in the same school room kindergarten, first grade, and you have juniors and seniors. They are all in the same room. That's what the telestial world is.

Student 1: Now, can I ask a question here?

Mike: Yes.

Student 1: If I read this (Moroni 7:16) in the context of the Holy Spirit, then it would say, *"For behold the* ~~Spirit of Christ~~ **Holy Spirit** *is given to every man, etc., etc., for every thing which invited to do good, and to persuade to believe in Christ, is sent forth by the* ~~power and gift of Christ~~ **Holy Spirit.***"*

Mike: That's correct. You could easily do that.

Student 1: But isn't the Holy Spirit sent forth by the power the Holy Spirit? That's what I'm getting out of this, which is kind of strange.

Mike: I don't know. Let me turn back to it there. I skipped ahead a little bit. So what's the question again?

Student 1: Okay, where it says *"the Spirit of Christ,"* if we put Holy Spirit there and further down it says, *"persuade to believe in Christ, is sent forth by the power of the gift of Christ."* So, that's the Holy Spirit too?

Mike: Well, Christ is a god who is using this channel to perform His work as the Mediator, Savior, and Redeemer of the world. God the Father, who is a god, uses this same channel to create worlds and to populate worlds. Any person that has a title of a god, whether a god with a small **g** or a God with a capital **G**, they are gods because they are able to use this channel to perform their ministry.

Student 4: Would this be like another priesthood then, or something of that nature, or what?

Mike: Yes, that's why Brother McConkie says he's having a hard time separating the Holy Spirit from the priesthood. That's why he's saying he thinks these could be the very same thing.

Student 4: That's what it sounds like to me, almost.

Mike: I don't know if that answered your question [student].

Here's the point: every person who comes into these telestial worlds, every child of God, comes with this gift of light. Now, something else to remember is that this light can be increased or decreased. What you want to do is to follow the enticing of this gift to increase Its power in your life. If you will use this gift, called the Light of Christ, It teaches you right from wrong. It's man's conscience. Man knows, inherently, what is right and wrong. If you follow this light, It will lead to a greater light. Now, that greater light is a man. And this man is the Holy Ghost. You can't access the Holy Ghost if you haven't had experience in recognizing and being obedient to the promptings of the Holy Spirit. Do you see what I'm saying now? So, the one sets the stage and is preparatory to the other. Everything in the Gospel of Jesus Christ moves from lower to higher, preparatory to fullness. Everything is moving upwards, and it is the same with the Holy Spirit. It begins quietly, and another name for this Spirit is the Still Small Voice. That's the Holy Spirit, not the Holy Ghost. And as you listen to this little voice, through your obedience and experience, It can become a revelatory channel where you can receive things that have no end. But, it begins with every person having a small little light that comes into this world with them at birth. Its basic function is to whisper, "This is right" and "That is wrong."

Now, let me read something to you out of Preach my Gospel on page 90. This is Brother Packer:

> *The Light of Christ should not be confused with the personage of the Holy Ghost, for the Light of Christ is not a personage at all. Its influence is preliminary to and preparatory to one's receiving*

> *the Holy Ghost...the Holy Ghost can work through*
> *the Light of Christ.*

I've got to tell you; this is not well understood in the church. 99% of the people who partook of the Sacrament today felt that *"they may always have His Spirit to be with them."* If you asked them, "Whose spirit?" they would say, "The Holy Ghost." And yet, the previous three sentences are talking about taking upon them the name of **Christ**, always remembering **Him**, and keeping **His** commandments. Whose commandments? Christ's. *"That they may have His spirit."* Whose spirit? **Christ's** Spirit to be with you. **Christ's** Spirit is not the Holy Ghost. That's what Brother Packer is saying. Now, *"its influence,"* the Holy Spirit, the light of Christ, *"Its influence is preliminary and preparatory to one receiving the Holy Ghost."* Did you catch that? I've got to tell you that this doctrine was not well understood throughout the church until two prophets, Marion G. Romney and Boyd K. Packer, started talking about it. We now have a greater understanding of these two things. How important is this to understand? Well, it was important enough that Joseph Smith came to visit Brigham Young from the spirit world. He came back from the dead to give Brigham Young a message that I'll read to you in just a minute. It is critically important, because how can you receive revelation, how can you call upon God and know what you worship, and how you worship if you don't understand these doctrines? At best, what we'll do is worship, according to the precepts of men and the philosophies of men mingled with scripture, where, if you get an answer at all, it's only going to be diluted. Now, Brother Packer goes on. He says, *"The Holy Ghost can work through the Light of Christ."* Here is a key. Christ works through the Light of Christ. The Father works through the Light of Christ because **It's** a channel. **It's** everywhere, and these gods use **It** to perform their missions.

Student 1: I think the thing that's a little bit confusing is when you say, "The Light of Christ." You know what I mean?

Mike: Yes.

Student 1: If all of the Godhead uses **It** and **It's** the Holy Spirit, why do they call **It** the Light of Christ, not the Light of God but the Light of Christ? So, that's something that confuses me, but I understand most of it.

41

Mike: That's a good question. Now, these are the questions that you receive through the Holy Spirit. The Holy Spirit inspires you with some of these questions. You, in turn, take some of these inspired questions to the Lord and receive an answer to that question. That's a good question. That's an excellent question. That's one you should be able to receive revelation on.

Brother Packer goes on to say that:

> *The Holy Ghost can work through the Light of Christ. A teacher of gospel truths is not planting something foreign or even new into an adult or a child. Rather, the missionary or teacher is making contact with the Spirit of Christ already there.*

So, if you're teaching an investigator about the principles and doctrines of the pre-mortal life, and you see a light go on in your investigators eyes and they look at you and they say something like this, (like they've said to me as a missionary) "You know, my church doesn't teach that, but I've always believed that I lived before I came here." Well, where did they get such a thought? It's because of that light that's in them. That, and other truths are found within them, and when they hear it, then it has a familiar ring to them. "It's something I've always believed." I can't tell you how many people have said that. "You know, I have never heard anybody teach that, but I have personally always believed that was true." And I tell them, "It's because it is true and that portion of truth resides in you, in the form of God's Spirit. What you are doing is simply coming into contact with truth that already exists inside you. And **It** came to you when you were born, as a gift from the Lord." So, when does the Holy Ghost come in? The Holy Ghost comes in when a person starts to come in contact with the doctrines of the Restoration, in our day. You're not going to have a person feel the influence of the Holy Ghost very much until they start knocking on the door of the Restoration, Joseph Smith, the *Book of Mormon*, etc., etc. They can receive revelation and do, all of the time, but it is coming through the Holy Spirit. The Holy Ghost comes when they open themselves up to receiving revelation about the Restoration of the gospel in the latter days.

Student 2: Does that mean that there was no Holy Ghost before the time of the Restoration?

Mike: Well, the Holy Ghost has always been on the earth whenever you have priesthood; and there's never been a time, even during the great periods of apostasy, that there has not been priesthood upon the earth. Whether in the form of translated men or godly men or whatever, there has always been priesthood. There has never been a time when the priesthood was not here on the earth. Wherever you have the priesthood, you have the Holy Ghost.

Let's take the population that's out there. I'm not going to say that the person can't feel the Holy Ghost if they're not knocking on the door of Restoration. I'm not going to say that but more likely not because one is preliminary to and preparatory to, the other. That's what Brother Packer just said, right? Preliminary to and preparatory to the others. So, here's how it works: a couple of missionaries knock on the door. Somebody inside sees them and recognizes them as missionaries; the white shirt, the black name-tags, or pretty girls with black name-tags, and they knock on the door. This person is on the other side of the door and has an impression inside, almost like a little voice that says, "Talk to them." Okay, so, she opens the door, and they introduce themselves. She's busy; she's got housework, the kids are screaming, she's got to get dinner on for her husband, and all of these are good reasons why she should not continue this conversation. And then all of a sudden she has another little prompting that says, "Let them in." These are Holy Spirit revelations. This is the Spirit of Christ. This is the Still Small Voice. This is teaching her right from wrong. Now, if she invites them in, and let's say they come in, they sit down and she has a beginning discussion about something of the gospel. The missionaries are teaching concepts, some truths, and principles.

Now she's going to have another voice that comes in and says, *"It's all true! What they're teaching you is true. I sent them here. You've been looking for them. They are coming from Me. They are My messengers."* That's the Holy Ghost. How do we know the difference? Because, the Holy Ghost instructs, teaches, fills in the blanks. It's more of a discussion, more of a commentary, more reasons **why** things are happening. The Holy Spirit, when **It** speaks to you, is a guide and a director. **It** simply says, "Do this; go here; don't go there; don't do this," and hardly, if ever, gives any reason for **Its** instructions. When the Holy Spirit speaks to you, you're going to have to have faith to move forward. If you move forward, you're going to open the door for a greater light to visit you. The greater light is the Holy Ghost. He comes as a visitor at this time. Meaning, He comes and He leaves. Comes and leaves. Okay? That's what's happening when the missionaries are teaching the gospel. The Holy Ghost is testifying of the truth.

Student 2: So, when we say that the Holy Ghost reasons things out, that's definitely different from our own voice, right?

Mike: Definitely different from your own voice. Your own voice is a different voice altogether. We'll talk about that one night, but we don't have time tonight. But, you're right, it's a different voice altogether. This is a man speaking to you. This is a man who is a God, and His ministry is to do the following things. If we were to take words and describe the Holy Ghost's ministry with words, they would be: testifies of truth, teaches and instructs, sanctifies, purifies, cleanses, and transforms. Those are words that describe the Holy Ghost. If we were to describe the Holy Spirit, we would say guide and direct.

Student 1: I don't know if it was from Catherine Thomas where I read that the Holy Spirit is a still, small voice. Where, on the other side, the Holy Ghost is not still. He can speak louder. That's what I read.

Mike: I like that.

Student 1: You know how you hear these stories that say, "I heard this voice. It was so clear." I think the Holy Spirit is not always clear unless you listen.

Mike: That's a good point [student]. I like that. I don't have any problem with that at all. To summarize a point here, it's my feeling that you are seldom if ever, going to have the influence of the Holy Ghost in your life if you have not been obedient to, and practice and become somewhat proficient in recognizing the Holy Spirit. If you reject the Holy Spirit (and the *Book of Mormon* says the way you do that is something called hard-heartedness and unbelief), it's my feeling that you'll be hard-pressed to ever have a visit from the Holy Ghost.

Student 1: That makes sense.

Mike: One is preliminary to and preparatory to the other. You can't have the Melchizedek Priesthood, in our day, unless you, first of all, receive the Aaronic Priesthood. Why? Well, because the Aaronic Priesthood is preparatory, in our day, to the Melchizedek Priesthood. These spirits appear to work in that same way. It appears that's the way God works in almost everything in the gospel that moves His children upward and closer to Him. It starts out small, in increments, and then as we are obedient, line upon line precept upon precept, here little there a little, we receive more until we can be in a full revelatory flow. So, let's take it to the next step. Here's the Holy Ghost coming and bearing testimony to the investigator, "It's true, it's true, it's true," filling in the blanks, teaching deeper principles and deeper truths. We have all seen that as missionaries. Now, if she enters into a covenant (the purpose of the investigation is to take her to a covenant) as she is invited by God, and the missionaries ask, "If you find out this is true, will you follow your Lord and Savior's example by entering the waters of baptism on such and such day?" If she chooses to do that and enters into the covenant, she's now opened herself up to a gospel RIGHT and privilege that's reserved only for those people who make covenants with the Lord. That something is called the Gift of the Holy Ghost.

Investigators cannot have the Gift of the Holy Ghost. They receive visitations from the Holy Ghost. He comes and goes during the investigation process. When they make a covenant, they now have the right to the companionship, not a visitor but the right to the companionship of the Holy Ghost. Does that make sense? It is now a greater light with more revelation, more truth and more knowledge flowing down through that channel. The Holy Ghost uses the Light of Christ, the Holy Spirit, and the Light of Truth to send that information through to God's children and impress it upon their minds. It becomes a channel and an agent for the Holy Ghost to use. So, the purpose of the Holy Spirit is to bring a man and a woman to a greater light called the Holy Ghost, which then leads to an even greater light. That light is called the Gift of the Holy Ghost and can then lead to something interesting which most people miss.

Go to section 109 in the *Doctrine and Covenants*. I remember when I came upon this. I'd read it many times, but the Spirit impressed it upon my mind. Section 109 is the dedicatory prayer of the Kirtland Temple. Now, think about things happening in increments, step-by-step, upward, upward, upward, line upon line. Then go to verse 14:

> *And do thou grant, Holy Father, that all of those who shall worship in this house may be taught words of wisdom out of the best books, and that they may seek learning even by study, and also by faith, as thou hast said;*
>
> *[15] And that they may **grow up in thee**, and receive a **fulness** of the Holy Ghost.*

Do you see how we started out? We started out with something still and small; something that everybody has, and then we move to something with a greater light, but more exclusive, brothers and sisters, more exclusive. As you go up, fewer and fewer people are going to be the recipient of greater and greater light. The reason for that is simply that the natural man loves darkness more than light. Most people won't come up to this. **It**'s a free gift to everybody to start with, but to come up and receive what God had reserved for you is going to require, sacrifice, diligence, faith, and obedience. Otherwise, you'll never have it.

So, at the top of the Holy Ghost spectrum is something called The Fullness of the Holy Ghost. Let me show you another thing that the Holy Ghost does. Let's go to section 121, verse 26. Now, notice something here. You tell me what you see in verse 26. Does somebody want to read that for us?

Student 2:

> *God shall give unto you knowledge by his Holy Spirit, yea, by the unspeakable gift of the Holy Ghost, that has not been revealed to the world was until now;*

Mike: So, tell me what we just saw there?

Student 1: The Holy Spirit and the Holy Ghost. They are two different...

Mike: But, every time you've read verse 26, before tonight, you thought it was two terms referring to the same thing, didn't you? You would look at it, and you would think that. You, with your understanding, should take a better look at verse 26 and try to understand what the Lord is telling us. *"God shall give unto you knowledge by his Holy Spirit, yea, by the unspeakable gift of the Holy Ghost."* Everything we've learned is that the Holy Spirit and the Holy Ghost are two different things. So, how can we reconcile verse 26 with everything that the prophets and apostles and the scriptures say, because, verse 26 sounds like two things talking about the same thing? Reconcile it for me, because this is one instance where you now take the doctrine and apply it to your understanding.

Student 3: Well, it almost sounds like if you're taught to do something, and if you do that, then you have more truth come to you.

Mike: All right, I like that. Look what else it says. Go to the second part. It's talking about knowledge in the first line, right? Now, skip down four lines, *"[knowledge] that has not been revealed since the world was until now;"* You don't get that knowledge from the Holy Spirit. You may get it from the Holy Ghost using the Holy Spirit to transfer it, but this is knowledge that is hidden from the masses of the world. Very few people are going to receive knowledge that has not been revealed since the world was until now. That is the Holy Ghost's prerogative. What He's doing now is revealing this hidden knowledge through the channel of the Holy Spirit.

Student 2: Wow! So, along with the restoration of the *Book of Mormon* and the other things, it's kind of a restoration of the Holy Ghost.

Mike: With everything else. Look at verse 28:

> *A time to come in the which nothing shall be withheld, whether there be one God or many gods, they shall be manifest.*

So, there are wonderful things in here. Go to section 84 and let's look at one more verse on this. And I will try to wrap it up, as we're almost done with our hour tonight. Look at section 84:43-45. You've read this before, but I want you to look at it with new eyes:

> *[43] And now I give unto you a commandment to beware concerning yourselves, to give diligent heed to the words of eternal life.*
>
> *[44] For you shall live by every word that proceedeth forth from the mouth of God.*
>
> *[45] For the word of the Lord is truth, and whatsoever is truth is light, and whatever is light is Spirit, even of the Spirit of Jesus Christ.*

You've got ask yourself a question: what are those words and how are they delivered? How do they come to us? Because you need to give diligent heed to them; *"For you shall live by every word that proceedeth forth from the mouth of God. For the word of the Lord is **truth**."* Think about what we've talked about tonight, *"And whatsoever is **truth** is **light** and whatever is **light** is the Spirit, even of the spirit of Jesus Christ."* Did you see the three 'L's? Did you see that? So, these verses are talking about what, the Holy Ghost or the Holy Spirit?

Student 2: The Holy Spirit.

Mike: It's talking about the Holy Spirit. Now, continuing with verse 46-48 (section 84), thinking back to Moroni 7:

> *[46]And the Spirit giveth light to **every man** that cometh into the world; and the Spirit enlighteneth every man through the world, that hearkeneth to the voice of the Spirit.*
>
> *[47]And every one that hearkeneth unto the voice of the Spirit cometh unto God, even the Father.*
>
> *[48]And the Father teacheth him of the covenant.*

None of this is talking about the Holy Ghost, brothers and sister, none of this. This is preliminary to and preparatory to the covenant that the Father has for those who follow this voice into His presence. Let's go to 1 Nephi, verse 16 and let me show you something I found in my studies today. During church, I was reading this, and the Spirit taught me something that I want to share with you that is fun. 1 Nephi 16 is talking about the thing called the Liahona. I want you to tell me what the Liahona symbolizes based on what we've talked about tonight. Verse 10:

> *And it came to pass that as my father arose in the morning, and went forth to the tent door, to his great astonishment he beheld upon the ground a round ball of curious workmanship; and it was of fine brass. And within the ball were two spindles; and the one pointed the way whither we should go into the wilderness.*

Now, what do you know of in today's world that is an instrument that points out direction? What do we call it?

Students: A compass.

Mike: Yes, a compass. So, what you've got here is a godly compass. One of the two spindles points the direction which you should go; go here, don't go there, go here, and don't go there. That's the definition of what, the Holy Spirit or the Holy Ghost?

Student 2: Holy Spirit

Mike: That's the Holy Spirit. The Holy Spirit is a compass. **It** is a director. In fact, Lehi calls **It** *the director.* But now we have a question about that other spindle because Lehi tells us there are two of them. So, let's find out about this. Let's go over to verse 16:

> *And we did follow the directions of the ball, which*
> *led us in the more fertile parts of the wilderness.*

See that director? **It**'s guiding them, **It**'s directing them.

Student 2: You said earlier that the Holy Spirit is the one that has no agency, the one to be acted upon. So, the Liahona works when they followed.

Mike: And when they had the faith! So, if you don't have the faith and you're not acting and showing faith, the Liahona isn't going to work for you. The spindle stops and then you're lost, okay? So, now watch. Go to verse 26:

> *And it came to pass that the voice of the Lord said*
> *unto him: Look upon the ball, and behold the things*
> *which are written.*
>
> *[27] And it came to pass that when my father beheld*
> *the things which were written upon the ball, he did*
> *fear and tremble exceedingly, and also my brethren,*
> *and the sons of Ishmael and our wives.*
>
> *[28] And came to pass that I, Nephi, beheld the*
> *pointers which were in the ball, that they did work*
> *according to the faith and diligence and heed which*
> *we did give unto them.*
>
> *[29] And there was also written upon **them** a new*
> *writing, which was plain to be read, which did give*
> *us understanding concerning the ways of the Lord;*

What's the **them**?

Student 4: Spindles.

Mike: There were two spindles, not just one but two of them. Now, remember one of them points the way, but both of them have written words on them periodically. Isn't that interesting? This is something the Spirit pointed out to me that I didn't see until today. Them—was a keyword—now watch, *"And there was also written upon them a new writing, which was plain to be read, **which did give us understanding**,"* Here's a keyword. The Holy Spirit does not give you understanding; the Holy Ghost gives you understanding. The Holy Ghost teaches, instructs, edifies, and fills in the blanks. It instructs you. It gives you understanding concerning the ways of the Lord. Continuing on:

> *[29] And it was written and changed from time to time, according to the faith and diligence we gave unto it. And thus we see that by small means the Lord can bring about great things.*

I believe that the two spindles are the Holy Ghost and the Holy Spirit and that the Holy Ghost, working through the Holy Spirit, can give information and understanding. That's why you have writings that are found upon both spindles. But **direction** is given only by one.

And, here is something else. If you weren't diligent in following the directions of the first spindle, I doubt that you would have ever seen any writing on the other or both of them; according to the pattern, if you are following patterns, and I believe we are. If you are diligent in following the first one, which is your director, or your compass and your guide, then the second one comes with additional information, greater understanding, greater depth, greater revelation, and can be seen on both of them. Because guess what? The Holy Ghost works through the Holy Spirit, so you find understanding written on both spindles. When you heed the one, the other gives you understanding and greater information. I thought that was just kind of fun.

Student 1: It's an interesting thing, to me, that's shown here. Maybe Lehi and Nephi looked at it, but Laman and Lemuel **never** looked at it because they were unbelievers.

Mike: Maybe. Let's end up with 1 Nephi, chapter 4. One of the things you can have fun with, as you study the *Book of Mormon* now, is with this greater understanding of this light, law, life, and truth, you can ask yourself the question: who is speaking here? Is this the Holy Ghost, or is this the Holy Spirit? What's going on here? And you should have some clues now as to how they operate so that you can discern that. Let's look at 1 Nephi, chapter 4, verse 5. This is Nephi, Sam, Laman, and Lemuel going back to get the brass plates:

> *And it was by night; and I caused that they should hide themselves without the walls. And after they had hid themselves, I, Nephi, crept into the city and went forth towards the house of Laban.*
> *[6]And I was led by the Spirit, not knowing beforehand the things which I should do.*

Now, you stop right there. What Spirit?

Student 1: The Holy Spirit.

Mike: Why would **It** be the Holy Spirit? You are right, but why would **It** be the Holy Spirit and not the Holy Ghost?

Student 2: It just gave directions.

Mike: Yes. It says *"I was led beforehand."* It's a guide, and it's telling him where to go. In verse 9 he finds Laban, right? Laban is drunk and is lying in the street. Nephi sees the sword of Laban and notices that it's of precious steel, etc. Look at verse 10:

> *And it came to pass that I was constrained by the Spirit that I should kill Laban; but I said in my heart: Never at any time have I shed the blood of man.*

So, the Spirit said what? He is looking at him, and the Spirit said, "Kill him." Period. Which one is it?

Students: The Holy Spirit.

Mike: It's the Holy Spirit. How do you know **It's** the Holy Spirit? Because **It** does not give any reasons. **It** just says kill him. Continuing on with verse 10, Nephi says, "Oh, my gosh! I shrunk back on that." Verse 10:

> *And I shrunk and would that I might not slay him.*
> *[11]And the Spirit said unto me again: Behold the Lord hath delivered him into thy hands. Yea, and I also knew that he had sought to take away mine own life; yea, and he would not hearken unto the commandments of the Lord; and he had also taken away our property.*

And you have this whole dialogue, now, as to why you should kill this man. So, the Spirit says, "Hey, he tried to take your money, he tried to kill you, he tried to do all this." And then look down at verse 12, this is what the Spirit says:

> *And it came to pass that the Spirit said unto me again; Slay him, for the Lord has delivered him into thy hands;*
> *[13]Behold the Lord slayeth the wicked to bring forth his righteous purposes. It is better that one man should perish than that a nation should dwindle and perish in unbelief.*

Who is the spirit that is speaking now?

Student 2: The Holy Ghost.

Mike: That's the Holy Ghost. How do you know this is the Holy Ghost? Well, because it's filling in all the blanks. It's giving the reasons why Laban's life should be forfeited. It goes down and lists the history of the last three attempts of trying to obtain the brass plates. All of this is the Spirit speaking to him. Then, He finally comes out and says that it is better for one person to die rather than a whole nation dwindle and perish in unbelief. And then, Nephi goes on and says, "I knew if I didn't have the plates, we would not have the whole law and we could not keep the commandments." Then in verse 18:

> *Therefore I obeyed the voice of the Spirit, and took Laban by the hair of his head, and I smote off his head with his own sword.*

Now, isn't that fun?

Student 2: It is!

Mike: If you take some principles now, and start looking at this, this doctrine will help you receive greater revelation than you've ever had before. You'll know how to ask and receive answers to questions, as you address Heavenly Father with greater knowledge. You'll say something like this, "Heavenly Father, instruct me by the power of the Holy Ghost, speaking through the Holy Spirit to my spirit that I might understand and obey." Now you're making requests based on true doctrine. Guess what? The truer the doctrine and the more direct your questions are, then the more your answers are going to come readily and powerfully. God will answer your prayers in your ignorance. He'll answer your prayers, but if you want to have a powerful revelatory experience, take what you're learning, and in your prayers, verbalize the truths that you're learning. Take a moment, get it in your mind, and in your prayers, and let it come out, and watch what happens. God will honor you for trying to approach him in greater truth and light, which is what you are doing.

Go to section 93. Now, all of these things that we've talked about tonight, we can take and apply them in closing up our lesson tonight. Think about everything we've said and then go to verse 19:

> *I give unto you these sayings that you may understand and know how to worship, and know what you worship, that you may come unto the Father in my name, and in due time receive of his fulness.*

Think about everything that we've talked about this last hour, *"I give unto you these sayings,"* for two purposes, *"that you may understand and know."* Notice those two words: Understand and know. The first purpose is, *"how to worship,"* and the second is, *"and know what you worship."* For what purpose? *"That in time you may come unto The Father in my name, and in due time receive of His fulness."* You see? Did you catch the two things? The Lord gives us this information that we may understand and know two things: **how** to worship and **what** you worship. The Lord wants us to worship Him in spirit and truth. Most of our worship, if you're like me, has been mixed with the precepts of man, and the philosophies of men mingled with scripture. And God, because of His mercy and grace to me in my ignorance, has answered my prayers and given me a revelation. But as I learn new concepts and as I embrace the truth, He expects me to incorporate that into my worship practices to Him. And as I do that, He honors me by greater, more powerful revelation, deeper understanding, a quickened mind, and enlarged intellect. You can't worship properly what you don't know. And remember that in the King Follett discourse, given April 2, 1844, just two months before Joseph was shot to death, he said the first principle of the gospel is, *"To know for certainty the character of God and that a man/woman can speak to God face-to-face as one man speaketh unto another."* And that's the first principle of the gospel: to know for a certainty the character of God. Why does He want you to know for a certainty? It's because you can then approach Him in spirit and truth. You approach Him in truth, and you bind Him; you've paid the price, you've sacrificed, you've studied through prayer and fasting, you've received revelation, and you're operating on truth. He honors that because of your sacrifices and then revelation flows. Any questions or comments?

Student 4: Thank you.

Mike: Our hour is up.

Student1: I thought I understood this Holy Ghost and Holy Spirit quite well, but I learned quite a bit tonight.

Mike: Well, I'm glad, and it's a good refresher for all of us. This is a good thing to know. And I think this is the revelatory foundation. You've got to have this as a foundation if you're really going to reach out and enjoy personal revelation. I testify unto you these things are true. God bless you.

References:
D&C 20:77 (Sacrament Prayer on the Bread)
D&C 88:5-13
A New Witness of the Articles of Faith, page 257-259 2 Nephi 2:
D&C 66:
Catherine Thomas quote
Moroni 7:6
D&C 93:36
Preach My Gospel, p 90
D&C 121:26
D&C 84:43
1 Nephi 16:10
1 Nephi 4:5
D&C 93:19

Chapter Two
Podcast 002 The Telestial World

Tonight I want to ask you a question. There's a question that has been asked throughout the world. It has been asked for thousands of years. The question is: "Why do bad things happen to good people?"

Student 1: Because we need the opposition.

Mike: Okay. There are three words that we want to concentrate on tonight: #1 adversity, #2 opposition, and #3 resistance. Now, look at the root word in all three of those: adverse, oppose and resist. If we were to take a common idiom, an American idiom, to describe adversity, it would be "going against the grain." "Going against the grain" equals adversity. So, is there such a thing as "bad things that happen to good people?"

Student 1: Yeah, if you want to call it that.

Mike: When we get through with today's lesson I hope that your idea, your way of thinking, and your belief, will be that there is no such thing as "bad things that happen to good people." According to the LDS view of adversity, trials, tribulations, opposition, and resistance, there is no such thing as bad things; ***there is only life!*** All right, I know that sounds a little bit weird, but nonetheless, that's the approach we are going to take on this.

So, let's start out by just looking in the universe. There are millions of worlds, innumerable telestial worlds that have people on them and look just like our world. The people that are on these planets are the children of the gods in the universe. Every one of these planets, just like this one, has people on them who are the children of mothers and fathers in heaven. These mothers and fathers have sent their children to these planets, telestial worlds, to go to school. It's just like sending our own children out to go to school. We prepare them at home. They learn all of the lessons they can at home, and then it comes time for them to leave and go to school so that they can further their education. It's just like that in eternity.

Now, I want you to understand that there are innumerable telestial worlds, in various stages of progression, in the universe at this very moment. Some of these telestial worlds only have two people on them. They have an Adam and Eve. Some of these telestial worlds have billions of people on them and are at the end of their progression getting ready for the second coming of a Messiah. Like our earth, they are waiting for their telestial world to end and become a terrestrial millennium. Some of these worlds are in a patriarchal stage. Some of these worlds are in a stage prior to a flood. Some of these worlds are in a stage of apostasy, where there has been truth, but truth has been lost because of transgression. And so, in the universe, we have many worlds which are in various stages of progression. The history of this world, from Adam and Eve down to the present, with all its various stages of progression, is found throughout the universe in millions and millions of different places.

This view sets the stage for something we are going to talk about here today. All of the children of these mothers and fathers in heaven are going to school on these worlds to learn how to become like their parents and to inherit everything that their parents have. There are not any of these innumerable men and women, gods and goddesses, kings and queens, priests and priestesses, mothers and fathers, that did not go through this very same thing that you and I are going through. They did not get to be where they are by any other way. So, when Eve, in the temple ceremony, looks at Lucifer and says, *"Is there no other way?"* and he looks at her and says, *"There is no other way."* Well, that is exactly true. There is only one pathway to godhood, and it passes through a telestial world somewhere. So literally, in order to get to heaven, you have to pass through hell.

In the temple ceremony, after Adam and Eve partake of the forbidden fruit, Eve turns to Adam and says this, *"It is better for us that we should pass through sorrow that we may know the good from the evil."* I want you to notice this comment she made. You see, her eyes are opening, and she is seeing things now. She is expressing herself in **wisdom**.

Remember that when they were being tempted, the thing that the devil and the opposition tempted Adam and Eve with was, *"It will make you **wise**. You must eat of this fruit for it will make you **wise**."* Did you notice that? Wisdom is something that is highly desirable by the gods. When I say gods, plural, I mean mothers and fathers. Latter-day Saints have a philosophy that parents in heaven are mothers and fathers in heaven, or in other words, another word for mother and father in heaven is god or goddess. Using priesthood terms, another name for a mother and a father in heaven is a king and queen, or a priest and a priestess. It's all the same thing. If you're a priest in heaven, you're a god. If you're a priest in heaven, you're a father. This whole plan is designed to bring their children up through a plan that allows them to inherit all that they have, and to become like them. This plan involves a telestial experience. So, if you want a description of hell, one of the things you could say is that a hell is a place where devils reside. Am I right? Isn't that one description of a hell? Hell is where you find devils, yes or no?

Student 1: Yes.

Mike: So, where is the third part that was cast out and became devils? Where are they right now?

Student 1: In hell.

Mike: Where are they? Where is that? What do we call it?

Student 1: I guess they are around here.

Mike: They are right here! They are in the telestial world. So, what does that make a telestial world? That makes it a hell. Now, don't get hung up on the word hell, because the Christian world has a different philosophy. They have a different idea of hell than Latter-day Saints do. To a Latter-day Saint, hell is a temporary place of restriction. The only place that we find in eternity that is permanent for wickedness is a place called Outer Darkness. All other places are temporary, and before they are resurrected, it's possible for people to progress and move from one place to another if they chose. So, now we come back to this telestial world, and we find out that this telestial world is a schoolhouse. All telestial worlds are schoolhouses, and the children of the gods are in school. School is in session, and the test is being administered.

Let's go to Abraham chapter 3 and look at some scriptures so that we can understand. In order to talk about our initial question, "Why do bad things happen to good people," we have to get a feel for this world that we are in because it's in this world that the so-called bad things are happening to good people. "Bad things happening to good people," takes place in a telestial world. Look in Abraham chapter 3. Now, here's the fathers and mothers in heaven, the gods, and they are talking about their children in verse 24:

> *And there stood one among them that was like unto God, and he said unto those who were with him: We will go down, for there is space there, and we will take of these materials, and we will make an earth whereon these may dwell;*

Now, look at this next verse, 25. Here's the purpose of earth life:

> *And **we will prove them** herewith, to see if they will do all things whatsoever the Lord their God shall command them;*

Another word for ***prove*** is test and *"herewith"* is referring back to this new earth in verse 24. *"We will **prove** them with this new earth,"* meaning: we're going to provide a place for them to go to be tested, *"To see if they will do all things whatsoever the Lord their God shall command them."* That's the purpose of this earth life.

So, Eve turns to Adam, as her eyes begin to open, and she's now obtaining **wisdom** through her experience in opposition. She says, *"Adam, it is better for us that we should pass through sorrow that we may know the good from the evil."* Now, the other thing that Satan tempted them with was, first, that you will obtain, *"wisdom,"* and second, that, *"you will have knowledge."* The two things that the devil hits Adam and Eve with on this new earth is something called **wisdom** and another thing called **knowledge**. It was because of the use of these two words, wisdom and knowledge, that caused Adam and Eve to partake of the fruit and fall. That's what happened. So, look at the telestial experience that you're in, and look at yourself as a child of a celestial mom and dad. You have heavenly parents who have sent you away to school so that you can have experiences in adversity, opposition, and resistance. These experiences, if properly learned and used, can lead to wisdom and great knowledge. Does that make sense?

Student 2: Yeah!

Mike: So, when Lucifer's hitting them with temptation, he is setting them up with the truth; wisdom and knowledge are desired by the gods. Those are two things that give the heavenly mothers and heavenly fathers their power. Now, these two words are very interesting. One leans towards the female side, and the other one leans toward the male side. As a matter of fact, in the scriptures, whenever the Lord uses the word wisdom, He always refers to it with the female pronoun. Wisdom is female. Knowledge is male. So, if you were to take a characteristic that applies to women that describe their core godly characteristic, it would be wisdom. If you were to take a core characteristic of men, it would be knowledge.

Student 1: Why is that so?

Mike: It's just the way that we are created. Men have the propensity to acquire knowledge and women innately have the ability to be wise. One without the other is incomplete. A man with knowledge is dangerous to the world. A man with knowledge, and without wisdom, isn't going very far. Hence, we have a need for a man and a woman to be united so that wisdom and knowledge can now produce the desired effect, which is to move a man and a woman toward godhood. One without the other is incomplete.

Also, to give you another male-female thing from the scriptures; Mercy is always female. Mercy is always referred to (you can read this in Alma 42:24) with the female pronoun. Justice is always male. You can see this application in a family. When a child is being disobedient and acting out, the father is the one who picks up and starts to apply and administer justice, and the mother is, more or less, going to intervene and seek for mercy. To do it right, a husband and wife need to be together in counsel and in wisdom and knowledge, so that justice and mercy work together, and one doesn't rob the other when it comes to administering family affairs. You can see this. You have a question, yes?

Student 5: I have a question regarding what you said earlier. Can you make this clearer? Satan said, "It will make you wise," because it's the truth. Then I heard a phrase a couple of minutes later, and you are saying that Satan is keeping the truth away from Adam and Eve? I should have asked this question earlier, but can you make that a little clearer for me?

Mike: Well, the process was this: he used two principles in order to get them to partake of the fruit. The first was to entice. The word 'entice' means to persuade; to entice them to partake of the fruit by saying, "It will make you wise." That's the one he gets Eve with. The second is when he says, "You'll be like the gods knowing good and evil, and you will have knowledge." So, those two things, those two terms, he uses to tempt them and persuade them to partake.

Student 2: And he's saying the truth.

Mike: It's true! It's true because, Satan always twists the truth and adds error, lies, and deception, mixed with truth. In fact, Satan's power comes from the fact that he uses partial truth. There is always a power associated with truth because the greater, the more unadulterated, and purer the truth means the greater the power and light. But even twisted truth mixed with error, the philosophies of men mingled with scriptures, and the precepts of men have power.

Student 5: Okay.

Mike: Temples are a true principle. God has always operated through temples. So, what does Lucifer do? He counterfeits these temples. He has his own temples. He has his own endowment ceremony. He has his own tokens, signs, names, and keywords and he uses those. They're all counterfeit from the truth, and those counterfeit, twisted, true principles have power within them. Dark power comes from the knowledge that Satan has acquired. He takes God's truths and twists and changes them. It has power because there is truth in all of it. [Moses 4:9-11] Let me give you an example, and I'm paraphrasing here:

> The Lord said, *"If you partake of this fruit thou shalt surely die."*
> And Lucifer comes up to Adam and Eve and says, *"You must eat of this fruit."*
> Eve says, *"I will not eat that fruit, for God said that in the day that I eat of it I should surely die."*
> Then, Satan says, *"Ye shall not surely die; but shall be as gods knowing good and evil."*

You see, *"Ye shall not die,"* is a lie. That's a lie. But, *"knowing good from evil and being like the gods,"* is a true statement. So in one sentence, he takes a lie and a truth; intertwines them and uses them to deceive, which is a satanic tactic. He does that all the time! You and I need to be able to have a strong enough knowledge of revealed, unadulterated truth, and to have a background in personal revelation so that we can keep from being deceived by this master deceiver.

Student 2: Is Satan capable of knowing the revealed truth that we just can't discern?

Mike: Well, go with me to Moses in the *Pearl of Great Price.* Moses 4:6. It appears that even Lucifer, in the Garden of Eden, loses some of the knowledge that he had. There's a little key here.

Student 3:

> *And Satan put it into the heart of the serpent, (for he had drawn away many after him,) and he sought also to beguile Eve, for he knew not the mind of God, wherefore he sought to destroy the world.*

Mike: Now, I want you to pay attention to the sentence, *"he knew not the mind of God."* That's an interesting statement. You have to ask yourself what that means. Did he forget something that he previously knew, or is his knowledge limited and he only grew to a certain point? I think it's a combination of both things. I think there are things that he has been made to forget, and there is a reason I believe that. There's a *Book of Mormon* principle that says you can digress in knowledge. Digression is the opposite of progression. It means that once you choose to reject light, once God gives you the opportunity for light, and you make a choice to reject it, something happens at that point. The light that you could have had if you'd been obedient, you now lose. And, the knowledge that you currently have starts going backward until you've lost it. So, you not only lose what you **could** have had, you lose what you **have** had. That's in Alma chapter 12 and in 3 Nephi and several other different places. So, based on his decision, I think that Lucifer, because of his rebellion, is going backward. I think he is losing what light he had. Keep in mind that this man was a very high General Authority type, an Archangel type, a massively progressed and knowledgeable person before he came out in rebellion against God. By the time he gets into the Garden of Eden, which is sometime after his being cast out for rebellion, it appears that he's going backward and forgetting, or losing whatever light he had had before.

Student 2: So, those who have a hardness of heart, they are given a lesser portion until they know nothing.

Mike: Yes.

Student 2: Then they become captive by the devil.

Mike: Yes, now let's go look at that. That's a good one. Alma talks about that, and it's a wonderful principle that applies to all of us if we're not careful. There's a term in the *Book of Mormon* called *hardness of heart.* You don't see it so much in the *Bible*, but it's all over in the *Book of Mormon.* The Lord wants us to have something the *Book of Mormon* calls the *mysteries of God.* He wants us to have these things. Now, these mysteries can only be found out through personal revelation. In these verses, the *mysteries of God* are also called the *greater portion of the word,* so when we talk about the *mysteries of God,* we're at the same time talking about the *greater portion of the word.* If there's *a greater portion of the word,* there has to be an opposite, the lesser portion. Let's go to Alma Chapter 12 verse 9:

> *And now Alma began to expound these things unto him, saying: It is given unto many to know the mysteries of God; nevertheless they are laid under a strict command that they shall not impart only according to the portion of his word which he doth grant unto the children of men,*

I want you to know that your Father in Heaven wants you to know all those things. He wants His children to know His mysteries. If God reveals to you his mysteries, you are obligated to share them, but you have to be careful who you share them with. You can only share what God reveals to you, to those who give diligent heed, and to those that He reveals to you by the Spirit. If you share something that God reveals to you and you shouldn't, you offend God, the heavens withdraw, the spirits grieve, and you shut off personal revelation. If you share something that God has revealed to you for the wrong reason, then what you're doing is offending the Spirit and you shut-off revelation. For instance, if you say, "Let me share with you what I learned," and your intention is, "I know more than you do, I am better than you, or I am more righteous than you are," then your intentions are wrong. You have to be careful when God reveals these things to you. Now look at verse 10:

> *And therefore, he that will harden his heart, the same receiveth the lesser portion of the word; and he that will not harden his heart, to him is given the greater portion of the word, until it is given unto him to know the mysteries of God he know them in full.*

Hardening in your heart is the difference between going backward and forward. This is the deal breaker. The hardened heart receives the lesser portion of the word, not the mysteries but less than the mysteries.

Now, brothers and sisters, what you hear in church every Sunday, what you hear from the pulpit, what you hear in Gospel Doctrine class, what you hear in priesthood, what you hear in Relief Society, what is taught in every Seminary class, and what is taught in every Sunday School class, is the lesser portion of the word.

If you want the greater portion, which are the mysteries of God, you can only receive those from your Heavenly Father through the process of personal revelation. That's the way it should be. What the church is doing, in teaching the lesser portion, is laying the foundation for the "convert level" in the church. Then, those folks can come into the church and have a foundation to build on. You can't obtain the greater portion by skipping the lesser portion. You can't do it. The problem with the church membership is that we've become satisfied with the lesser portion. We think that's all there is. We are really content, and we say, "All of this makes me so happy! I feel so good. I never knew the answers to that!" And so, we sit back and become satisfied with the lesser portion. It's just one way that we harden our hearts. If you become apathetic and say, "I've got this, I'm so happy with it, I don't want any more," then that's hardening your heart, and God will honor that, and you won't get any more. In fact, you'll start to go backward because of what's found next in verse 11:

> *And they that will harden their hearts, to them is given the lesser portion the word until they know nothing concerning his mysteries; and then they are*

*taken captive by the devil, and led by his will down
to destruction. Now, this is what is meant by the
chains of hell.*

Do you see that? *"Until they know nothing."* You go backward concerning the mysteries. So, all of us stand in a place where God offers us something. Different people are being offered different things. Not everybody's been offered the same thing because we're all in school but in different grades. It's a one-room schoolhouse. And in this one room schoolhouse, called the telestial world, you have kindergartners, first-graders, third-graders, junior high, high school and some graduate students, all in the same classroom. That's the telestial world. Whatever it is God offers you, at whatever level you're at, and how you respond, determines whether you are going to go forward and grow in light, or go backward and diminish until you lose what you have. It's all based on the choice that you make when God offers you something. Questions or comments on that?

Student 5: That's why I realized that when we are teaching, we should emphasize to the students that they need to study for themselves, personally, so they can get personal revelations that can lead them to something more.

Mike: Exactly, and you must not be satisfied. Joseph Smith was so frustrated with the Latter-day Saints. I have quote after quote where he says he's tried to get the Latter-day Saints to understand this principle, to accept that principle, and they just put up stakes and say, "No, I don't want to go any further than this. I'm happy where I am." Whenever Joseph introduced a new principle or doctrine, they were just so caught up in the traditions of their fathers that he said, "They flew to pieces like glass." Joseph's number one frustration was that what God had revealed to him was available to every Latter-day Saint, but the majority of the Latter-day Saints rejected it and said, "We don't want to know."

Now, you can see that over in *Doctrine and Covenants*, section 84. I want to show you something here. This is where you have to be careful. There's a fine line, brothers and sisters, in being open to new doctrine, in being open to things that the Lord reveals to you, and the fear of being deceived. We are really afraid of being led off into a different path and being deceived, and so the fear of deception keeps us from obtaining future revelation and growing in knowledge. In section 84, we can see an example of this with the people of Moses. When Moses brought the children of Israel out of Egypt, and Egyptian bondage, one of the first things he wanted to do, and the Lord wanted him to do, was to sanctify that whole nation of people and prepare them to come up and enjoy an encounter with God. God told Moses to bring the whole nation, who was numbered in the millions, up to where they would have an experience in the presence of God, where God would come down from heaven, and show himself to them. [You can read about this in Exodus chapter 19, 20 and 21] Now, it's referring to that here, so God told Moses to go down to the people and have them prepare themselves for three days. Have them wash their clothes, clean their bodies, and husbands and wives refrain from sexual relations. On the third day, I want you to bring them up to the mountain, and I will come down and show myself to the congregation.

Think about that! This is an opportunity for over 1 million people to actually see God face-to-face and He would come down and talk to them! Now, this God is a glorified being. He is a being of light and power and glory. Whenever a being of light and power and glory comes into a telestial world, it upsets nature. Nature is upset because the telestial world is not the dwelling place of glorified, exalted men and women. Whenever you have a god come down from a celestial level into a telestial world, nature will react in the form of earthquakes, tidal waves, fire, and volcanoes. You ARE going to have a reaction, and that's exactly what happened. God came down the mountain to the Temple place and Mt. Sinai is on fire. The ground is shaking. It's thundering and lightning. There are smoke and fire, and it scared the dickens out of all those people. They ran away and stood afar off. [Exodus 20:18-19] And so, there's Moses standing by himself, probably with Aaron and some of the priests, and there are a million-plus people who got out of there. They said, "Whoa! We are not staying here! This is terrible!" It scared them to death.

So, guess what happens? They all leave, and Moses says, "What are you doing?" The people turned to Moses and said, "Listen, YOU go up and talk to God. We're scared. YOU go talk to Him. Then YOU, Moses, come and tell us what He said." So, they rejected the invitation, which God himself offered these people. As a result, let's go down to *Doctrine and Covenants* section 84 verses 19-26:

> *[19]And this greater priesthood administereth the gospel and holdeth the key of the mysteries of the kingdom, even the key of the knowledge of God*
> *[20]Therefore, in the ordinances thereof, the power of godliness is manifest.*

The greater priesthood is the Melchizedek Priesthood, and Moses and God wanted to give it to the whole nation. He wanted to give them *"the keys of the knowledge of God."*

> *[21]And without the ordinances thereof, and the authority of the priesthood, the power of godliness is not manifest unto men in the flesh;*
> *[22]For without this* (the priesthood and the ordinances or the Melchizedek Priesthood) *no man can see the face of God, even the Father, and live.*

This is what God wanted to give the children of Israel. It was a priesthood that brought them into the presence of God and redeemed them from the fall. Now look at the next verse:

> *[23]Now this Moses plainly taught to the children of Israel in the wilderness, and sought diligently to sanctify his people that they might behold the face of God;*
> *[24]But they hardened their hearts and could not endure his presence; therefore, the Lord in his wrath, for his anger was kindled against them, swore that they should not enter into his rest while in the wilderness, which rest is the fulness of his glory.*
> *[25]Therefore, he took Moses out of their midst, and the holy priesthood also;*
> *[26]And the lesser priesthood continued,*

That's what happened.

Now, look in our day where there are great parallels. Joseph Smith restored a doctrine that was designed to bring the Latter-day Saints into the presence of God to behold His face. But, the Latter-day Saints rejected it. As a society, they rejected that. This is why Joseph was so frustrated. So, guess what happened? God took Joseph out of their midst. He allowed Joseph to be murdered. Look at the parallels. The program that Joseph wanted to restore was canceled out, and the Latter-day Saints received another program in the form of an administrative, organizational, *New Testament* church, which is what we have today. It is wonderful, and it's true, but Joseph had something higher in mind and the Latter-day Saints, just like the Israelites in the day of Moses, would not accept it. Therefore, the Lord allowed something lesser to stay until the Latter-day Saints are prepared for something greater, in a future day. Do you understand?

The children of Israel said unto Moses, "You go up and talk to God. We don't want to talk to Him. You go talk to Him, and you tell us what He said." Today, what are the Latter-day Saints doing? The Latter-day Saints say, "Thomas [Monson] you go talk to God, and you tell us what God said." They do this instead of seeking that *personal audience* with the Lord that He wants us to receive. We are kind of in a middle ground where we have prophets and apostles mediate for us because we are not ready to rise up and live a life that sanctifies us to the degree that we can have a *personal audience* with Christ and enter into His presence, while in this life. There are a great many Latter-day Saints that will do nothing; they will not act but will only respond to what they're told to do by their leaders, and if their leaders don't tell them to do it, they absolutely will not do it.

As a society, we condemn ourselves because we are acted upon but fail to act. Prophets and apostles are necessary. The Church of Jesus Christ of Latter-day Saints is God's church. It's fulfilling a purpose, but the purpose is to get us to a temple. Church membership, brothers and sisters, is designed to get you into the temple. In the temple, you're being initiated into something **higher** than membership in The Church of Jesus Christ of Latter-day Saints. Membership in the Church is not even mentioned in the temple, but membership in the Church is necessary in order to get into the temple. Do you see the preparatory steps?

So, the children of Israel end up with an Aaronic Priesthood order, which is designed to move them through ordinances, initiations, and ceremonies into something greater, that eventually brings them into the presence of God while in this life and redeems them from *The Fall.* But they never did do that. The whole history of Israel is one of an Aaronic Priesthood-level, a preparatory gospel that had baptism, faith, and the ministering of angels, but it never ever did get them to the point where they had the priesthood and the power to bring people into the presence of God. It never happened. So, from Moses up until Jesus Christ, we have a group of people who never ever were able to make the step from *Aaronic Priesthood (preparatory)* to *Melchizedek Priesthood (entering)* God's presence. And even Jesus, brothers and sisters, even Jesus was not able to bring the *New Testament* church, as a society, into that group. Albeit, there were some *New Testament* members that did rise up, enter through the veil, and become members of The Church of the Firstborn, and did have a personal audience with Christ and the spirits of *just men made perfect*. The *New Testament* saints did obtain the Church of the Firstborn and the fullness of the gospel, but the *Old Testament* people never did.

Now, here's something interesting. In America, you had an *Old Testament* group of people from 600 BC up to Christ, and even though they were here in America, they were *Old Testament*. Am I my right? They're *Old Testament* because they were practicing the law of Moses and doing all those things that the children of Israel were doing on the Eastern side. Guess what? The American Israelites did obtain the presence of God. So, their law of Moses practice and Aaronic Priesthood fulfilled its purpose and the Nephites rose up and obtained Melchizedek Priesthood status. Even though they practiced the law of Moses, they said, "The Law is dead unto us. It has fulfilled its purpose, and we are alive in Christ."

This is why the whole Nephite society was wiped out because they had more given to them and sinned against the greater light than Israelites did. This is why the Nephites were extinguished from the earth because they had too much given to them and they sinned against greater light. As a result, there are no Nephites on the earth. All we have is a record of a dead people. Why? They had obtained the Melchizedek redemption through faith in Christ. The law of Moses did work for them, but it never worked for the children of Israel on the eastern continent. It never did! They wanted it to, but Moses tried and failed. Melchizedek tried and had some limited success. Enoch tried and had some pretty good success. Adam tried and failed. Every patriarch all the way through the *Old Testament* tried to bring the people up to behold the face of

God while they were still alive, but the history of the world is pretty much one of never achieving that level.

Now, the question comes up, and we have to ask, how are we doing as Latter-day Saints? We have the same program today. It's still open to us. Every man, woman, and individual member of the church have the opportunity to enter into the presence of the Lord while still alive in this life. You can have a personal audience with the Lord Jesus Christ before you die. In fact, it's desirable, and the only thing that's keeping us from doing that is what? Yes, us! The key is *hard hearts* and *unbelief.* We just don't think it's possible. We're in the same position that Joseph and the Latter-day Saints were in, in the early days. I'm not trying to be hard on them because this is the most difficult thing that we will overcome in this life, my brothers and sisters, this unbelief. We read about these things happening in the scriptures. We believe what happened to the brother of Jared. We believe what happened to Moses. We believe what happened to Joseph. But we just absolutely cannot see it happening to us. That is called *unbelief,* and it stops the whole thing.

Do you now have a feeling for what this telestial world is? It's our schoolhouse. The purpose of the gospel of Jesus Christ is to help us graduate from this school, learn the lessons, obtain a degree and have an advantage in the world to come. And by the way, the world to come is not celestial. The world to come is terrestrial/millennial. If you were to ask 100 Latter-day Saints, what is the world to come (mentioned in section 130, versus 21 and 22) almost all of them will say, "Oh, that's the celestial kingdom." **No**, it's not the celestial kingdom.

Go over to section 130 and let me show you. Somehow, as members of the church, we've totally skipped over the whole thousand-year world. We're jumping right over it as members. Section 130 verses 18 and 19:

> [18]Whatever principle of intelligence we attain unto in this life, it will rise with us in the resurrection.

Do you see what we're doing? We're trying to gain knowledge and intelligence.

> [19]And if a person gains more **knowledge** and intelligence in this life through his diligence and

*obedience than another, **he will have so much the advantage in the world to come.***

Remember what Lucifer says? You will have knowledge. I always thought the world to come was the celestial world. I'm a teacher with 40 years experience, and I looked at it in this same way. Most Latter-day Saints look at it like that. No, it's not. You don't go from telestial to celestial. You have to go from telestial, to terrestrial, to celestial. There's a sequence. We don't drop out the whole terrestrial world. The **terrestrial** world is the **millennial** world, and that's the one that is coming. Right now, we're on the edge of moving from a telestial to a terrestrial world. What you should be trying to do in this life is gain an advantage from your experience here, so that when you go into the terrestrial/millennial world, you will have a greater advantage. You want to seek for an advantage. The whole name of the game is to do something that gives you an advantage in the next phase of your progression. You want to move up with advantages. You don't want disadvantages. You don't want to go into the terrestrial world disadvantaged. As a matter of fact, if you are disadvantaged, you probably won't go there.

Student 2: I just had a realization. That's why our individual situations here, in this world, are based on our performance in the first estate.

Mike: Exactly! So, your advantages in the next world are based on performance here. And listen to this, brothers and sisters! Think about it: there are about 7 billion people on the earth right now. How many of those 7 billion people will, in their lifetime, have an opportunity to talk about the things we talked about tonight? How many? Do you think it's a lot or a little?

Students: A little.

Mike: Do you know why it's a little? Do you want to know why some will and some won't? Because some of them came here with an advantage! And because they came here with an advantage, they come into favorable contact with this information. In other words, what you did before you came here has resulted in you sitting here tonight, and listening to these wonderful doctrines and principles. It is because you have an advantage over everybody else. You have the advantage because of your diligence and obedience in the previous world.

Student 5: I have a question. So, in the previous world, had these already grown like other advantages? You know, we see a lot of intelligent people who do amazing, unbelievable things; like scientists, rocket scientists, and such. All of that applies to this?

Student 2: It applies to all of those gifted people?

Mike: They absolutely are gifted people. And they developed those gifts in the world before they came here. The purpose of the development of those gifts, whether science, social studies, music, or whatever it is; these people come to this world and bless God's others children with their achievements, with their knowledge, and with what they've gained. It's all a process of blessing God's children. Some people in the premortal life chose to place their emphasis on music. Some people in the premortal life chose to place their emphasis in judicial affairs and government affairs. Some people chose to place their emphasis in medicines and in healing in the future world. Others chose to place their emphasis in gospel principles and priesthood principles and ordinances, etc. Just as we choose different things in this life, so the same things happened in the previous life. Then, you come here into this world, and you bring those things with you. All of that helps you progress and also blesses all of The Father's other children that are exposed to your gifts, your talents, and the knowledge and wisdom you brought. All of it ends up blessing everybody, but there is something called *choosing the better part*. It's Lehi that comes out and says, "I have chosen the better part." There are lots of good things, but Lehi chose something better. And I would submit to you that the better part has to do with the priesthood, the Holy Spirit, the principles of the gospel, the knowledge of the gospel, and the mysteries of godliness. That's the better part. Some chose that, and some didn't.

Well, we've been at it an hour and just kind of rambled on a little bit to see where the Spirit would guide us. My purpose with this was to give us a different view of what this life is affording us, what we're doing here, what's happening here, and what is to be desired for us to accomplish while we are here so that when we move into the next phase, the world to come, we can do so with an advantage. The purpose of the gods sending their children to this earth is not to become great musicians. The purpose for them to send their children here is to not to become marvelous mathematicians, and judges, or lawyers. The purpose of sending them here is to become gods, but their children choose which direction they want to go. Some choose *the better part.*

References:
Abraham 3: 24-25
Alma 42
Moses 4: 9-11
Moses 4: 6
Alma 12: 9-11
D&C 84:19
Exodus 19, 20, 21

Chapter Three
Podcast 003 Adversity

Last week we talked about the telestial world. I want to chat a little bit more about the purpose for coming into this world, which is to experience adversity. We mentioned three words last week: Opposition, adversity, and resistance. All three of these words seem to indicate an adverse effect; we're going to have to push hard against something in order to accomplish a goal. Everything in this world opposes everything else. It's a world of opposition. The reason it's a world of opposition is that it's the only place where man can come and exercise moral agency, or what we call *free agency*. By the way, the word free agency is not a scriptural term. Nowhere in the scriptures is it referred to as free agency. These telestial worlds have opposition, and opposition is absolutely necessary in order for us to exercise agency. Otherwise, as it says over in 2 Nephi chapter 2:11, *"For it must needs be, that there is an opposition in all things,"* and if it were not so, everything would remain in a state of **one**; there would be no opposing views, no opposing circumstances, no growth, no progress, and everything would be frustrated with no purpose in its creation, nor in the end thereof.

So, let's talk a little bit about adversity. I've got a couple of quotes I want to read to you tonight. This is one of my favorite quotes on adversity, opposition, trials, tribulations, and comes from Brigham Young in the Journal of Discourses, page 345. He says this:

> *All intelligent beings who are crowned with the crowns of glory immortality and eternal life, and eternal **lives**, must pass through every ordeal **appointed** for intelligent beings to pass through to gain their glory and exaltation. Every calamity that can come upon mortal beings will be suffered to come upon **the few** to prepare them to enjoy the presence of the Lord. If we obtain the glory that Abraham attained, we must do so by the same means that he did. If we're ever to be prepared to enjoy the society of Enoch, Noah, Melchizedek, Abraham, Isaac, and Jacob, or of their faithful children, and of the faithful prophets and apostles; then we must pass through the same experience to gain the knowledge, intelligence, and endowments that will prepare us to enter into the kingdom of our Father and God. How many of the Latter-day Saints will endure all of these things and be prepared to enjoy the presence of the Father and of the Son? You can answer that question at your leisure. Every trial and experience you have passed through are necessary for your salvation.*

We need to pay attention to that. You have to pass through every ordeal appointed for intelligent beings to pass through. There are several things in that quote that I think are interesting. These ordeals that we go through are APPOINTED. Another quote which I'm going to read to you in a minute, says they are ordained ordeals. They belong to you. They are unique. Brother Neil Maxwell said:

> *There are two kinds of adversity in this world.*

There is the common adversity that everyone goes through and is a part of just being here in this fallen world.

And then there's what he calls "ordained tutorials," that are specific, that just belong just to you and that you knew about before you came here. These are designed to have a specific effect upon your progress.

So, what we can learn is that if you want to go where Abraham, Isaac, and Jacob are, you're going to have trials that will try **you** to the same extent that they were tried, or you can't hope to have an inheritance with them, wherever they are. That doesn't necessarily mean you'll be called upon to offer up your son, but it will be, for you, as great a trial as it was for them. These are called "Abrahamic trials." Moroni talked about it. He said that you would have the *trial of your faith*. There would be something called the *trial of your faith*, not trials but **THE** *trial of your faith,* and that trial would bring you to know God in a way that you could not know otherwise. Now, whenever we talk about knowing God here, in these discussions, we're talking about a level *above* what we talk about in testimony meetings on the first Sunday of each month. We're talking about **knowing God**, not knowing about him but **knowing Him**; in the way that Joseph Smith talked about knowing Him. That means you will have an encounter with God while you're in this life.

Now, these things have names. An encounter with God, an encounter with the God of the terrestrial world, an encounter with the God of the Millennium, is called the *Second Comforter*. The God of the terrestrial world is Jesus Christ. Joseph Smith taught that it is desirable to seek after and have that experience. You can't have that experience unless you can be trusted. If you were to have an encounter or visitation with the son of God, with an angel, with the spirits of *just men made perfect*, or any heavenly being, and turn against that, then your condemnation would be so great that it would frustrate the very purpose of the visitation in the first place.

So, God has to be able to know if He can trust you with this information. Can He trust you with this experience? The only way He can know is to put you in a position of opposition, and adversity, and trial, to see if you remain faithful to Him in the midst of all these adverse situations. One of the purposes of adversity is to find out if He can trust you enough with sacred things so that when He reveals Himself to you, you will not violate that trust and bring upon yourself damnation. It is true that where much is given, much is required. If you sin against the greater light, you receive greater condemnation. Another purpose of adversity and trial is to put you in a position where you can prove to God that you are willing to do all things whatsoever He commands of you, and then He can give you more, line upon line. If He reveals Himself to you and you violate that trust, not only do you condemn yourself but you go backward in your experience. You go backward in knowledge. You go backward in power. Everything goes backward because you violated a trust. There are two things God wants to know: can He trust you, and can you prove that by showing that you trust Him. So, its trust going both ways; you trust Him, and He trusts you. The Lord says in Proverbs 3:5-6:

> Trust in the Lord with all thine heart; and lean
> not unto thine own understanding. In all thy ways
> acknowledge him, and he shall direct thy paths.

So, you need to be able to trust Him. Once He knows that you trust Him, He will bless you with information and with spiritual experiences that will increase your spirituality and your standing. This will accelerate your pathway back into the presence of the Father. The whole purpose of this is to move us along the path so that we can successfully complete this journey. This is from Brigham Young again, talking about general Christianity. He says:

> They cannot dwell with the Father and His Son
> unless they go through those ordeals which are
> ordained for the Church of the Firstborn. The

76

> *ordinances of the house of God are expressly for the*
> *Church of the Firstborn.*

The Church of the Firstborn is not the Church of Jesus Christ of Latter-day Saints. The Church of Jesus Christ of Latter-day Saints is an outward organization; it's a general organization; it's a preparatory organization that's trying to prepare you to come up to and obtain something higher. If the Church of Jesus Christ of Latter-day Saints is an outward organization, then the Church of the Firstborn is an inward organization. If the Church of Jesus Christ of Latter-day Saints is preparatory; the Church of the Firstborn is the church that is presided over by Christ himself. One of the things the Lord wants us to do is to come into and obtain membership in the Church of the Firstborn. The first ordinance you experience in the temple is called the *Initiatory.* You're being **initiated**, through this ordinance called the *Initiatory,* into the Church of the Firstborn. That's what initiatory is; it's an initiation. So, the purpose of the Church of Jesus Christ of Latter-day Saints is to bring men and women out of the world into the membership of this church and immediately begin to prepare them to come to something higher, the temple. All of these experiences, all of this adversity, all of this opposition, are designed to test us and prove us along the way so that God knows that He can trust you. Notice in that last statement it said, *"These ordeals are ordained for the Church of the Firstborn."* All of the ordinances of the house of God are expressly for that purpose.

Here is one more quote. Again this is Brigham Young. He says:

> *To have the promise of receiving eternal **lives**, so*
> *sealed upon our heads with no power on earth, or*
> *in heaven, or beneath the earth can take from us, is*
> *to be sealed up to the day of redemption and to have*
> *the promise of eternal lives, the greatest gift of all.*
> *The people do not fully understand these things and*
> *have them not in full vision before their minds. If*
> *they did I will tell you plainly and honestly, there is*

not a trial which the Saints are called to pass through that they would not realize and acknowledged to be their greatest blessings.

LIVES, there's a difference between eternal life and eternal lives. So, now we have a unique perspective of suffering, of trials, of tribulations, of adversity, of opposition, and of resistance. In reality, if we understood these things, we would understand that they are the very things that bring us our greatest blessings.

So, we look at things differently. Last week I asked the question, "Why do bad things happen to good people?" It's the great philosophical question of all time, and the answer to that is that there is no such thing. There is no such thing as *bad things happening to good people*. All there is is LIFE. And now we have a different perspective that there some trials and tribulations that are specifically ordained for us in this life to bring about specific results. The more you can handle, the more that you can show that you can be faithful in tribulation and trial, the more the Lord will move you upward in the scale of things. These trials will be **increasing** so that you can eventually enter into the Church of the Firstborn and dwell with all the Holy Fathers in the presence of God, *to go no more out.* So, it has a purpose. All of this has a purpose. Now, let us stop for just a moment and ask if you have any comments or questions about that? That is the unique perspective of the Latter-day Saints restored doctrine on opposition, resistance, and diversity. Are there any questions or comments or thoughts?

Student 3: I've been thinking about being a Zion people and becoming Zion individuals. So, this is all toward helping us become a Zion individual, right?

Mike: Exactly! We have an assignment ahead of us as members of the Church. It's unique in a way that our mission is to establish a society, a Zion society, and do it successfully like it's never been done since Adam came out of the Garden of Eden. The Lord Jesus Christ has to have a group of people who are sanctified and prepared to receive Him when He comes to this Earth.

Student 3: Or He will not come.

Mike: According to some of the writings of the early Brethren, He will not come; that is correct. We are told by the early Brethren that the time of the Second Coming is a fixed date. Therefore, if we, who have the opportunity now to establish this Zion society, and can't do it, then He will find somebody who can. He is going to raise up people who will. He won't come until there are a people prepared to receive Him. If He comes as Lord of Lords and King of Kings, He has to have a group of people on Earth that are referred to as lords, kings, queens, priests, and priestesses in order to receive Him.

Student 3: Does that mean members of the Church of the Firstborn?

Mike: That means that a Zion person, a person who has risen up and attained that status, is a person who has been able to stand in the presence of the Lord. It's going to come to that point. But eventually, in the Millennium everybody's going to be in His presence. It's a place where everyone will know the Lord because everybody in the Millennium will be enjoying the *Second Comforter* experience. However, it's a unique opportunity for those who are here within the veil at this time, while the earth is preparing for these changes, to rise up and attain that status before the Second Coming; to be that group of people that the Lord can come to personally. When you get enough of those kinds of people that the Lord comes to personally, they will then form a group or society, and He comes to that society of people. At that point, we'll have a call come out from the president of the church (I assume) for those people to gather and begin the process of building this New Jerusalem, but it has to be here before He comes. I feel that right now, there is a spirit of preparation hovering over the Latter-day Saints, for men and women to rise up to this ideal and attain this stature before the Lord. You can't do it without tremendous adversity, though. Those who come into the presence of the Lord in this life and have that personal audience with Him, are people who have been tried and tested to the maximum. Because, if you have that experience, brothers and sisters, and if you sin against it, the condemnation is tremendous. It's tremendous. If you rise up and receive a fullness of the Melchizedek Priesthood and then turn against that, you become a son of perdition, and the Lord's not here to cause His children to fail. He's here to exalt people, not to damn them. So, the only way He can tell if you're to be a part of that society and if He can trust you is to put you in the depths of these trials and tribulations, and then you come through those refined as gold.

As a matter of fact, at this point in my life, I have a different view of the tribulations of the last days. We all know what's coming. You can read the scriptures. If you go to *Doctrine and Covenants* section 29, section 88, section 101, and section 45 where each one talks about the great signs and upheavals prior to the Second Coming. I used to think that those were experiences that took place because of man's wickedness and the anger and vengeance of God. I now have a different view on that. I have the view that these very things, these upheavals, are provided so that those who are foreordained to become members of the Church of the Firstborn can go through these trials. Through that process, they can become sanctified, transformed, purified, and cleansed from all sin so they can stand in the presence of God and enjoy that company. I believe that's the primary purpose of the great upheavals in the latter days.

Student 1: Maybe, it's both.

Mike: Maybe it is both! There's no question about it. In the scriptures, He talks about a day of vengeance, where He takes vengeance upon the ungodly, and the wicked are burned to stubble, etc., etc. But, for those who are foreordained for something greater, these experiences provide the ground for that to take place. So, that's a whole different way of looking at these things.

Let's look at a couple of scriptures. The scriptures talk about these kinds of things. Does somebody want to read that for us? 2 Nephi 2, verses 1 and 2.

Student 3:

> *And now, Jacob, I speak unto you: Thou art my firstborn in the days my tribulation in the wilderness. And behold, in thy childhood thou hast* **suffered afflictions** *and much* **sorrow**, *because of the* **rudeness** *of thy brethren.*
>
> *[2]***Nevertheless***, Jacob, my firstborn in the wilderness, thou knowest the greatness of God; and he shall consecrate thine afflictions for thy* **gain**.

Mike: Okay. So, let's look closely at that, and you'll see four words that are mentioned; *suffered, afflictions, sorrow, and rudeness.* Those are all opposition words. They are all words that pertain to a telestial world. Now, look at verse 2. *Nevertheless,* means "in spite of." He's saying, "In spite of these four things, you know the goodness and greatness of God *and he shall consecrate thine afflictions for thy* **gain**." So, all of the sorrow, all the suffering, all of the afflictions, and the rudeness that you experience in the telestial world are designed to give you spiritual, eternal *gain.* That's what they're designed to do.

Now, let's look at another one. Let's go to section 98 of the *Doctrine and Covenants*. Section 98 was at a time when the Latter-day Saints were being driven out of Missouri. Some of them have been murdered, some of the sisters have been raped, children have been killed, and their property has been burned and stolen. They were driven right out of the country across the river right into to another county. Each step they took drove them further and further away from Independence, Jackson County, Missouri, which was to be the place of the New Jerusalem. We understand the background now, so go to *Doctrine and Covenants* 98, verses 1 through 3. This is a sad time for the Latter-day Saints:

> *Verily I say unto you my friends,* **fear not***, let your hearts be* **comforted***; yea,* **rejoice** *evermore, and in*

*everything **give thanks**;*

*[2]**Waiting patiently** on the Lord, for your prayers have entered into the ears of the Lord of Sabaoth, and are **recorded** with this **seal and testament** – the Lord **hath sworn** and **decreed** that they shall be granted.*

*[3]Therefore, he giveth us this **promise** unto you, with an immutable covenant that they should be fulfilled; and all things wherewith you have been afflicted shall work together **for your good**, and to my name's glory, saith the Lord.*

Now, there are five things the Lord tells us to do in the midst of adversity. Look at what it says. Don't be afraid, be comforted, rejoice evermore, give thanks for everything, and wait patiently. Now, look in verse 2 at the words he uses to seal upon us blessings in the midst of adversity. He says these things are *recorded* with; a *seal*, a *testament*, hath *sworn and decreed* and **promised**. Those are all words that show that if we will fear not, be comforted, rejoice evermore, give thanks in everything, and wait patiently on the Lord, then the Lord has five words to describe *"all things wherewith you have been afflicted shall work together **for your good**, and to my name's glory, saith the Lord."* I've written in a little note on my scriptures, "our trials become sacred ground." When the trial occurs, if you're faithfully involved, where you are, the time that you are, and the place that you are, become sacred ground, even if your trial results in the shedding of your own blood. **Sacred ground.** Comments? Does that sound okay? Did you catch those words there? See how the Lord's spells that out?

Let's go to the one that's most famous. Let's go to section 121 in the *Doctrine and Covenants*. It's interesting that when the Lord talks about blessings for adversity in the scriptures, it's usually at a time when the person to whom He's referring is in the midst of his deepest darkest distress. You saw that in section 98. The Lord's great promises concerning trials and tribulations came at a time when the Latter-day Saints were being driven from pillar to post. They had already been driven out of New York. They'd been driven out of Ohio to Missouri. They're going to be driven out of Missouri into Nauvoo, Illinois and eventually out of Illinois and right out of the United States. And in each one of these cases, the Latter-day Saints are experiencing great trials and great tribulations.

Section 121:1-6 is in the Liberty Jail. The first six verses are a prayer where Joseph is crying out to the Lord because of the adversity and the afflictions of his people. Look at verse 3, talking about the people:

> *Yea, O Lord, how long shall they suffer these wrongs and unlawful oppressions, before thine heart shall be softened toward them, and thy bowels be moved with compassion toward them?*

So you see, this prayer asks, how long are the Latter-day Saints going to suffer? Now, let's look at the answer in verse 7 and 8. Does someone want to read that for us?

Student 1:

> *My son, peace be unto thy soul; thine adversity and thine afflictions shall be but a small moment;*
> *[8]And then, **if** thou endure it well, God shall exalt thee on high; thou shalt triumph over all thy foes.*

Mike: Now, there's a great principle! Let's look and see what we can learn there. *"Peace be unto thy soul; and adversity and afflictions shall be but a small moment."* What's the principle to learn from that verse when we're in the midst of suffering from trial and adversity? What's to be learned there?

Student 3: It will pass.

Mike: Yes. All of it is temporary. You live in a temporary world. Everything in this world is temporary. Everything has beginnings and endings. Over in James 4:7, the half-brother of Jesus Christ, James the apostle says, *"Resist the devil, and he will flee from you."* Even the dark ones, the evil ones, don't have any staying

√ power. If they can't get you within their time-frame, they back off, go away and try to attack you from another angle. So, you resist, and he will flee. Everything has an end to it. Think about this for a minute. Think back in your life when you were severely tried. Just kind of go back and find someplace in your life where things were dark, and as a friend of mine says, "You were up to your eyebrows in alligators." Now, for the sake of our discussion, we'll assume that it's over and you're no longer in that circumstance. When you look back on it after it's over, does it ever seem as bad as when you were in it?

Student 1: No.

Mike: And I would answer the same. Looking back at my life, things don't seem as bad now, as they did when I was up to my eyeballs in it. It's at best, temporary and will end.

Now, look at verse 8. The big word in verse 8 is only two letters long, **IF**, and I have that circled. **IF** is a small word with a big meaning, *"If thou endure it well."* See, the indication is that you're going to endure it no matter what. I have to chuckle at members of the church because I've done this all my life. We say, the first principles of ordinances of the gospel are; faith in the Lord Jesus Christ, repentance, baptism by immersion, the laying on of hands for the gift of the Holy Ghost, and what's the 5th one? Endure to the end, right? That's **incomplete** doctrine. Enduring to the end is **incomplete** doctrine. Why? It's because, of course, we're all going to endure to the end. That simply means that you are going to live until you die. Everybody's going to live until they die, so everyone is going to endure to the end. The end is the end of your mortal life. Everybody's going to do that. What's the big deal? We need to change that phrase and say that the fifth principle is *to endure to the end in righteousness*; not just endure. You need to add that in there, otherwise, it just means that you'll be alive until you die and there's no meaning to that. There's no depth in that. So, it comes out, *"if thou endure it well, God shall exalt thee on high; thou shalt triumph over all thy foes."* And the last foe is death. It is physical and spiritual death.

So, your adversities, brothers and sisters, can do one of two things to you depending on how you endure it. You can either endure it well or not endure it well. But, you are going to endure it because you're going to be in it until you're out of it. It's either going to be one of two things; it's either going to make you **bitter**, or it's going to make you **better**. You're in control of the lesson you can learn and the experience you can derive from the adversity and trial that you pass through. And remember what Brigham Young said, *"Some of these trials are ordained ordeals that are specifically designed to move you into the Church of the Firstborn and give you full membership in that Zion society."* It's up to you. So, how are you going to do this and what's the purpose of our lesson tonight? The purpose is for us to take a different look at adversity, trial, opposition, and resistance and develop a restored latter day doctrinal view of it which helps us so that when we're in it, we endure it well. That's the whole purpose. Because, if you don't endure it well, and it a makes you bitter instead of better, what's the purpose of it? What was gained?

Student 3: Nothing.

Mike: Nothing was gained. So, if nothing is gained from the experience, you leave this world traveling into the next world, the world to come, without an advantage. We don't want to do that. You want to move from this world into the next world with an advantage.

Let's look at one more, let's look at *Doctrine and Covenants* section 122. Joseph Smith is still in Liberty Jail. Liberty Jail for Joseph Smith was the trial of his faith. Did you know that? Every person who rises up and attains the Zion of Heaven has an encounter with the Lord and knows the Lord in a unique and intimate way; you don't know about Him, but you know Him. Every person that does that has to travel this path. You can't circumvent this. So, the greater the glory, the greater the experience, the greater the encounter, the greater the opposition, the greater the adversity, and one goes with the other. One travels the same path. You're on the same path as our ancient fathers; Abraham, Isaac, and Jacob; who are now gods and sit upon thrones. (See section 132) It's the same path, the very same path. The first six verses of section 122 talk about the tribulations that Joseph Smith travailed. Verse 7 is kind of a capstone. It builds to a crescendo:

> *And if thou shouldest be cast into the pit, or into the hands of murderers, and the sentence of death passed upon thee; if thou be cast into the deep; if the billowing surge conspire against thee; if fierce winds become thine enemy; if the heavens gather blackness, and all the elements combine to hedge up the way; and above all, if the very jaws of hell shall gape open the mouth wide after thee, know thou, my son, that all these things shall **give thee experience**, and shall be **for thy good.**

So, the lesson is that trials and tribulations give us experience and are for our own good.

Now, many experiences are going to come in this world of opposition. Are they going to be good for you? Are you going to learn from them? Are you going to gain from them? Are they going to make you better? Will they make you bitter? **You** determine that. Having this view of adversity will help you make the determination that you are going to be better as a result of this, and not be bitter. That's the whole purpose of this knowledge. People who end up shaking their fists at God because of the things they suffer don't have access to this knowledge. You and I do. So, we should have a better view, and as a result, be able to **endure things well**. And, as you come out of the experience, it ends up being for your good.

Go to Section 11, verse 7 in the *Doctrine and Covenants* and let me show you something. Experience is the mother of wisdom. Wisdom is a gem desired by all who seek godhood. Now, remember that wisdom cannot come without experience. So, the **child** of experience can be wisdom, should be wisdom, and it's desirable for it to be wisdom. Now, look what it says:

> *Seek not for riches but for wisdom; and, behold, the mysteries of God shall be unfolded unto you, and then shall you be made rich. Behold, he that hath eternal life is rich.*

"Seek not for riches but for wisdom; and, behold," here's your sequence; if you obtain wisdom; *"the mysteries of God shall be unfolded unto you."* Ok, *"and then,"* meaning after you have attained the mysteries of God, *"then shall you be made rich. Behold he that has eternal life is rich."* What is the end result of opposition? The sequence is experience, wisdom, the mysteries of God, eternal riches and eternal life. That's the sequence. Can I be so bold as to suggest that your greatest wisdom comes from your greatest suffering? I do not believe there is any wisdom to be obtained sitting on a park bench in the sunshine. I believe that wisdom is found in dark, trying, opposing, and resisting situations. That is when wisdom comes. Any thoughts and comments? Does this make sense?

Student 3: It does.

Mike: Let's go back to the idea that there are *bad things that happen to good people*. That's a comment made by people who don't have a knowledge of the restoration doctrines of adversity, opposition, and trial. They don't have the knowledge that we do. So, there are **no** bad things that happen to good people; there is just life. And the trials of life are designed to do what? Yes, make you godly. It's all designed to make you godly. Richard Bushman wrote a book a few years ago called *Joseph Smith: Rough Stone Rolling.* Have any of you read that book?

Student 1: No, never heard of it.

Mike: Okay, the title of that book, is taken from a comment by the Prophet Joseph Smith when he said, *"I'm like a huge, rough stone rolling down the mountainside."* He referred to himself as a huge, rough stone rolling down the mountainside. As that stone rolls down the mountainside, it strikes up against other rough rocks and chips off pieces of the rock. He describes it as;

> Hitting up against priestcrafts, against oppositions, against adversity, against mobs, and violence and being driven, etc. as all hell is breaking off a piece here and there until I become a polished shaft in the quiver of the Almighty.

That polishing comes from striking up against opposing forces, and breaking the rough edges off of you and polishing you, as you go down the hill. Joseph said, "I'm like a rough stone rolling."

Student 1: Did you ever hear the little story of the refiner's fire?

Mike: No, go ahead.

Student 1: Well, I will send it to you.

Mike: Okay.

Student 1: It's about a lady and some others who went on a trip. But, it is talking about something similar like this, you know? It's really nice. I'll send it to you.

Mike: Thank you, I'd like to see it.

As we try to wrap things up a little bit, here is a quote by President Kimball who knew quite a little bit of suffering, disappointment, and circumstances beyond his control. Remember, President Kimball had a lot of physical trials. That raspy little voice of his came as a result of having his vocal cords cut out because of throat cancer. He had to learn to speak again. And his voice became famous among all the Latter-day Saints. It was a reminder of the things that he suffered. He said this in his book *Faith Precedes the Miracle*:

> *Being human, we would expel from our lives physical pain and mental anguish and assure ourselves a continual ease and comfort. But if we were to close the doors upon sorrow and distress, we might be excluding our greatest friends and benefactors. Suffering can make saints of people, as*

they learn patience long-suffering and self-mastery.

One of the greatest friends we can have is physical pain. So, brothers and sisters, where *"much is given much is required."* The Lord wants to see that He can trust you and then He has great blessings for you.

Go to section 121, and let me show you about the day that we live in, as we wind up our discussion. I don't believe I've ever heard this quoted anywhere. We quote the first parts of 121, and we quote verse 40, *"Hence many are called, but few are chosen,"* but here's a part I don't believe I've ever heard quoted in a general conference or taught in a lesson. Let's go to verse 26:

> God shall give unto you knowledge by his Holy Spirit, yea, by the **unspeakable** gift of the Holy Ghost, that has not been revealed since the world was until now;
> [27]Which our forefathers have awaited with anxious expectation to be revealed in the last times, which their minds were pointed to by the angels, as held in reserve for the fulness of their glory;
> [28] A time to come in the which nothing shall be withheld.

If you are scripture students, you should ask yourself a question: why does the Lord refer to the Gift of the Holy Ghost as unspeakable? You should ponder that. This knowledge that he's going to give you through the Holy Spirit and the unspeakable gift of the Holy Ghost *"has not been revealed since the world was until now."* Of course, the date of section 121 is 1839, so there's something that is available to us right now that has never been revealed until now. Look at the next verse. *"Our forefathers,"* think about your ancestors, *"have waited with anxious expectations for this knowledge to be revealed in the last times."* Now, the forefathers are dead. So, they're waiting for something to be revealed that wasn't revealed in their lifetime but will be revealed to their children; *"which their minds were pointed to by* angels." In other words, these forefathers who were dead before this knowledge came upon the earth, had visions and had dreams, and were shown the restoration of this knowledge to their children. They did not personally enjoy it themselves. But, they received promises from the angels and holy beings that this knowledge would be poured about upon their children. And look what it says, *"held in reserve for the fulness of their glory."* So, whatever it is their children are going to receive, which are shown by angels, is necessary for their glory in the eternal heavens. Interesting stuff, *"A time to come in which nothing shall be withheld."* Nothing! This is our day.

I was teaching the High Priest Group today in our class, and we were teaching the lesson by Brother Hunter on receiving help from on high. I told them that we live in a day where things are reserved for us that have never been available ever in the history of the world. They are reserved for us, and we're not tapping into those things that have our name on them. They belong to us, and we are not accessing them because we fail to ask, seek, and knock. Receiving these hidden things that have been held in reserve is conditioned upon you asking. All you have to do is ask, seek, and knock, and the Lord opens up the door for these things. Some of the things that are in there are continued in verse 28:

> *Whether there be one God or many gods, they shall be manifest.*
> *[29]All thrones and dominions, principalities and powers, shall be revealed and set forth upon all who have endured valiantly for the gospel of Jesus Christ.*

And then the last sentence in verse 31 says that all of these things:

> *shall be revealed in the days of the dispensation of the fulness of times.*

That's what's available to us because this is that dispensation.

I would say that there are great events coming upon us with the trials and tribulations that have been prophesied. I'm saying that in a positive way because Mother Earth is being prepared to transition from a telestial to a terrestrial world. She is getting ready to leave this solar system with this sun, and these other eight planets. This earth is being prepared to move back in space closer to the center of this galaxy where it was first created. The next place it will move back to will be a third of the way closer to the center than it is now.

Student 1: Will that only happen when we are done with our responsibilities? Will that happen when we're not ready?

Mike: If you're not qualified to make that transition, you'll be taken from the earth by fire. Your body will die in a fire, and your spirit will go into a prison place where you will not be able to enjoy the terrestrial world that's coming. It's interesting that Lorenzo Snow once heard a man ask the Prophet, Joseph Smith, "Who are you?" Joseph said, *"Noah came before the flood, I come before the fire!"* So, everything that we have here is designed to help us transition from one place to another. We want to make the move with the earth. The earth is a living being, a living breathing soul. It breathes. It's a soul. It has a body and a spirit. It's female. It has a voice. It can speak, and it is an obedient planet. Not all planets are obedient. The one that we are on is obedient. It fulfills the measure of its creation and transgresses not the law. And that law is the law of the Celestial Kingdom. As children of God, we should want to stay with this earth as it cycles back in its upward movement, back toward where it was first created. This is where it will become a celestial world and dwell in the center of this galaxy with other innumerable celestial worlds that have gone through the same process. We need to be able to make the trip.

Student 1: Does that also include the spirits in the spirit world?

Mike: Yes, I've got questions on how that will work, but yes, it would. Eventually, those spirits, in the spiritual world, who are not allowed to live on the earth's face during the terrestrial/ millennial reign, will have to come out of that spirit place, be resurrected and inherit a planet prepared for them, which will be a telestial world.

So yes, although, I'm not sure how that works. They are a part of this earth's probationary state. Even the millennial reign, brothers and sisters, is a probationary state; it's just extended to a higher order. In other words, a probationary state means it's possible for persons to fall. We know that the Millennium is a probationary estate because, toward the end of the Millennium, there will be a war and many, many people fall. The earth is in a probationary state until it dies and is resurrected as a celestial world, and crowned as a celestial world; until that happens, it's in a probationary state. It is just moving from a lower to a higher position.

People don't want to talk about any of the coming tribulations. They say it's *doom and gloom*, which I think is nonsense. It's not *doom and gloom*! We are talking about the transition of a telestial world into a terrestrial world. The whole purpose of these last-days scenarios and trials that the scriptures talk about is to transition from the telestial world into a terrestrial world. We'll be going from a mortal, corrupt, dying place into a place where there will be no more physical death or disease. Those who abide that day on the earth and are able to make that transition are going to be blessed to enjoy one thousand years of the presence of the Son of God in a millennial, terrestrial, translated, not resurrected but translated state. Because the Millennium is in a terrestrial world, it is a translation state. Terrestrial doctrine is translation doctrine; resurrection doctrine is celestial doctrine. One comes before the other. So, here's our review: look at this suffering and opposition with some optimism! It is the very thing that will make you a god. It is the very thing that will qualify you to make the transition from a dying telestial, sick and tired world, into a translated, wonderful world of light where there's no need for a planetary sun. When this earth moves out of this solar system and goes back to wherever its terrestrial abode is for one thousand years, there won't be a sun in the sky. The sun that will light the terrestrial world is the Son of God and His glory. The physical sun that we see in the sky now is a temporary light for the telestial world. We're so far out from the center of that galactic light, which is a bulge of innumerable celestial worlds that the light from the center of the galaxy can't reach us, so we have to have an artificial light that we call the sun. Our sun is a symbol of **the** SON. You see, it's a symbol. So, all truth is circumscribed into one great whole. Everything fits! Does that make sense? Does that feel right?

Our lesson today was on adversity, and the purpose for it and I'm so thankful for this knowledge. I've had some adversity in my life, and so have you, but we're going to have all that we can handle in a coming day, and we're going to need to have this knowledge, which gives us power. Knowledge is power. When you have a knowledge of spiritual things, it bestows upon you spiritual power. That's what it's going to take to get through what's coming. To circumvent and navigate the coming day of adversity, you're going to need all the power that you can get to do it.

Resources:
Nephi 11
Discourses of Brigham Young, page 345 Neal Maxwell
D&C 45
D&C 29
D&C 88
D&C 98:1-3
D&C 101
2 Nephi 2
D&C 121
D&C 122:7
D&C 11
Faith Precedes the Miracle, Kimball

Chapter Four
Podcast 004 Mighty Prayer and Personal Revelation

I want to talk about prayer and personal revelation. Reading in the *Joseph Smith Translation* of Matthew chapter 24; the word that comes up over and over that the Savior uses is *deceive*. I think we all agree that we are living in an age of the world where deception is rampant. How do we avoid deception? How can we discern right from wrong? How can we tell light from darkness, especially when it comes to receiving revelations? How do we know that the revelations we are receiving are coming from the right source? How do we discern that our thoughts are coming from the right source? In section 8, verse 2 of the *Doctrine and Covenants*, the Lord comes out and says:

> *Yea, behold, I will tell you in your mind and in your heart, by the Holy Ghost, which shall come upon you and which shall dwell in your heart.*
> *[3]Now, behold, this is the spirit of revelation...*

So, the Lord says that when He speaks to us, He speaks to our **mind** in the form of thoughts and to our **heart** in the form of feelings. And yet, how can you tell if those are coming from the Holy Ghost, or if they're coming from a deceptive source; the devil as an angel of light, for example?

I want to start out tonight by reciting a statement from the Prophet Joseph Smith. This is the *Doctrinal History of the Church*, volume 4, page 587, and was given while the Saints were in the

Kirtland Temple era. There was a lot of confusion about various spirits and spiritual phenomena that were deceiving the Saints. I think the one we're most familiar with is the one of Hiram Page where he had a stone and was receiving revelation through the stone for the Church. The Prophet Joseph Smith had to correct him personally, and these kinds of things happened several times throughout the early history of the Church. This is about the same time that section 50 of the *Doctrine and Covenants* was given. In the first part of section 50, it talks about false spirits that have gone abroad in the earth. So, the Prophet Joseph Smith asked a couple of questions:

> *Who can describe an angel of light? If Satan should appear as one in glory, who can tell his color, his signs, his appearance, his glory, or what is the manner of his manifestation?*

He's asking, "What if you were to have an angel of the devil appear to you as an angel of light? How can you tell the difference?" For example, Korihor in Alma 30 was led astray and led a good portion of the Zoramites and others astray. He was deceived. Going on, the Prophet Joseph Smith says:

> *Who can drag into daylight and develop the hidden mysteries of the false spirits that so frequently are made manifest among the Latter-day Saints?*

Now, right there is a warning for us. Even though this occurred in the Kirtland Temple period, I submit that deception has not decreased since that time. If anything, it's become more refined and has increased to where Latter-day Saints now, must be even more diligent in trying to decide if this is coming from the right source or from the wrong source. The prophet goes on and says:

> *We answer that no man can do this without the priesthood and having a knowledge of the **laws** by which spirits are governed.*

Isn't that interesting? If you're going to be able to detect Satan appearing as an angel of light, you have to have a knowledge of the **laws** that govern the priesthood and the spirits that are abroad on the earth. Then he says:

> *For no man knows the things of God but by the spirit of God, so no man knows the spirit of the devil and his power of influence, but by possessing*

intelligence, which is more than human, and having unfolded through the medium of the priesthood, the mysteries and operations of his, Satan's, devices.

Student 4: Are you quoting page 587?

Mike: Yes, the *Doctrinal History of the Church*. It's also in the *Teachings of the Prophet Joseph Smith*. Now, look at this next quote from Joseph Smith. There are eight things here, and I want you to ask yourselves these questions as I read it. Are these things godly, or ungodly? Are they light, or are they dark? He goes on and says:

Without knowing [1] the angelic form; [2] the sanctified look; [3] and gesture, the sanctified gesture; [4] and the zeal, which is frequently manifested by him for the glory of God; together with a [5] prophetic spirit, [6] the gracious influence; [7] the godly appearance; and [8] the holy garb; which are characteristic of his proceedings and his mysterious windings.

Now, if you look at those eight things and ask yourself if they are they godly or ungodly, most of us would say they are godly. And yet, the prophet is using these eight things to describe an angel from the dark side appearing as an angel of light. Isn't that interesting? So again, those eight things are angelic form, sanctified look, sanctified gesture, zeal, gracious influence, prophetic spirit, godly appearance and holy garb, or clothing. Now, he goes on, and he says this. And this I'd double underline:

*A man must have the **discerning of spirits** before he can drag into daylight this hellish influence and unfold it unto the world in all of its soul destroying, diabolical, and horrid colors.*

Do you see what novices we are if we don't have divine help? The thing we need to realize about being in this telestial schoolroom, with the opposition we have here in the form of dark spirits, devils, and unclean spirits is: we're helpless by ourselves.

Student 4: We are oblivious.

Mike: And we ARE oblivious.

Student 4: We are oblivious, and we don't talk about it. We just think there are bad things going around us, but we're really being attacked. I have to go back to when you talked to me in July last year, and I had the definite impression that I need to learn more about this.

Mike: And so did I.

Student 4: Yeah, you told me that.

Mike: Notice the keywords here: **priesthood** and knowledge of **laws** which govern these spirits. Now, that right there is an interesting statement. Let me finish this little quote from the Prophet Joseph Smith:

> *Nothing is a greater injury to the children of men*
> *than to be under the influence of a false spirit when*
> *they think they have the spirit of the Lord.*

Can you think of anything that would be more damning than that?

Student 4: We've probably been there, Mike. You and I have probably been there.

Mike: Probably.

Student 4: We probably thought we were doing the right thing, but we were amiss.

Mike: One of the gifts of the Spirit is the gift of the *discerning of spirits*. There are two different gifts that sometimes we think are one and the same. One is the *gift of discernment*, and the other is a separate gift, the *discerning of spirits*. I feel that if the Savior warns us about great deception in our day, both in and out of the Church, it will behoove us to make it a matter of prayer. We should pray for this great gift of the discerning of spirits so that we can know for a surety that the revelations we are seeking are coming from the right source. Isn't it interesting that the Lord gives us a commandment to seek His face continually and to live in a state of personal revelation? Yet, at the same time, we have the adversary who can so closely counterfeit and copy the real thing. By ourselves, without this knowledge and priesthood keys and the keys that govern the spirits, we don't stand a chance! With that in mind, I've been looking for some keys on how to tell, when receiving revelation, whether it's coming from the Holy Ghost/Holy Spirit or from an alternate source. We're not going to discuss "your own voice" or "the voice of your mind" in this lesson. We'll only talk about the two voices, the voices of light and the voices of darkness.

Let's go over to section 50 of the *Doctrine and Covenants* and look at a couple of things there. In the section heading the Lord gives us some keys:

> *The Prophet states that some of the elders did not understand the manifestations of different spirits abroad in the earth,*

And further on in the heading:

> *So-called spiritual phenomena were not uncommon among the members, some of whom claimed to be receiving visions and revelations.*

And I have no doubt in my mind that they were. So, the question comes up, what is the source? That's the question: how can you tell the source? Well, I can tell you one answer you can find, if you go to section 50: 23. We can get one key:

> *And that which doth not **edify** is not of God, and is darkness.*

When I looked it up in Webster's 1828 dictionary, which is the dictionary that Joseph would've had; the word *edify* means, "to build, to illuminate, to enlighten, to instruct, especially in spiritual things."

Student 4: What's the definition in today's dictionary?

Mike: I didn't look up today's definition. I always look in the 1828 dictionary. I always keep that icon on my app so when I'm reading the scriptures I can go to the dictionary that Joseph had access to.

Student 4: Where do you find that?

Mike: You just look for the Webster's 1828 dictionary in your iTunes store and click on it. It's a free dictionary and doesn't cost anything.

Also, edification always moves you toward improvement of a spiritual nature. Edify has the same root word as edifice, which is a sacred building; i.e. a temple. It's tied in conjunction with construction or building something that moves you, illuminates you, enlightens you, and moves you toward spiritual improvement. That's a good word to look at; edify. That's a good one.

I have another quote here by the Prophet Joseph Smith that I thought was really good. It's in the *Teachings of the Prophet Joseph Smith* on page 98. Several years after the Prophet Joseph Smith was killed, he appeared to President Brigham Young, and he said this:

*Tell the people to keep the spirit of the Lord and it will lead them right. The still small voice, will teach you what to do and where to go. Tell the brethren to keep their hearts open so that when the Holy Ghost comes to their hearts, they will be able to receive it. They can tell the Spirit of the Lord from all other spirits. It will whisper **peace** and **joy** to their souls. Their whole desire will be **to do good**. If they follow the spirit of the Lord, they will go right.*

So, what have we got thus far? We've got words like edification, peace, joy, and your whole desire will be to do good.

This last week I was reading in the very back of the *Joseph Smith-History*, an account written by Oliver Cowdery, about the day that John the Baptist appeared to Joseph and Oliver and conferred the Aaronic Priesthood. It's the very last paragraph. I saw some things that were amazing. I want to read this to you, he says:

*I shall not attempt to paint to you the feelings of this heart, nor the majestic beauty and glory which surrounded us on this occasion; but you will believe me when I say, that earth, nor men, with the eloquence of time, cannot begin to clothe language in as interesting and sublime a manner as this holy personage. No; nor has this earth power to give the **joy**, to bestow the **peace**, or comprehend the **wisdom** which was contained in each sentence as they were delivered by the power of the Holy Spirit! Man may deceive his fellow-men, deception may follow deception, and the children of the wicked one may have power to seduce the foolish and untaught, till naught but fiction feeds the many, and the fruit of falsehood carries in its current the giddy to the grave; but one touch with the finger of his love, yes, one ray of glory from the upper world, or one word from the mouth of the Savior, from the bosom of eternity, strikes it all into insignificance, and blots it forever from my mind.*

So, here we have some keys from Joseph Smith, Oliver Cowdery, and from the Lord that there are things that apparently the devil cannot counterfeit or duplicate. Whenever he speaks, there is no edification because the Lord bluntly comes out and says that there's no edification that comes from the darkside. So, (1) to be edified, (2) there is joy, (3) there is peace, and (4) there is wisdom that comes as a result of the Holy Spirit whispering to us.

Student 6: When we are led by the Spirit, we also will feel corrected by the Spirit, and it leads us to forgive and repent. In my mind, the evil one would never lead us there. See what I am saying? I don't think he would lead us to forgiveness, repentance, and those types of things.

Mike: I agree with that. Now, those of us who have been endowed in the temple have additional tools at our disposal to discern a false messenger from a true messenger. In the Garden of Eden, Adam received a token and a sign that he uses in the lone and dreary world, in the telestial world, to detect true from false messengers. How do you detect an angel of darkness from the angel of light? If you look in *Doctrine and Covenants* section 129, what it says is not complete enough to do the job because it is revealed in its entirety in the Endowment Session. Even though the date of Section 129 is February 9, 1843, and even though the temple wasn't complete at this point, the Endowment Session, with that token and sign, was revealed by the Prophet Joseph Smith in May of 1842. It had been given in the Joseph Smith Brick Store, and there is a record that some parts of the Endowment were given in the Mansion House and in other places. So, how do you detect an angel of darkness from the angel of light? Section 129, verse 8 says that if you have a person appear to you:

> *If it be the devil as an angel of light, when you ask*
> *him to shake hands he will offer you his hand, and*
> *you will not feel anything; you may therefore detect*
> *him.*

Now, what we've received in the temple completes that, and I don't think we can talk anymore about it. But, what is taught in the temple gives us a more a complete way of discerning darkness from light. If I were in a position where I had a person standing in my room, wrapped in light, 3 feet off the ground, telling me he was an angel sent from the presence of God, I would rehearse to him and do exactly what I've been taught as a part of the Temple Endowment. In other words, section 129 does not give me enough information. I would want to do everything that I've been taught in the temple; use every word, use every motion, use everything to discern him and detect him and send him on his way. Comments or questions on that?

Student 4: It's pretty cut and dry. You just have to learn it and be familiar with it so that when the time comes, you can do it.

Mike: Yes. It would behoove those of us who are temple attendees to go ahead and memorize certain parts of the temple ceremony and commit those things to memory. This is my opinion. I think that as we move down through the corridors of time closer to the coming of the Lord, this deception will become so profound that if you don't have what Joseph was talking about, the priesthood and a knowledge of the laws that govern these spirits, I just don't know how we will make it successfully on our journey.

Student 6: Don't you think that when we receive something like that, we would have peace and joy? We would not have peace and joy if it weren't from the Lord. It's the feeling of peace and joy that we feel when we have this happen, that makes us want to go and do everything right and good, like what you were talking about earlier.

Mike: I agree with that. That's why I think one of the things that are necessary, that Joseph keeps mentioning over and over, to keep from being deceived is that you have to have knowledge. Knowledge is the key that we need to have possession of.

Student 6: So, the peace and joy you're talking about; we need more than peace and joy?

Mike: Peace, and joy, and desire to do good. Your whole desire will be to do good to your fellow man. Wisdom and edification are the words that we zoned in on tonight. Let's go over to *Doctrine and Covenants* 11 and see what the Lord says. One of those things that he said is that you need to have wisdom beyond your own ability when the Lord sends a true messenger. Verse 7:

> *Seek not for riches but for wisdom; and, behold, the mysteries of God shall be unfolded unto you, and then shall you be made rich. Behold, he that hath eternal life is rich.*

Do you see what follows after obtaining wisdom from the Lord? The mysteries of God are unfolded to you. It's a sequence. I think that when we guys get married, with our wives, we have a built-in source of wisdom because, in the scriptures, wisdom is always female. And I believe that's the core central virtue of women: they are wisdom. Men seek after knowledge and women have the ability to dispense wisdom that comes as a part of their core values. So, a man with a good woman, if he relies on her and treats her the way he should, has access to some godly wisdom within the marriage relationship.

Student 4: We were reading out of *Triumph of Zion* coming down here today. In chapter 9, 'The Final Scene,' it talks about the importance of women and the priesthood, and women and the temple, and it says exactly what you just said. Women have that wisdom and knowledge and expertise. So, they carry all that information, and the wife becomes the better source for exaltation when we work together than when we work separately.

Mike: That's a good comment! If you look into the scriptures and were to pick a story that illustrates wisdom, what would be?

Student 6: Adam and Eve.

Mike: Adam and Eve is one. I was thinking of another one in the *Old Testament*; the wisdom of who? Solomon, right? Remember Solomon? Did you ever stop to think why he was so wise? He had 300 wives and 700 concubines!

Students: Ha-ha-ha!

Mike: That's a joke.

Let's talk for a few minutes about prayer, and we will wrap it all up. This last week I had a chance to teach the High Priest Group in our ward. We were talking about prayer and revelation. As we were chatting about that, I told them that there are different layers and different steps involved in every principle of the gospel. Everything in the gospel is moving us from where we are at a lower place and striving to move stair step-by-stair step to something higher. You take any concept, any principle of the gospel, and you'll find if you look for it, that everything moves upward by degrees. I believe it's the same in prayer. I really tapped into this when I was on my mission. Margie and I were on a mission in New Jersey, and this is where this started formulating in our minds a little bit, and we even started to practice some of the things we were learning. And I felt for some time that the prayer that we vocalize in the Church is a primary prayer, a basic, elementary, fundamental form of prayer. We know that the missionaries are going to teach investigators at the end of the first discussion how to pray because most people don't have an understanding even of this fundamental, foundational method of prayer. You fold your arms, close your eyes, bow your head, and then you address your Heavenly Father. You thank Him for the things that you enjoy, ask Him for the things you need, and then you close your prayer in the name of Jesus Christ. That's foundational. It's appropriate, and it has its place, but there's something else in the scriptures. Go with me over to 2 Nephi chapter 4. This is where I started to see these things and as I focused on this, I found it everywhere. It's one of those situations where you open the door and all of a sudden you understand and say, "My gosh! How did I miss all of this?" Here are some of the blessings that Nephi says in verse 21:

> *He hath filled me with his love, even unto the consuming of my flesh.*
> *[22]He hath confounded mine enemies, unto the causing of them to quake before me.*
> *[23]Behold, he hath heard my cry by day, and he hath given me knowledge by visions in the nighttime.*
> *[24]And by day have I waxed bold in **mighty** prayer before him; yea, my voice have I sent up on high; and angels came down and ministered unto me.*

I want you to notice the blessings that come to him. Nephi is talking about an order of prayer that is above what most of us are tapping into. He calls it **mighty prayer**. Look what comes as a result of mighty prayer: knowledge by visions in the nighttime and angels coming down and ministering to him. Look at verse 25:

> *[25]And upon the wings of his Spirit hath my body been carried away upon exceedingly high mountains. And mine eyes have beheld great things, yea, even too great for man; therefore I was bidden that I should not write them.*

I take that literally. I don't think that it is symbolic. I believe he was physically moved by the Spirit of the Lord from one place to another. See all of these things that have happened as a result? And right in the middle of all these tremendous things is this concept, *"by day have I waxed bold in **mighty** prayer before him."* That's your key. What is this mighty prayer? What is the difference between the prayer that we speak at a foundational level and this concept of a higher order which literally brings down the powers of heaven? Do you have any thoughts on that?

Student 6: Isn't it the power of the Holy Ghost that helps us to ask and know what to say? Isn't that where we get that mighty prayer so that we can connect in ways that we couldn't otherwise?

Mike: I agree with you. It is tied in with the Holy Ghost, but here's a key that we miss. In verse 23 and 24 he says, *"He hath given me knowledge by visions in the night-time. And by day have I waxed bold in mighty prayer."* Notice the hour of his prayers; the mighty prayer is a concept practiced during the day. Now, let's go on over to 3 Nephi chapter 19, and get some feelings for this. If you're looking for a prayer that rends the veil and that calls down the powers of heaven, you're not going to do it with foundational beginning prayer. We have got to rise up to a higher order of things. You can really see this order in 3 Nephi 19. This is the second day that the Savior appears to these Nephites. The first day there were 2,500 people, and they stayed up all night long noising abroad that He was going to come the next day, so there's no telling how many thousands of people were at the Bountiful temple place on the second day. The disciples had taken the congregation, divided them into 12 groups and each one of them presided over their group. They all knelt down and prayed. Verse 6:

> And the twelve did teach the multitude; and behold, they did cause that the multitude should kneel down upon the face of the earth, and should pray unto the Father in the name of Jesus.
>
> [7]And the disciples did pray unto the Father also in the name of Jesus. And it came to pass that they arose and ministered unto the people.
>
> [8]And when they had ministered those same words which Jesus had spoken– nothing varying from the words which Jesus had spoken–behold, they knelt again and prayed to the Father in the name of Jesus.

Now, this ties into what you were saying, [student]. If I had spent a day with the Savior and was now a witness of His physical, bodily resurrection as those 2,500 were that day, and I had touched His hands, heard Him teach, and knew He was coming back the next day; what would I be praying for?

Student 6: To hear Him—to absolutely **hear** Him!

Mike: Okay, well, here's the interesting thing. Look at verse 9 for the key.

> *And they did pray for that which they most desired; and they desired that the Holy Ghost should be given unto them.*

Now, all of these people are members of the Church. You had to be among the more righteous part of the people to even survive the holocaust that took place over there in chapters 8, 9, and 10. So, these people are all members of the Church. They are already baptized members of the Church.

Student 6: In last week's class, I was trying to get this verbalized; didn't you say that when Jesus comes, the atmosphere of Mother Earth gets stressed. Something like that. What did you say?

Mike: Whenever you have a glorified, resurrected, and exalted being come into a telestial sphere, nature is going to react to that. I don't know if it's going to be rejoicing or mourning. When this whole thing started to take place in 3 Nephi, and there were earthquakes, volcanoes, and tidal waves, there were people who said, "The God of nature suffers." That concept of the earth reacting to the presence of an exalted, glorified being that comes into a telestial sphere is bound to cause some kind of reaction. But, they're praying for the thing they desire the most, the Holy Ghost. These people have already been baptized; they've already received the Holy Ghost. And if you read about these twelve apostles, they were also raising the dead. Timothy was raised from the dead. Nephi raised his brother. They had priesthood power. These are people who are righteous, and yet what are they praying for at the beginning of the second day? The thing that they desired most was the Holy Ghost. I asked myself the question, "What is it that they know about this topic that I don't?" Because that's probably not the thing, I would be praying for and yet, they were. We won't go there right now, but in section 121 the Lord refers to the **unspeakable** gift of the Holy Ghost, so, somehow the Holy Ghost is tied in with this higher order of **mighty prayer**.

Let's go back to 3 Nephi 19:24 where we'll find a couple of clues:

*And it came to pass that when Jesus had thus prayed unto the Father, he came unto his disciples, and behold, they did still continue, **without ceasing**, to pray unto him; and they **did not multiply many words**, for **it was given unto them what they should pray**, and they were filled with desire.*

Pray **without ceasing** is one key. **Not multiplying many words** is another key. And the heart of it is that *it was given unto them what they should pray*. So now, we start to see that this mighty prayer is a prayer that is dictated, guided, and the very words of the prayer come through revelation. You are so involved and so in tune with the Spirit that the Lord tells you what to say and what to pray for. You don't *multiply many words*, or in other words, there are no vain repetitious sentences, you don't consume your prayer upon your lusts, and you don't ask amiss. This prayer is pure revelation.

The next verse says that as a result of that prayer, the people were turned white in their countenance and they were as white as the garments of Jesus. There could be nothing on earth that was as white as these people were. And then verse 28 the Lord comes out and says:

Father, I thank thee that thou hast purified those whom I have chosen, because of their faith, and I pray for them, and also for them who shall believe on their words, that they may be purified in me, through faith on their words, even as they are purified in me.

This whole process of mighty prayer is a sanctifying, purifying, cleansing type of prayer. When you find yourself in this type of a prayer-order (that's what I call it, a prayer-order) you are literally changed. It changes your very nature. You're sanctified, cleansed, purified, and transformed. So, what do we need to do? Let's look at a couple of examples. Look at Enos, Jacob's boy, for example.
Student 6: Now that's a Zion people! They were a Zion people.
Mike: They were. They had risen up to that level. Listen to what Enos says...
Student 4: I have a question before you start that. Of all these people who were there when the Savior appeared, I don't remember seeing where some of them were translated, or taken up. Any ideas about that?

Mike: Say that again.

Student 4: Were these people translated?

Mike: You know, I don't know. I don't know that they were. I know that three of them are going to be. I don't know if others were. But it is possible for you to have the powers of translation without having undergone that change. It's possible for you to have some of those powers without the actual change, a temporary type thing.

Student 6: "Have the power," what does that mean?

Mike: They have the power over the elements of the earth; the power over time and space; the power to be transported from one place to another; to not to be restricted by the physical body in the telestial world; they kind of rise above that.

Student 4: These people lived in harmony and love for 200 years, right?

Mike: Right.

Student 4: So, is this maybe one of the unspeakable things that they didn't talk about? About how they were able to overcome these things and maybe it's none of our business that they were translated? It's just more that they were so valiant because it was 200 years before they started falling away? What really took place in those 200 years?

Mike: Yes, that's a great question. I don't know. The only ones that we know about in that whole Nephite congregation were the three disciples that were actually caught up into heaven and underwent some kind of physical change. When they came back, they weren't telestial mortals anymore.

Student 4: When they come by here, I'll ask them!

Mike: Yeah, ha-ha-ha! So, here in Enos 1:3 is one more example, Enos the son of Jacob, says:

> Behold, I went to hunt beasts in the forests; and the words which I had often heard my father speak concerning eternal life, and the joy of the saints, sunk deep into my heart.
>
> [4]And my soul hungered; and I kneeled down before my Maker, and I cried unto him in **mighty prayer** and supplication for mine own soul; and all the day long did I cry unto him; yea, and when the

night came I did still raise my voice high that it reached the heavens.

You see, that's mighty prayer! I don't think it has to do so much with the amount of time praying as much as it was that he is able to tap into a higher order of prayer by using some keys and knowledge.

Student 4: We just talked about it. It would be given unto him what to say. Don't you think maybe that's what was happening, that it was given unto him additional things to pray for? Because, here he is: his dad is a prophet and sees the last days, his dad's brother is a prophet and sees the last days, and here Enos comes along and maybe has some unbelief, so he was going into this grove, or wherever it was, and that began. And because of the findings of his fathers, I felt he was given utterance about what to say and what to do to find himself and overcome the natural man. Does that make sense?

Mike: It does. Let's go to the *Bible* dictionary and look under *prayer* to study a couple of other things. There is some great information there on how to tap into this mighty prayer. First of all, let me just say that there is a difference when the scriptures say, "Pray unto the Lord," versus, "Cry unto the Lord." Every time you hear *mighty prayer*, the word *cry* is there. That's something to ponder. What does it mean to **cry** unto the Lord, versus **pray** unto the Lord? I think there's a secret there, a little mystery that we can uncover. In the *Bible* dictionary, it also talks about posture. So, then ask yourself a question, is posture an important part of your prayers? If you want to move into a higher order of prayer, does posture have anything to do with that? If you read under *prayer* in the *Bible* dictionary, you'll find several interesting things. For example, anciently they prayed in three different posture positions: standing, kneeling, and prostrate upon the ground, always with outstretched arms and hands, always! Now, if you look at us, in our form, if body language means anything, and you have to decide if it does; we fold our arms. Folding arms is a closed position, versus open arms. You don't want to close-out, you want to open-up and **receive**. The key word there is to receive. You want to stretch out and rise up to something higher, something different. Remember the old saying, "If you always do what you've always done, you always get what you've always got." So, if we are willing to experiment and try something different, even if we don't know what we're doing, we may tap into something significant.

Student 6: Prostrate was when they totally lay out on their stomach on the ground.

Mike: Face on the ground.

Student 6: Yes, face down.

Mike: And stretched out, with their arms opened up. Interestingly, if you read the accounts of the Savior in Gethsemane, you'll see that He went into, and then came out of, Gethsemane 3 times. You have to read all the accounts. Luke says He *"kneeled down, and prayed."* In Mark, it says He *"fell on the ground."* In Matthew, it says He *"fell on his face,"* right down on His face. So, it's interesting.

Student 4: What about the true order of prayer?

Mike: Well, that's even a higher order of prayer than what we're talking about. I guess what we're talking about is telestial, terrestrial, and celestial orders of prayer. We have our foundational, fundamental type prayer that every person is taught when they come out of the world, and go into the Church. Then the scriptures seem to teach us something higher: cry unto the Lord and be involved in mighty prayer. And then there's an even higher order of prayer that can help us do things in our devotion that we can't talk about here. But, those of you who have been in the temple know of these higher forms. I guess the point is that there are ways to step up and attain something more significant.

Now, I just want to tell you that if you're waiting for somebody to tell you to do these things, you're going to be waiting a long time. See, I think the formula that Joseph had, applies to us as we seek to improve our devotion. *"If any of you lack wisdom, let him ask of God that giveth liberally and upbraideth not."* What you have to do when you gain the knowledge of this information is then take it to The Lord and seek the further knowledge that you lack. If you start to move into the mighty prayer area, you'll have revealed to you by the Holy Ghost, what it is that you specifically need to be involved in to draw nearer unto the Lord and obtain the blessings that He has that have been reserved for you. It's such a personal, intimate thing. Right now, when I say prayers, I pray with my arms folded and my head bowed in church. But, that's the only place I pray that way; for meals and in public. Other than that, I pray with outstretched arms. During the day, I will face the sun if I can, because I feel that it is a symbolic representation of facing the Son coming up out of the east. I've had some wonderful experiences of standing in the sunlight with my face turned up, eyes closed, and my arms outstretched as I talked to my Father in the name of Christ. I've had some great experiences with that. So, these are just some things to think about, mighty prayer.

Student 6: That takes trust! You have to have faith and trust in Him as you do that. What I'm saying is that you have to have faith and trust **in order** to do that.

Mike: You do. And here's something else that I've learned: it's literally true that **He does not upbraid.** I can testify to you that He does not upbraid. I looked up the meaning of upbraid in the 1828 edition of the dictionary (to reproach, to chide, to reprove with severity) and it's interesting. He will not chastise you, reprimand you, or rebuke you. He will not withdraw His Spirit, He will not curse you, and He will not send curses and plagues upon you **if** your heart is right.

Student 6: Right.

Mike: And if you will *step-out* and take a leap of faith when you lack wisdom, trusting in Him that giveth liberally and upbraideth not, it will be given to you. I discovered that when I've *stepped-out* and have done things without being asked to do them, I am following Brother Bednar's admonition. He said this in a Brigham Young University-Idaho Devotional, January 6, 2004:

> *It is one thing to perform the outward actions of obedience; it is quite a different thing to become inwardly what the commandments are intended for to us to become.*

He's talking about commandments and actions that are outward and inward, two sets.

> *It is one thing to obey the institutional, public, and shared commandments associated with the Lord's kingdom on earth-commandments such as the law of chastity, the law of tithing, and the Word Wisdom;*

Those are your outward actions of obedience that are tied to the institutional, church, public and shared commandments.

*It is an even a greater thing to receive and respond to the individual, private, and personally revealed commandments that result from continual and faithful obedience. Such instructions typically are **proactive and anticipatory in nature.***

Proactive means that you're *stepping-out* and you're doing something without being told what to do. You're acting instead of being acted upon, which is the core message of Elder Bednar's ministry. I feel that this is one his core messages. What I'm saying is that if we want to do, or have things happen to us differently than we've had in the past, we're going to have to do things differently. We just can't continue to do the same things over and over hoping for different results. You can't do that. So, as the Spirit prompts us, through our study and acquisition of knowledge and revelation, to *step-out* and do something, you need to trust in the Lord and have the courage to do it, knowing that he will not upbraid you. Now, I've done that and here's what I learned; I learned that Heaven smiles when you do these things. You may get it wrong, but you do sense a smiling, heavenly presence. If you were to put words to what I've felt, in my case, it would be, "Atta boy, Mike!"

In the temple, you will see a process where angels and messengers are sent down from the gods to observe man in the fallen world. They're told to go down to observe conditions, generally, and bring back information. And so, they return and report; back and forth, back and forth. When you do something like this that is out of the mainstream, (and you've got to be inspired to do it) you're going to attract the attention of both Heaven and Hell. And you're going to have messengers who are going to go back and say to the powers that be, "You need to come and look at this. You need to come and take a look because this is something worth your notice." And if you haven't got it right, what the powers of heaven will do is gently and lovingly correct you in such a quiet, subtle manner that if you need to stop doing what you're doing, you will lose all desire for and it won't even enter your mind. If you need to simply correct it a little bit and tweak it, then the Holy Ghost will teach exactly what to do. So, those are some ideas, in prayer, that you might want to do. If you listen to this lesson about revelation and mighty prayer and the Spirit touches you to try something different, then have the courage to try it and don't be afraid because **He does not upbraid.**

References:
D&C 8:2-3
Doctrinal History of the Church, volume 4, page 587. D&C 50:23
1828 Dictionary
Pearl of Great Price, Joseph Smith – History Teachings of the Prophet Joseph Smith; page 98 D&C 129:23
D&C 11:7
Nephi 4:21 – 25
3 Nephi 19
Enos 1:4
BYU-Idaho devotional, January 6, 2004

Chapter Five
Podcast 005 Angels and Precious Promises

We've had questions that have come up throughout the week on various things. One of the questions had to do with the ministry of angels. I would like to give some input on that. Let's go over to Moroni chapter 7, for just a minute, and let's see what the Lord has said about receiving angels. There is a difference between visions and visitations. In a vision, you see and hear something. In a visitation, you see, hear, and touch something. Moroni was talking about angels in chapter 7, verse 29. Let's get some information on this. It says:

> *And because he hath done this, my beloved brethren, have miracles ceased? Behold I say unto you, Nay; neither have angels ceased to minister unto the children of men.*

Now, this is the takeoff verse on the ministry of angels. These verses give us more information than anywhere else in the scriptures on angels. Verse 30:

> *For behold, they* [the angels] *are subject unto him* [Christ] *to minister according to **the word of his command, showing themselves** unto them of **strong faith** and a **firm mind** in every form of godliness.*

It says *"to minister according to the word of his command."* That verse teaches us something, and you see it in the temple. You can see that very hierarchy, movement, and governance: God the Father speaks to Christ, Christ speaks to messengers, and messengers come to man and then return and report to Christ. And you will want to double underline *"showing themselves."* Now, that's a visitation. That's not behind the veil. That's where they come, and you see them, you talk to them, they appear to you face to face, and you speak to them as one person speaks to another. There's your formula from the *Book of Mormon*, on attaining the *ministration of angels.* You need to study and pray and ask yourselves, what does it mean to have that kind of strong faith? What does it mean to have a firm mind **in every form of godliness?** Now, look at verse 31:

> *And the office of their ministry* [the angels] *is to call men unto repentance, and to fulfil and to do the work of the covenants of the Father, which he hath made unto the children of men, to prepare the way among the children of men, by declaring the word of Christ* **unto the chosen vessels of the Lord**, *that they may bear testimony of him.*

That verse identifies that those who have strong faith and a firm mind in every form of godliness, are considered the chosen vessels of the Lord and are able to receive the *ministry of angels.* In the temple, we're told that messengers come and teach us in the ways of life and salvation. Paraphrasing Adam, he said, "These are true messengers. I exhort you to give strict heed to their counsel and advice, and they will teach you in ways of **life** and **salvation.**" There is another clue. Look at verse 32. This is really interesting. We have a group of people who, because of their faithfulness and a firm mind in every form of godliness, are able to entertain angels. They are called the chosen vessels of the Lord and verse 32 says:

> *And by so doing, the Lord God prepareth the way that* **the residue of men** *may have faith in Christ,*

There are two groups we are talking about in regards to the ministration of angels. Those who receive them face to face are called the "chosen vessels." Then, those "chosen vessels" are obligated to share the message they received from that ministration and bear testimony of it. The people they share the message with are referred to as "the residue of men." Now, there is a little clause in there. You have to be careful who you share with, according to Alma 12:9-11. But, the message they bring to you is not designed to just stay with you. The message is designed to prepare "the residue of men" that they may have faith in Christ. Moroni 7:32 continues:

> *That the Holy Ghost may have place in their hearts, according to the power thereof; and after this manner bringeth to pass the Father, the covenants which he hath made unto the children of men.*

This is great information on the ministry of angels.

When you receive a true messenger, and he shows himself unto you, you're going to have to be able to discern whether he is a messenger of light or a messenger from the dark. As we mentioned in a quote last week, the prophet Joseph Smith said that you need to have the priesthood and the gifts of the Spirit in order to discern the laws which govern these spirits. There are certain laws by which spirits, messengers, angels, translated beings, spirits of *just men made perfect*—all of these godly men and women who work for and on behalf of the Father and the Son—are discerned. You've got to be able to determine what source they are actually coming from. In order to do that, it's going to require you to attempt to touch them. You're going to have to be able to make an attempt at a touch. That's why a vision is only seeing and hearing something, and a visitation is seeing, hearing and **touching** something. It's in the **touching** something that part of the discernment happens to tell whether or not they come from the Lord, or whether they're imposters.

Let me share with you a couple of things that I've learned through experience and that have proven to be true. Messengers from the dark side can be discerned because they have no respect for the agency of man. The laws of agency and the laws of the priesthood—they have no respect for that governance. For example, angels from the dark side are intruders. We can use certain words to describe them. They are intruders, trespassers, imposters, counterfeiters, and have absolutely zero respect for the agency of man. That's one of the ways you can discern which side they come from.

On the other side, though, we have angels from the Lord that we just read about in Moroni 7. This is my opinion, so I'm not going to say that they *are*, but it's almost *as if they are* bound by certain laws. I have a feeling that they are. These would be the laws that the Prophet Joseph Smith said we need to understand and have a knowledge of so that we can work with, discern, and receive the benefits from these messengers. One of the laws that they respect, that they hold utmost, is the law governing the agency of God's children. I'm going to give you my opinion. When it's doctrine, I will just say it, but when it's my opinion I will always let you know that this is now Brother Stroud's experience. My opinion is that they need to have permission by you and the invitation extended from you to come and administer to you. It's one of the ways that you can discern light from darkness when it comes to messengers that are abroad on the earth, both good and bad. Elder Holland gave a talk called, *Place No More for the Enemy of My Soul*, and in that talk, he says that we need to ask for angels to come and help us.

Student 1: So, what you're saying is if we have a difficulty or some distress, we can ask for angels?

Mike: That's what I'm saying. And I think that it's largely a source of power that we're not tapping into simply because we don't have the knowledge that is available. You know the prophet Joseph Smith made a statement that I'd like to read to you quickly. It's one of my favorites:

> *A man is saved no faster than he gets knowledge, for if he does not get knowledge, he will be brought into captivity by some evil power in the other world as evil spirits will have more knowledge and consequently more power than many men who are here on the earth. Hence it needs revelation to assist us, and give us knowledge of the things of God.*

If I understand it correctly, he is saying that if we leave this world ignorant of certain laws and keys that govern beings in the eternal world, and we had an opportunity to obtain that and we didn't, those spirit beings will have power over us as we reside in the spirit world, upon death. We won't have the necessary knowledge to have preeminence over them. Hence, he says we need revelation to assist us to give us knowledge of the things of God.

Student 4: Where is that quote from?

Mike: *Teachings of the Prophet Joseph Smith.* You can look it up, *"A man is saved no faster than he gets knowledge."* Google that in your individual Urim and Thummim, called the Internet. You can find anything you want.

Student 4: What page?

Mike: You'll have to look that up. I don't have the page number right now. Here is another quote from the same book:

> Knowledge is necessary to life and godliness... Knowledge is revelation. Hear all ye brethren, this grand key: knowledge is the power of God unto salvation.

Brothers and sisters, in talking about angels, I'm saying that we're perhaps not tapping into a significant power source to help us in our mortal sojourn here in a telestial world. I can also tell you, and I think you all believe this, that things are not going to get easier. They're going to become more difficult, more confusing, and more chaotic as we move through the coming days, months, and years. We're going to need to have all the help we can get.

So, this is what you need to do. Most of the messenger angels that minister to us are our family members. They are either family members who are coming that have not been born yet and you are either their mother, their grandmother, or their great grandmother; or they are they your ancestors, loved ones, who have been here and have preceded you in death, and are in the spirit world looking back. Those are usually the messengers that the Lord uses to help us because they're assigned to us by family ties and foreordained ordinances. You and I are on the battleground, so those who haven't been born, who are coming through us, through our bodies, and those who have been here before us and we have come through their bodies, have vested interest in us successfully completing our period of time in this schoolhouse. Does that make sense?

Student 6: Yes.

Mike: So, we need to be more actively involved in asking for their help. Now, we need to remember two things: permission and an invitation. I have learned that from personal experience, so I can testify to you that that is true. They want to help but many times don't because we don't make the invitation. Comment?

Student 1: Well, my dad was into genealogy quite a bit. Before he died, we talked together. I asked him if he will come back and help me do the genealogy if he had permission. So, in other words, I could **ask** for him to come and help me?

Mike: I think you can, and it's interesting that you said, "If he had permission," which I think we interpret that all too often as meaning permission from God or from eternal beings. And that may well be, but it may be that the main permission has to come from us. We're in a state of opposition. We're in a state within the veil, and we are in a state where they will not intrude. I have discovered that seldom does God intrude in the agency of man. I won't say that he can't, but my experience from what I've learned is that He seldom does. We have to put our trust in Him, who knows the beginning from the end, in the wisdom of Him who knoweth all things. And He does.

Another thing to remember is that these angels, just like in this world, are people with different skill sets, different talents, and different gifts of the Spirit. Even though they are not in the mortal world at this time, as mortals in the telestial world, they are still in a state of probation. They are still progressing, and part of their progression is that they have experience, knowledge, and the gifts that they've developed through the gospel of Jesus Christ, just like you and I are doing. When you invite them, identify and be specific as to the kind of help you need. If you're struggling with addiction, if you're struggling with spiritual warfare, with dark spirits, if you're struggling with interpersonal relationships or marriage difficulties, you can specify help from angels that have skills in those different areas. In other words, brothers and sister, the more specific we can be in our request and our inquiries, the more readily they are going to be answered. Vague questions seldom elicit a clear response. Any thoughts or comments?

Student 4: My great-great-grandfather died, and he appeared to his wife one evening, just at dusk, and he said, "I have come to talk to you and make amends for old things. And I've gotten **permission** to come and see you." He said, "I'm sorry, I have had a hasty temper throughout my life, but I always loved you from my youth." And then, of course, he went on to say many more things, but that was my evidence that I've had that he asked permission from those on the other side for him to come here. At the end of the revelation, he said to her, "I will come and get you, and you'll know when I come because you will say, "Behold the chariot of fire and the horsemen thereof." The children testified that's what happened when she died.

Mike: Interesting. Again that concept of permission comes up. Well, brothers and sisters, I have had personal experience where we have asked for specific help on behalf of people who were in dramatic need, and that help was given in astounding ways. In one case we asked for angels who had specific gifts in healing the physical body of diseases and ailments, just before a daughter of mine went into surgery. As they wheeled her in, just before she went under the anesthetic, there were six men who surrounded the operating table—two on each side, one at the foot, and one at the head—that stood next to the doctors and nurses and counseled them in the operation, which she came through successfully. So, I know that this is a true principle and I tell you this in the hope that we can all access this power. It's my testimony that, more than ever before, we're going to need the help of these beings and they may be hindered from helping us simply because we don't ask.

Last week we talked about adversity, and we talked about prayer. In the *Bible* dictionary, I recommend you read the whole section on prayer. It is one of the great jewels in the *Bible's* dictionary. Under the heading of prayer, it states, that there are blessings already foreordained and reserved for you, as it were, blessings that have your name on them that are not being realized in your lives simply because they are conditioned upon you asking for them. That's a sobering thing, and that was a great awakening for me. I started realizing that:

> *Ye have not, because ye ask not.*

That was James 4:2. And as Nephi said, *"Wherefore, [we] must perish in the dark."* (2 Nephi 32:4) Something as simple as asking is all that is needed to unlock the powers of heaven and start to have a flow in your life that will give you power and knowledge. Anyway, I give that to you.

Student 1: Mike, it's difficult.

Mike: Pardon?

Student 1: It is difficult because we don't want to ask amiss.

Mike: Usually you can tell if you ask it amiss. We need to quote the second part of that scripture in James. James 4:

> *[3]Ye ask, and receive not, because ye ask amiss, that ye may consume it upon your lusts.*

You can tell if your prayers are amiss. You can measure if what you're asking for is being consumed upon by your lusts by asking yourself if your desires are unrighteous desires, vain glory, etc. I think most of us don't ask amiss. I think the problem with most of us is we don't ask, let alone ask amiss; we just don't ask. I know that's the way it's been in my life. When I learned this little secret, several years ago, then the heavens started to open up, and the veil thinned out, revelation increased, ask, seek, knock... ask, seek, knock. Of course, the knocking part: the place for you to knock is *at the veil*. So, asking proceeds seeking, seeking proceeds knocking and knocking parts the veil and you see as you are seen. Understand?

This takes us into what I would like to talk to you about tonight. I'd like to talk to you for the remaining time, on something in the scriptures called 'precious promises.' I hope the Holy Ghost will give us utterance on this. I want to teach this in a way that is understandable in the little bit of time that we have left here. I pray that the Holy Ghost will be with us. This is a significant doctrinal principle. Joseph Smith said this about Peter, the Apostle, *"Peter, the apostle, penned the most sublime language of all of the apostles."* How's that for a quote? Go to 2 Peter, chapter 1, verse 1:

> *Simon Peter, a servant and an apostle of Jesus Christ, to them that have obtained like precious faith with us through the righteousness of God and our Savior Jesus Christ:*
> *[2]Grace and peace be multiplied unto you through the knowledge of God, and of Jesus our Lord,*
> *[3]According as his divine power hath given unto us all things that pertain unto life and godliness, through the knowledge of him that hath called us to glory and virtue:*
> *[4]Whereby are given unto us exceeding great and* **precious promises***: that by these ye might be partakers of the* **divine nature***, having escaped the corruption that is in the world through lust.*

Think about what we just read about **knowledge** in the quotes by Joseph Smith. This is a group of people who have obtained something that the majority don't obtain and never will. Now, look at verse 4, *"Whereby,"* in other words, through this knowledge, through this glory, *"whereby are given unto us exceeding great* *and precious promises:*" that is the part that you want to underline. *"That by these,"* these promises, *"that by these, ye might be partakers of the divine nature."* Now, brothers and sisters, this is the only place in all of the written scriptures were the phrase **divine nature** is mentioned. It's the only place where you find that. In order to become a partaker of **divine nature**, you have to obtain these exceeding great and **precious promises**. When you do, look at the last part of verse 4, you *"escape the corruption that is in the world through lust."* It puts you in a position where you are above the temptations of the devil. It doesn't mean that he will stop tempting you, but it will have no effect. Do you think it is possible for you to get to a point in this life where Satan's temptations have no more effect on you?

Student 1: Yes, yes I do!

Mike: It is possible because if you go to the temple, you'll notice that at a certain place in the temple allegory, it tells us these things. The Father and the Son send down messengers, and They say, "Cast Satan out of their midst." Remember that? And the messengers come down and do that. At that point, Adam and Eve are above falling. Something has been given to them. They did obtain something whereby they cannot fall. Now, let's go a little bit further and go to verse 5. He lists some of the things that you will obtain through these precious promises and being partakers of the divine nature. The divine nature, brothers and sisters, is God's character. It is who He is. It is His core. It is everything about Him in perfection and fullness. Those are the two words, perfection and fullness. So, as we read some of these attributes, some of these characteristics of God's nature, know that they reside in the Father and Son in fullness and in perfection. In us, we may obtain a portion, but in Them resides a fullness. Okay? So, let's look at some of the things that Peter lists. He says:

> [5]*And beside this, giving all diligence, add to your* **faith virtue**; *and to virtue* **knowledge**;
> [6]*And to knowledge* **temperance**; *and to temperance* **patience**; *and to patience* **godliness**;
> [7]*And to godliness* **brotherly kindness**; *and to brotherly kindness* **charity**.

So, besides escaping the corruption of this world through lust; *"And beside this, giving all diligence, add to your faith,"* is the first thing you notice. If you will notice up in verse 1, these people have already obtained a precious faith. They are already there. They have a faith, which the *Book of Mormon* calls it an unshaken faith. You can't shake it. Then you add to that faith, look at the next thing "*virtue,* " and another word for virtue is power (if you're looking at the 1828 version of the Webster dictionary, which is the dictionary Joseph had). So, you've got faith, virtue, knowledge, temperance, and then patience, godliness, brotherly kindness, and charity. Now, there is a list. Can I tell you it begins with faith and ends with... what?

Student 4: Charity.

Mike: Charity, which is the greatest of all the gifts, attributes and characteristics of the Father and the Son. If you are in possession of charity, brothers and sisters, you have all the others spiritual gifts there. If you are in possession of patience, you may not have charity. If you are in possession of kindness and gentleness and meekness, you may not have charity. But, if you have charity you have all of these things. This is a list that begins with faith and ends with charity. Now, watch the next verse, this is where it gets interesting:

> *[8] For if these things be in you, and abound, they make you that you shall neither be barren nor unfruitful in the knowledge of our Lord Jesus Christ.*

How many times did you see the word **knowledge** used in these verses?

Student 3: A lot.

Mike: Verse 9:

> *But he that lacketh these things is blind, and cannot see afar off, and hath forgotten that he was purged from his old sins.*
> *[10]Wherefore the rather, brethren, **give diligence to make your calling and election sure**: for if ye do these things, **ye shall never fall**:*

Verse 10 is significant and is a triple-underliner verse. "*Wherefore the rather, brethren,* " in other words, after everything that I've said to you, "*give diligence to make your calling and election sure.* " That is the **only** place in all of the scriptures, including the *Book of Mormon* and the *Doctrine and Covenants*, that the words "*calling* *and election made sure"* is written. No wonder Joseph said that Peter penned the most sublime words of all the apostles; *"For if ye do these things, ye shall never fall:"*

Most people stop right there, but I want to go to the next verse:

> *[11] For so an **entrance** shall be ministered unto you abundantly into the everlasting kingdom of our Lord and Savior Jesus Christ.*

If you attain this thing called **calling and election made sure**, with it, you receive a promise of an entrance into the kingdom of the Lord Jesus Christ, and you cannot fall. You will come to a point where Satan has no power over you. What we need to be thinking about and paying attention to is obtaining **precious promises** from the Lord. Remember, you cannot obtain anything if you don't know about it, and if you do know about it, you still can't obtain it, if you don't ask for it. The reason knowledge is so enthroned in these verses is that knowledge is the basis of action. How can you seek for something that you don't know anything about? In tonight's lesson, the thing I hope you are learning about angels, and spirits, and precious promises is that you will change your prayer vocabulary. Be more specific in using the words used by these holy prophets, which are given to them by angels delivering messages for Christ under the directions of the Father, and that you would use those words in your prayers. If you will start using the words: obtaining **precious promises**, making your **calling and election sure**, to inherit an entrance into the everlasting kingdom of the Father—if you start using verbiage like that, words that you feel inspired to use, I can promise you that you're going to start receiving things that you haven't received before. It's all hinged on asking specifically and being guided by the Spirit in your request. Questions or comments?

Student 4: I like it.

Mike: Let's go over and look at another couple of places. I want to take you to several different places. *Doctrine and Covenants*, section 2. This is a little section that we don't pay a lot of attention to, but now that we're talking about promises let's read it. These are the exact words of the Angel Moroni to Joseph Smith, on the evening of September 21, 1823. This was given before the *Book of Mormon* even came out of the ground. In the heading of section 2, it says that *"Elijah is to reveal the priesthood."* and then *"The* *promises of fathers are planted in hearts of children."* You ought to be perking up when you see the word promises. I want you to ask yourself a question because this is the verse that we use all the time in genealogy work, Malachi 4:6, that Elijah will come and restore the priesthood:

> *And he shall turn the heart of the fathers to the children, and the heart of the children to their fathers, lest I come and smite the earth with a curse.*

That's the one we talk about. Now, look at it a little different. Let me show you two different ways. The one we quote in Malachi never mentions promises. It just says turn the hearts of the fathers to the children. Am I right?

Student 6: Yeah.

Mike: That's the one we use all the time in genealogy, right? Now look at section 2, verse 1 in the Doctrine of Covenants:

> *Behold, I will reveal unto you the Priesthood, by the* **hand** *of Elijah the prophet,*

Why do you think he puts in there, *by the hand*? What do you know as a result of tonight's discussion that might give added light on that? So, Elijah appears to Joseph...

Student 6: To know if he's a true messenger?

Mike: Yeah, you want to know if he is a true messenger. Remember last week I quoted eight things that a false messenger can give you that, at face value, appear godly. How are you going to tell if this is a true messenger? Because when Elijah comes, he gives his hand. And why does he give his hand? It's because he has been asked to. Where does that come from? Section 129, in 1843, when Joseph was starting to reveal, in the Red Brick Store, the ordinances of the Temple Endowment. *"I will reveal unto you,"* notice that 'I will' is future. It didn't happen until 1836, and we are in January 1829. Continuing on with verse 1:

> *By the hand of Elijah the prophet, before the coming the great and dreadful day of the Lord.*

Now, here's the part that is different.

> *[2] And he shall plant in the hearts of the children the promises made to the fathers, and the hearts of the children shall turn to their fathers.*
>
> *[3] If it were not so, the whole earth would be utterly wasted at his coming.*

You have to ask yourself a couple of questions: who are the children? Who are the fathers? Before we do that, let's look at one more. Let's go to *Joseph Smith—History*. And here we have a different reading of it. It's a little different, and we never quote these things and never look at this. In *Joseph Smith—History* we want to go to verse 38. This is Moroni, and he's quoting the scriptures out of Isaiah, the book of Joel, out of Acts and many, many other scriptures. Joseph said in another place that he quoted as many as 35 other scriptural sources. Then Joseph says, "Which I won't mention at this time." But, what did he say? Let's go to verse 38. Here's one of them that he quotes and it's out of the book of Malachi. But he quotes it just a little bit different. Okay? We're in the *Joseph Smith – History* and let's read verse 36 first:

> *After telling me of these things* [meaning the Urim and Thummim], *he commenced quoting the prophecies of the Old Testament. He first quoted part of the third chapter of Malachi; and he quoted the fourth or last chapter of the same prophecy, though with a little variation from the way it reads in our Bibles.*

Did you catch that? What you're getting here from an angel is different from what you read in the *Bible*. Now, let's look at *Joseph Smith—History* verse 38:

> *And again, he quoted the fifth verse thus: Behold, I will reveal unto you the Priesthood, by the hand of Elijah the prophet, before the coming of the great and dreadful day of the Lord.*
>
> *[39] He also quoted the next verse differently: And he shall plant in the hearts of the children the promises made to the fathers, and the hearts of the children shall turn to their fathers. If it were not so, the whole earth would be utterly wasted at his coming.*

Now, as with all scriptures, there are different levels of truth. One of the levels of truth is the one that we quote all the time in Malachi, and it is true that the hearts of the fathers will turn to the children. And we quote the fathers as being our deceased ancestors who have preceded us and are now in the spirit world, and that this thing that Elijah is restoring, and whatever he is doing, is going to create a welding link between them who have gone on and us who are still here. And that is true. I don't have any problem with that. Except, I question what the promises are that are made to the fathers. What are the promises made to the fathers in the hearts of the children? What are these promises? Well, we go back to Peter, and there are several different kinds of promises. Lehi received a promise that he would obtain a land of promise. Joseph in Egypt received a promise that a great seer would come through his loins. There are all kinds of promises, but Peter talks about exceeding great and precious promises. And the one that he talks about has to do with obtaining a promise from God, from His own mouth, that you will inherit a place in His kingdom. This is called *making your calling and election sure* by a process called *the more sure word of prophecy.* **Having their *calling and election made sure* and receiving the Second Comforter are the promises that were made to the fathers.** Our *New Testament* tells us that there is a whole group of Saints, members of the *New Testament* Church, which obtained the Church of the Firstborn.

Go over to section 107 in the *Doctrine and Covenants.* Let me show you something that is interesting. We have so much more available to us that we are not tapping into because we lack the knowledge to ask for it. Let's go to verse 18 and 19. This is what we're talking about here. Think about the promises to obtain the blessings mentioned in these verses:

> *[18] The power and authority of the higher, or Melchizedek Priesthood, is to hold the keys of all the spiritual blessings of the church–*

Among the spiritual blessings of the church are the promises that we can obtain them from God Himself, through His own mouth. I want to emphasize that. We have the right to have God speak to us. We may not see Him, but we will hear His voice, and His voice will call you by your name, and it will be the name that you're most often known by in this world. And when He calls you by your name He's going to promise you an inheritance/entrance into His kingdom. And He will do that because you have been tried and tested in all things and found to be true and faithful.

Now, look what he says. The blessings are here in verse 19. What are the spiritual blessings?

> *To have the privilege of receiving the mysteries of the*
> *kingdom of heaven, to have the heavens opened unto them,*

Brothers and sisters, are there some things that you would like to ask God that you have always wondered about? Are there things you have wondered about, and others have said, "Those are the mysteries. You ought to leave those alone." By the way, that is counter to true doctrine. You have the opportunity to receive *"the mysteries of the kingdom of heaven, to have the heavens open unto them,"* there's the second blessing. Can I tell you that this is one that builds upon the other? You can't have the heavens open unto you until you've obtained knowledge of the mysteries. Knowledge of the mysteries gives you knowledge and keys that unlock the doors that part the veil and you can now have a conversation with those who live on the other side. So, this is a process. This is something that builds on it. Look at the next part of verse 19:

> *to commune with the general assembly and church*
> *of the Firstborn,*

Do you know who those people are? It is the City of Enoch! They are the Church of the Firstborn. They are translated beings that live in Enoch's Zion. Now, there are members of the Church of the Firstborn here on the earth. Let me tell you this, brothers and sisters, when you obtain these promises that Peter is talking about, when you obtain an entrance and a promise to an inheritance in the everlasting kingdom of Christ the Lord and the Father, you become a member of the Church of the Firstborn. Now, you hold dual citizenship, dual membership. You hold membership in the outward church below. We used to have a hymn that we sang in the church; it was written by Eliza R. Snow and called, *The Outward Church Below*. And the outward church below is The Church of Jesus Christ of Latter-day Saints in the telestial world. The inward church above is the Church of the Firstborn, and that is translated beings, and angels, and gods, with a small **g**, that minister to people in the telestial world and help them rise up to where they are. Look at the rest of this, verse 19:

> *To commune with the general assembly and church*
> *of the Firstborn, and to enjoy the communion and*
> *presence of God the Father, and Jesus, the mediator*
> *of the new covenant.*

Now, those are the blessings and promises that we have. Those promises are made to every one of us here. Every one of us has access to those exceeding precious promises. Now, let me ask you a question as we kind of wrap things up here. You want to obtain those promises from the Lord while you are still here in this life. That is what you want to do; seek for that. These promises have their greatest potential, greatest power, while you're still a mortal in the telestial world. Can you imagine? How would it affect your life; your day in and day out interaction with your fellow man and in the telestial world; your interaction with your husband or wife; your interaction with your other family members and church members? How would it affect your life if God had spoken to you personally, calling you by name, and you heard his voice; and He promised you with his own mouth, accompanied by the confirmation of the Holy Spirit of promise, that you are now sealed up to eternal life and have an inheritance in the Celestial Kingdom of God with the Father and the Son? What would that do? How would you act? Would that make a difference in how you lived your day in and day out life as sojourners and wanderers in this telestial world? Would it make a difference? Would you do things differently? Would you view things differently? Would you love people differently? Would you forgive more fully? Would you judge more righteously if you had obtained those promises? What difference would it make? And, if it would make a difference, why not seek for it?

Let's go to Ether chapter 12 and let me give you an example of something. When you obtain these promises, you also obtain power over the natural world. When you obtain these promises, you are now living in a telestial world, but you have become a terrestrial being. It's also possible that with these promises you can receive translation through the Melchizedek Priesthood. It's possible because translation is a doctrine that belongs to the terrestrial world. And these promises that we're talking about are promises that elevate you into the terrestrial world. You are still living here, but you are now a terrestrial being and have access to terrestrial knowledge and power. Part of translation and terrestrial knowledge is that time and space don't control you as they do here now.

So, in Ether chapter 12, Moroni is talking about the brother of Jared, and he is pondering as I have pondered. And it's because of my pondering that the Lord led me to this, to help me see this. Moroni is talking about this man, who saw the finger of God. Go to verse 17 and think about the promises:

> *And it was by faith that the three disciples* [the three Nephites] *obtained a promise that they should not taste of death; and they obtained not the promise until after their faith.*

Now, that is the format for us. If you want to obtain these promises you're going to be tried; the greater the promise, the greater the glory, the greater the trial. If you want to be an Abraham, a father of many nations, a prince of peace, you are going to have to undergo an Abrahamic test. Will it be that you are commanded to kill your son? Probably not but I will tell you that whatever it is, it will be as difficult, as challenging, and as wrenching to your heart strings as it was to Abraham. As Joseph Smith said, *"God will wrench your very heartstrings"* so that when you pass that trial, you will have an inheritance with Abraham, Isaac, and Jacob; and more importantly than that, you will feel comfortable being there. Look what else Moroni says in Ether 12:18:

> *[18]And neither at any time hath any wrought miracles until after their faith; wherefore they first believed in the Son of God.* [That's where we all are] *[19]And there were many whose faith was so exceedingly strong, even before Christ came, who could not be kept from **within the veil**, but truly saw with their eyes the things which they had beheld with **an eye of faith**, and they were glad.*

Did you pick up something there? If you are seeking for these things, brothers and sisters, before you physically obtain them you have to see them in your mind. If you want to have "ministering of angels," in your meditation and prayer practice and pondering, you have to visualize entertaining an angel. If you want to hear Christ's voice call you by name, you have to visualize that. It's called *seeing things by the eye of faith.* And every one of these people who physically obtained a promise, first of all, saw it *with the eye of faith* before they obtained it physically. And when they obtained it physically they were glad. There is a sequence. See? Yes, now it gets better, watch:

> *[20]And behold, we have seen in this record that one of these was the brother of Jared; for so great was his faith in God, that when God put forth his finger he could not hide it...*

Now, I thought about that, and I wondered, "Could I do that?" And I thought that I probably couldn't do that, but if I'd had the experience the brother of Jared did **before** he sees Christ, then I think I could. Now, this is where I want to take you tonight. We read the record over there in Ether 3, and we just think that nothing preceded that tremendous manifestation where He stretches forth his finger and touches the stones and then Christ asks if he saw more than that. The brother of Jared in this astounding faith says, *"Nay Lord, show myself unto me."* I've read that over the years, and I thought, "Wow! Where did he get that kind of confidence? Where did that come from?" And then the Lord showed me. I stumbled upon this and either I was mentored by somebody, or the Lord showed me. I don't know who it was, but the answer is in the middle of verse 20:

> *that when God put forth his finger he could not hide it from the sight of the brother of Jared, **because**...*

Now, you ought to circle the word **because** and triple underline it because here comes the mystery of godliness:

> *of his word* [Christ's word] *which he had spoken unto him,* [the brother of Jared] *which word he had obtained by faith.*

What is the word? **What is this *word*?** Well, the word is *the precious promise.* Before the brother of Jared sees Christ physically, he had obtained **promises** from the voice of the Lord; the word of the Lord came to him; he didn't see Him, he heard His voice. He'd obtained the promise, and because of that promise, when this situation unfolds on the mountain, the brother of Jared has unbelievable confidence and faith. Why? Because he's already heard the voice of Christ speaking to him and obtained **precious promises** before he ever smelts out the 16 stones.

Student 6: I've never heard that before, Mike. That's amazing!

Mike: Isn't that amazing? Now, look at the next verse. Do you want to get a mystery? These are the mysteries of godliness! This is the knowledge that opens the veil, brothers and sisters. Look at the next verse, and we will close on this:

> [21]And after the brother of Jared had beheld the finger of the Lord, **because of the promise which the brother of Jared had obtained by faith,**

There's the key!

Students: Wow!

Mike: There is the key:

> the Lord **could not** withhold anything from his sight; wherefore he showed him **all** things, for he could no longer be kept **without the veil.**

Student 6: That is amazing!

Mike: Think about this, brothers and sisters. This is the pattern for us. The Prophet Joseph Smith said this:

> God hath not revealed anything to Joseph, but that He will make known unto the Twelve, and even the least Saint may know all things as fast as he is able to bear them.

Everything you read about in the scriptures has to be available to you in 2016, whether it's *Old Testament, Book of Mormon, Doctrine and Covenants, Church History*—I don't care what it is. It has to be available to you, or God is a liar because He says, "I am no respecter of persons, I change not, and there is no such shadow of changing in Me." It has to be available to us, or God cannot say that without lying.

So, what is it that we need to get to this point? We need knowledge, and a man or woman is saved no faster than they get knowledge. Now, there is more on this. I would just invite you to go and look it up under *promises of the Lord* and do some study on this, okay? There are great promises. I'll close by giving you the last and great promise. Go to section 88, and this is what the Lord calls the last and greatest of all promises. We want to look at verses 67, 68 and 69. We will close with this scripture. Think about these promises:

> And if your eye be single to my glory, your whole bodies shall be filled with light, and there shall be

no darkness in you; and that body which is filled
with light comprehend all things.
[68]Therefore,

Now, that word, *"therefore"* means: **because** your body is filled with light; **because** you can comprehend all things; **because** your eye is single to my glory:

Therefore, sanctify yourselves that your minds
become single to God, and the days will come that
*you shall **see** him; for he will unveil his face unto*
you, and it shall be in his own time, and in his own
way, and according to his own will.

Now, brothers and sisters, we think that that's talking about the Second Coming. We think that's talking about after death. But, let me tell you that the criteria of; *eye single to His glory, fill your body with light, sanctify yourselves, let your minds be single to God*; all of that is not necessary if He's going to a show Himself **after** the period of time in the terrestial world. It's not necessary. **Millions** of people are going to see His face, hear His voice, testify, bow the knee, and confess with the tongue at that time. These verses are us, here, **behind the veil,** in the telestial world, NOW! Not sometime after death. Not in the Resurrection. Not at the Second Coming. NOW! And look what he says, 69:

Remember the great and last promise which I have made
unto you;

What is the great and last promise he has made? What is it in verse 68? *"The days will come that you shall see him; for he will unveil his face unto you."* This is the great and last promise.

Now, go look at verse 74:

And I give unto you, who are the first laborers in
this last kingdom, a commandment that you
assemble yourselves together; and organize
yourselves, and prepare yourselves, and sanctify
yourselves; yea, purify your hearts, and cleanse
your hands and your feet before me, that I may
make you clean;

That's what we do in the Church: assemble, organize and prepare ourselves. The purpose of the Gospel is to sanctify, purify and cleanse. Do you see the difference between the Gospel and the Church? The church brings us together. We organize ourselves.

We prepare ourselves. We assemble ourselves. And then the Lord's gospel sanctifies, purifies your hearts, make sure hands and feet clean, *"that I may make you clean."* What this all for? Why? Verse 75:

> *That I may testify unto your Father, and your God, and my God, that you are clean from the blood of this wicked generation;* **that I may fulfill this promise, this great and last promise**, *which I have made unto you, when I will.*

And what is that? Well, it all begins with faith, builds up to charity, peels the veil, you hear His voice, you obtain promises, and then you see the face of Christ. It builds up your confidence. This is why you have to have *the more sure word of prophecy* before the *Second Comforter*. You have to have God's voice speak to you, calling you by name because, in that, you develop unshakable faith, a confidence that cannot be moved. And that enables you to peel back the veil and enter into the presence of the Savior... **In this life**!

Student 6: This is very exciting truth!

Mike: It is something to ponder on. If you have questions, brothers and sisters, email them to me. And I'll answer your questions or comments. Then what I'll do is share them with you at the beginning of each lesson so others can also learn from what you have to say and what your thoughts are.

Resources:

Moroni 7:29-32
April 2010 Conference Elder Holland
Teachings of Presidents of the Church: Joseph Smith, (2011), 261–70
James 4:2, 3
2 Peter 1
D&C 2
Teachings of the Prophet Joseph Smith, 264–68
D&C 129
Joseph Smith History; 36, 38 – 39
D&C 107:18
Ether 12:17-21
D&C 88:11

Chapter Six
Podcast 006 Accusations and Advocacy

Let's start out by going to Revelation chapter 12 in the *Bible*. I hope that we can have the Holy Ghost with us tonight. I pray for that so that we can discuss this concept. I was in the High Priest Group today, and taught a lesson on Joseph Smith the Prophet, by President Hunter, which had to do with developing a new appreciation for the Prophet Joseph, and for the things that he restored. One of the things that he restored had to do with what we call the *doctrine of advocacy*. We will talk a little bit about that; in other words, Christ being our advocate with the Father. That is a great Atonement principle and great Atonement doctrine, but to understand the *doctrine of advocacy*, which is also a legal term, we need to think about some other legal terms. A lot of the gospel of Jesus Christ uses legal terminology: judge, advocate, pleading, bar of justice, guilty, not guilty, innocent, and **accuser**. All of these things are legal terms that you will find within the school of legal thought in our country and in the world.

One of these is the *doctrine of advocacy*. I want to chat with you a little bit and put all of these together tonight, and see what the Lord is trying to teach us with these various terms. In the heading of Revelation 12, it says:

> *[John] sees the war in heaven in the beginning when Satan was cast out – He sees the continuation of that war on earth.*

What began as a war in heaven was not ended when the Garden of Eden was established and Adam and Eve were placed in the garden. It is simply being extended on earth, and that war won't end until after the Millennium. It actually began in the premortal life, and goes all through the telestial world, through the Millennium, and doesn't end until the end of the Millennium, when Satan and his hosts are allowed one final battle against Christ and His saints. In verse 9 it says:

> *And the great dragon was cast out, that old serpent, called the Devil, and Satan, which deceiveth the whole world: he was cast out into the earth, and his angels were cast out with him.*

And they are here providing the opposition for man. They oppose everything that is light and good and righteous. Now, look at verse 10:

> *And I heard a loud voice saying in heaven, Now is come salvation, and strength, and the kingdom of our God, and the power of his Christ:*

It's an interesting reason to place that colon after Christ. We need to have the salvation and strength of God and the Kingdom of God, *and **the power of his Christ*** because of what comes after the colon:

> *For the accuser of our brethren is cast down, which accused them* [the brethren] *before our God day and night.*

So, one of the names of Lucifer is *the accuser of the brethren* and the brethren are those who align themselves with Christ and the Father. Now in verse 11:

> *[11]And they overcame him by the blood of the Lamb, and by the word of their testimony; and they loved not their lives unto the death.*

They, meaning the brethren, overcame the accuser *by the blood of the Lamb and by the word of their testimony; then there is a semicolon.* The placement of these colons and semicolons in the scriptures are very important. Look at what comes after the semicolon; *"and they loved not their lives unto the death."*

> *[12]Therefore rejoice, ye heavens, and ye that dwell in them. Woe to the inhabiters of the earth and of the sea! for the devil is come down unto you, having*

great wrath, because he knoweth he has but a short time.

That is a great scripture if we want to learn some things about Lucifer, his tactics, and what he's trying to accomplish. We need to understand his strategy, his nature, and his tactics. Remember you can come to know a lot about Jesus Christ by His opposition. In other words, Christ can be known better through His adversary. The more you understand Lucifer and the powers of darkness, the better you can comprehend Christ and the powers of heaven. Things are made better known through their opposing factors. If you want to understand light better, come to understand darkness. If you want to come to understand Christ better, then you need to understand His enemy. Now, there's some truth in that. Comment?

Student 6: Brother Stroud, I've understood, all my life, that we are **not** to invite the adversary. You know, don't go there; **not** to do that. Now, you're saying here that by studying the adversary you get to know Christ better. How do I make that work?

Mike: Well, that's a good question. For example, one of the great principles that I've learned has brought me power. It has been a guiding principle in my life. Through my study, I have learned what is meant when we talk about devils and unclean spirits. I have read about that all of my life and I always thought those two terms were referring to one group or class of individuals. By looking deeper into it, and studying and pondering the scriptures mentioning those terms, I've come to understand something that I never did know before; that those are two different groups of people with different agendas and different powers and must be dealt with specifically but in different ways. If I had not taken the time to look into that, I would not have discovered and had revealed to me, and had given to me, great insight and power to deal with these spiritual forces of darkness. This knowledge has been a great blessing in my family, and in my life. As it turns out, I have been able to be an instrument for good, in the lives of others, because I understand this doctrine. So, it's not the same thing as going into it and becoming fascinated with the occult. It's not a titillation of dark things, and wondering if Ouija boards and spiritual mediums work. We're in warfare. In the heading of Revelation chapter 12, it talks about the war in heaven. I think it's a great and wonderful question. As I've studied the scriptures, I discovered that the one word that our Father in Heaven and Christ use to describe the telestial world experience that their children are going through is WAR. Now if you're in warfare, which I testify that we are, it becomes really helpful for us to understand the battle strategy and the plans of the enemy. The more you understand them, the better off you are in overcoming and fighting the battle.

Student 1: So, how do you do that?

Mike: Well, it's mainly tactical. Let me give you my experience on that. First of all, understand this principle: that we're in a warfare and we need to know all that we can about the tactics and strategy of the person who wants to defeat us in this war. If you come to that point where you accept that principle, then the Holy Spirit will take you by the hand, and bit by bit will lead you in the things you need to know, personally, to help you fight the good fight and come off victorious. I don't know that there are any particular books or manuals that we can get on it. It's not like the war book written by the great Chinese warfare expert, who wrote the book *The Art of War*. We don't have anything like that. However, a good portion of the *Book of Mormon*, especially in 2 Nephi, was spent showing us the tactics of *the evil one*, how he works, how he leads you carefully by the neck, with a flaxen cord until he carefully grasps you with his strong chains forever. You see, there's information that we have to help us understand that he never comes at us with the large heinous, horrendous, sins of this world. He just doesn't do that, because he understands that each one of God's children has something within them called *enmity*. Do you remember that from the Garden of Eden? *"I will place **enmity** between thee and the seed of the woman."* Enmity has many different meanings. One of them is a natural abhorrence that God's children have in this life, for darkness and evil and those kinds of things. So, it's just a matter of listening. When the Spirit touches you and awakens you in a particular area, then move forward and follow the promptings and it will lead you to learn things that you personally need to know in order to come out victoriously. Does that help?

Students 1 and 6: Yeah.

Student 4: Hey Mike? You had some handouts that really helped me. It was about understanding the different voices we have in our mind; the voice of the Spirit, the voice of the adversary, and our own voice. I have those handouts, and they have been really helpful.

Also, did you get the article I sent you today? It was about the seven missionaries that were sent to England to open up the missionary work?

Mike: I'm familiar with that story, but I didn't get the article. You mean the missionaries in the early days of the Church that were attacked by evil spirits in Preston, England?

Student 4: Yeah. I just thought that was a good example of how real it is. And with Joseph Smith it was real. Right before God appeared to him, darkness took over his life for awhile, until Christ appeared to him and drove Satan away. Joseph admitted a lot of times where he struggled with this. And Oliver Cowdrey was chased out of his house three times because of evil spirits.

Mike: Yeah! Thank you. I appreciate those comments. Let's go back to verse 11. They overcome the *accuser of the brethren* by three things: [1] The blood of the Lamb; I think that we can say safely that that is by accessing the power of Christ's Atonement to empower you in many ways. Coming off victorious is the name of the game in this battle.

So, we have the power of Christ's Atonement, and [2] *the word of their testimony.* Isn't that interesting? That's the brethren now, remember that we're talking about the brethren that are accused. Now, I think that the brethren who are accused by Lucifer are any one of us here in mortality, that have a stewardship in the lives of God's children. That would be from as lofty a place as the First Presidency and the Quorum of the Twelve, right down to fathers and mothers in their homes, where they have a stewardship to rear and protect their children in righteousness, and bear testimony.

I found this last one interesting: [3] *they loved not their lives unto death.* This warfare can cause your death. I think that in the *Sixth Lecture on Faith*, which is called *Sacrifice*, by the prophet Joseph Smith, where he said that if you're not willing to sacrifice everything, including your life, for the cause of Christ, for the restored truth, then you're not worthy to enter into Their presence. Now, whether or not you are going to be required to do that is another question. You have to be **willing** to give up and sacrifice **everything**, and in some cases, many people were given that opportunity. It says *they loved not their lives unto to death.* In other words, a place with Christ and the Father was more precious to them than remaining alive in the telestial world. They willingly gave up their lives for Christ, on the great battlefield of the telestial world.

I want to come back to this thing: *the accuser of the brethren.* That is Lucifer's title. That is one of his names. As Christ is an **advocate** *of the brethren,* which is also a name of Christ, a name/title; *the **accuser** of the brethren* is also a name/title of the evil one. I remember that Margie and I were on a mission in New Jersey, I believe it was, and we came across this information, and the Spirit taught us this principle. This is at the heart of what I want to discuss with you in the next few minutes.

To the degree that we are **accusatory** in this life, to the degree that we **accuse** others, we take upon ourselves a satanic role. Now, the opposite of accusation is forgiveness. And what we will do as a result of this lesson tonight is that we will look inside ourselves over the next several days and you'll be amazed just how often we slip into this **accusatory** condition. It is really common among the fallen men and women in the telestial world. In fact, this is one of the main things that we, through the *blood of the Lamb* and the *testimony of the brethren,* have to overcome if we want an inheritance with the Father and the Son. That is not easy because we really don't think too much about it. Another word for the accusation is another legal term called indictment. If you bring an **indictment** against somebody, by law, it requires some kind of a hearing. And the accuser or the person who is bringing the indictment is doing such so that the **hearing** can be convened and their cause can be listened to and **judged**. So, every time that we bring an accusation against somebody, part of that process is not to have it end with the accusation. It only begins a process that ends up bringing in **somebody,** before a judge, in a hearing, where innocence or guilt can be determined. That's the purpose of an indictment or an accusation. Now, what I want to present to you tonight is that this is satanic.

Matthew Chapter 7 is the Sermon on the Mount. In the last chapter of the Sermon on the Mount, the Lord comes out and says *"Judge not that ye be not judged."* First of all, making an accusation is making a judgment based on a person's innocence or guilt, right or wrong, and you're going to have to have a hearing that ends with a judgment from somebody in authority, in behalf of, or against the person making the accusation, or the indictment. You see what we're talking about here? Now, Joseph Smith took Matthew 7, and he said, *"Judge not that ye be not judged, for with what judgment ye judge, ye shall be judged."* And then Joseph Smith said, *"but judge righteous judgment."* Let's go over to section 121 and see what the Lord says about the only time righteous judgment is made. These kinds of things should help us. Remember that *true doctrine, understood, changes behavior.* It isn't enough to simply say, "You shouldn't do that, it's wrong." It's important that we see what the Lord has to say about it. If you're going to take it upon yourself to judge a person, to reprove a person, to correct a person, to chastise a person, verse 43 becomes the rule to make sure what you're doing is righteous. Remember what Joseph said, *"judge righteous judgment."* Well, here's the key to that in verse 43:

> *Reproving betimes with sharpness, when moved upon*
> *by the Holy Ghost;*

To reprove means to judge. Our judgment, in order to be correct, in order to fulfill what Joseph said, *"judge righteous judgment,"* needs to be in tune with the Holy Spirit, and the *mind of Christ* and the Father, which is the Holy Spirit, according to the *Fifth Lecture on Faith.* You need to have the *mind of Christ* in you so that whatever you think, do, or say is in accordance with His mind. At that point, whatever judgment, chastisement, or correction that you make will be done right. Otherwise, you end up being in danger of judgment yourself, because you don't judge righteously.

Verse 43 ends by saying that after you have made this correction, judgment, reproof, or chastisement:

> *And then showing forth afterwards an increase of*
> *love toward him whom thou hast reproved, lest he*
> *esteem thee to be his enemy;*

So, what we're saying here is that there is a way for you, in your stewardship, to correct, reprove, chasten, and instruct, without being accusatory, or condemning the person. That is the trick. Now, the natural man wants to just make a statement and accuse a person: "You're wrong. You do this. You don't do that, You're just that kind of person, You have always been like this, and you will never change. This is your fault." Those kinds of things are dark.

My wife and I were talking about this today, and I'd like to give you an example of how you help somebody correct themselves without being accusatory. A lot of times our accusations are based on the lack of information. I would say **most** of the time they are. This last week, I was taking a horse I've been working with, to go out with a friend of mine, and to move some cows at the Flyin' Box Ranch, just east of Springerville. I've been training this horse now for number weeks. I got him all saddled up and was waiting for my friend to come by with his trailer so we could load the horses up and go out and move these cows around. I noticed that he was favoring his leg. I had told Margie before, that he was a little gimpy on that leg and that I was going to take him out.

She asked, "Why are you going to take him out on this round-up, gathering up these cows, when you know that his leg is hurt?" She said, "I don't think it's right that you should ride him out there if he's not well. You can make that leg worse." Now we had this discussion back and forth, and she didn't come out and say, "You're wrong. You shouldn't do this. You know better than that." She simply said, "Help me understand why you're going to take this horse out when you know he's lame, and it may cause him further injury?"

Now, this is a 10-year-old horse, and I said, "A lot of times a horse can have a little bit of arthritis in his knee and that little bit of exercise out on the trail, will take it out. I really won't know how bad it is until I'm on his back, and we're moving cows. And if it does not seem to correct itself, then I will simply take him back, unsaddle him and put him in the trailer, and do something else."

And she said, "Oh, well. That makes sense." In this discussion back and forth she could've come out and said, "You know better than that Mike. You're going to hurt that animal. I thought you knew more about horses than that to take a horse that's lame out on a cattle drive. That's hard work." She didn't do any of that. Rather than accusing, she simply said, "Help me understand why you're doing this?" And so, when I explained it she said, "Well, that makes sense."

When I got him out to the trailer, I noticed a knot on this knee that hadn't been there before. When I bent down and touched the knee with my hand, he picked up his leg. So, when my friend came by, I simply said, "I can't take this horse. I don't think it will be a good idea to take this horse out there." I unsaddled him, took him out to the pasture, and turned him loose. I got another ranch horse and went on that drive with the other horse. The point was, she didn't have to come out with a railing accusation and say, "You know better than that." The reason she handled it that way was because both of us have been working on not falling into this trap of accusing people and going to the dark side. It's tricky to do, but it can be done.

Let me give you another example over in John chapter 8. My premise tonight is that at our level of gospel understanding, we need to avoid making accusations and condemning others. When we do that, we literally fall into the role of *the accuser of the brethren,* and we don't want to do that. None of us want to do that. I find it interesting that as I study the gospel, I don't find the Lord accusing people and I don't find Him condemning. His ministry was not to condemn or accuse. His ministry was to forgive, to edify, and to lift. In that process, we're allowed to have our own experiences in the journey of life and learn from those experiences and have those experiences be for our own good; all things we have studied before.

Let's go down to John 8:2-11. You know this story. It's Jesus, and He's in the temple. In verse 2 all the people come in, and then verse 3:

> *[3]And the scribes and Pharisees brought unto him a woman taken in adultery; and when they had set her in the midst,*
> *[4]They say unto him, Master, this woman was taken in adultery, in the very act.*
> *[5]Now Moses in the law commanded us, that such should be stoned: but what sayest thou?*
> *[6]This they said, tempting him, that they might have to accuse him. But Jesus stooped down, and with his finger wrote on the ground, as though he heard them not.*

Now, look at this verse. *This they said, tempting him, that they might have to **accuse** him.* Do you see the role that is going on? They are not concerned at all with this woman's spiritual welfare.

They are more than prepared to take her outside the gates of the city and put her to death, as was the law of Moses. They came to Him, tempting Him that they might find a way to accuse Him. *But Jesus stooped down, and with his finger wrote on the ground,* **as though he heard them not.** Now, that's an interesting thing to ponder! You see, it wasn't just a one-time request. He just kind of ignored them, and then they continued with this: "What do you say? This is what Moses said. You're a rabbi, and you profess to be the Son of God. So, what do you say about this?"

> *[7]So when they continued asking him, he lifted up himself, and said unto them, He that is without sin among you, let him first cast a stone at her.*

You know the story. Each one of them has rocks that they start to drop, and they condemned their own selves, *convicted by their own conscience,* and they left one by one. Verse 10:

> *[10]When Jesus had lifted up himself, and saw none but the woman, he said unto her, Woman, where are those thine* **accusers**? *hath no man* **condemned** *thee?*

Now, here are the words that we can learn from, accusation and condemnation. That is satanic.

> *[11]She said, No man, Lord.*

There is no accuser, no condemner.

> *And Jesus said unto her, Neither do I condemn thee: go, and sin no more.*

That is a great lesson in what we're trying to talk about here tonight.

Now, there are different levels of godliness that you can go into here. Remember we are all at different levels of progression. One level is that when you are wrongfully accused or persecuted, or someone seeks to condemn you in any way, then let's go to section 64 in the *Doctrine and Covenants* and see what the Lord requires **of us**. What does the Lord require of us in that situation? Section 64, verse 8:

> *My disciples, in days of old, sought occasion one against another,*

What do you think that was?
Student 6: Accusing!

Mike: Yeah! They are accusing one another. So, here we are right smack in the middle of what we're talking about. I don't know what the situation was, but then it says they:

> *Sought occasion against one another and forgave not one another in their hearts; and **for this evil they were afflicted and sorely chastened.***

You see? This is good stuff. Now, we get into the heart of it. If you seek occasion against one another, whether you are the accuser or the accused, doesn't justify you:

> *[9]Wherefore, I say unto you, that ye ought to forgive one another;*

That's what the Lord says. If you're the one, who has been wrongfully persecuted or accused, and you are truly the victim, and you're guiltless in this, then the Lord says you have an obligation to forgive those who accuse, condemn, or persecute you:

> *For he that forgiveth not his brother his trespasses*

See? The Lord's spells it out here. If you are the victim, you:

> *standeth condemned before the Lord; for there remaineth in him* [the victim] *the greater sin.*

I want to share with you tonight, why that is such a great sin. Why is it that the victim can find themselves in a position that the sin is greater than the original persecutor, or the original reviler, or the original accuser?

Student 1: I don't understand when you say "the victim." I don't see that in verse 9.

Mike: In verse 9, it says if you *forgive not [your] brother his trespasses*. If your brother is trespassing against you, then you're the victim. Do you see that?

Student 1: You're right.

Mike: The Lord says in verse 10:

> *I, the Lord, will forgive whom I will forgive, but of you it is required to forgive all men.*

Now, to help you in the process, the Lord gives you a state of mind to adopt. The attitude or state of mind is in verse 11:

> *And ye ought to say in your hearts—let God judge between me and thee, and reward thee according to thy deeds.*

Now, what is that? Punishment. You're not in the position to bring a claim against this person. God sees all. You forgive, and to help you to forgive in a difficult situation, you take upon yourself this attitude and frame of mind. You ought to say in your heart, *"Let God judge between me and thee and reward thee according to thy deeds."* In other words, *"Justice is mine saith the Lord and I will repay whom I will repay,"* and you walk away and muster up that forgiveness, knowing that God will punish that person for unrighteously accusing, condemning, or persecuting you. Are we okay there?

Student 1: Yeah.

Mike: In this situation you become **justified**. There is another legal term: **justified**. In the scriptures, the term justified means found blameless, or guiltless before the accuser. That has to require a hearing and a judge, so if someone makes an accusation, it has to go all the way through to somewhere, at some point. If it doesn't happen in life, it will happen in eternity. That accusation has to be answered by law, with a hearing before a judge. And if the accuser is wrong, and you truly are the victim, then as a result of that hearing, and that accusation, and that judgment, that accuser will be punished for what they have done to you. You are justified because you have forgiven them, but your forgiveness of that person does not free them from the demands of your accusations. Did you catch that? That's an important part.

Let me say it again. **Your forgiveness does not free them from their actions.** They are still going to have to account for what they did to you. That's why it says the Lord will judge them and reward them according to their deeds. Somewhere down the road, even though you have forgiven the person, that person will have to answer before God, before a judgment, for their sins against you. Comment?

Student 4: It occurred to me that Joseph Smith was going to court all the time. I think he knew the law of the land, but he also knew the law of heaven. In different appearances in court, he pushed because he had witnesses so they wouldn't *really* put him away. And yet, he never spoke ill of the persecutors or the accusers, and he forgave them. And he knew their sins would be upon their heads for what they've done because they wouldn't let go of it. They would hang on to it.

Mike: And as a result, there would have to be some future hearing on that case, where a judgment is passed, and punishment meted out, right? Section 64 says that at least you're justified. Being justified before the law means this; when you see the term justified, or just man, or justification, that means you are found guiltless and blameless before God and any judgment for what you've done.

Student 4: Does justification come before sanctification?

Mike: It does.

Student 4: Thanks a lot.

Mike: It does come before that; you can't be sanctified unless you're justified first. Now, when you forgive a person of their wrongs, even if you have to come up to the level of saying, "God is going to take care of it, and I'm not troubling myself with it any longer," you can bet your bottom dollar that there will be a future hearing, and that person will be held accountable by God for what they did and punished for their sins, if they do not repent. If you walk away from that and you don't seek for some kind of retaliation or some kind of vengeance, and you turn it over to God, at that point you are **justified**. And that's a good place to be. Remember, if you die in a state of justification, the demands of justice have no claim on you, and the Atonement of Christ absolves you. There's another legal term. The Atonement **absolves** you from all guilt and responsibility in the matter. That's not a bad place to be, but my point is that justification is a lesser step than where we want to be. What we see here in section 64 is a wonderful place to be, and it is way up above the natural man because most people cannot find it in their hearts to forgive. Do you know how hard it is for the natural man to say, "I'm sorry. I was wrong. Can you forgive me? I love you." Do you know how hard it is for the natural man to say those words? And a lot of people will grow up, their whole lives carrying a grudge for something, and that's so tragic. And if they die in that state, they die in a state of being unjustified. That's why the Lord in Matthew 7:2 says:

For with what judgment ye judge, ye shall be judged:
and with what measure ye mete, it shall be measured
to you again.

If you want to be forgiven of your sins, then do what? Forgive others. If you want mercy, then show mercy.

Student 6: This is fantastic. This is really, really good.

Mike: So, all of these things are to put us in a state where we can learn to forgive, become justified, to move on, and develop a love for our fellow man. But, I want to end the lesson tonight with something much deeper and much more significant.

Turn to section 45 in the *Doctrine and Covenants.* Beyond forgiveness, there is another step. This first step of being forgiving is truly Christ-like, but the next step is **Godly**. The next step puts you in a place where the Elohim dwell. This is a part that very few people discover, and Margie and I discovered this while we were on a mission in New Jersey. Let's go to section 45. We're going to read verses 3, 4, and 5. This is deeper and more significant. This puts you within the society of those who dwell among the Elohim, the fathers and mothers in heaven, who dwell in heaven to go no more out. Verse 3:

Listen to him who is the advocate with the Father,
who is pleading your cause before him—

Now, if you go over to England today, and even here in the United States, you will have signs outside of Law offices saying *Law firms* or *Lawyer.* In England, the word for lawyer is **advocate.** So, an advocate is representing somebody before the law. Isn't that right, isn't that what lawyers do? Now, think of the Father as the judge. You are the aggrieved party, and you have an Advocate between you and the Father, Who is the judge. This is a very, very graphic legal image that is portrayed here. You can see how this works. Now, listen to what the Advocate says when He pleads the cause of the **plaintiff.** By the way, we are all plaintiffs because we haven't earned anything in this life except one thing. You'll notice that the word *earned* is not found anywhere in scriptures, but I will tell you that there is one thing that we have earned and that is to go to hell!

So, we need somebody to plead our case. Listen to what the Advocate says:

[4]Father, behold the sufferings and death of him who did no sin, in whom thou wast well pleased; behold the blood of thy Son which was shed, the blood of him whom thou gavest that thyself might be glorified;

Notice in the advocacy and in the pleading, there is something that is interesting. In a court of law, in this world, the lawyer pleads your cause as he stands before the judge. He is drawing the judge's attention to you, the plaintiff. The attorney in a legal case, in a world case, in the telestial world, never refers to his own life, his own circumstances, in order to plead the cause of the plaintiff. He never does it. He is drawing the judge's attention to the accused, or to the plaintiff. Notice that here, in this scripture, He draws the attention to Himself. Not once in verse 4, does the advocate mention the plaintiff; not once. He says look at Me, remember My blood, remember Gethsemane Father; remember Golgotha Father, remember the blood, remember the life, remember the ministry, and everything He does when He pleads the cause before the Father is pointing toward His atoning life. In the next verse that *"wherefore"* means because you're looking on Me, because you remember what I did, because you were there with Me in Gethsemane, because of the cross:

[5]Wherefore, Father, spare these my brethren that believe on my name, that they may come unto me have everlasting life.

That is a beautiful picture, isn't it? Isn't that a beautiful, wonderful scripture?

How does that apply to the accuser, which we talked about tonight? If you bring no accusation against those, who abuse you, if you instead forgive them and then go to the next step, what's the next step? You pray for them. You plead their cause before Christ, and the Father like Christ pleads for your cause to the Father. When you do that you have taken upon yourself the role of a God. You become in your own way, a savior for that person who has accused and seeks to condemn you. You become a savior for them because if you make no accusation, and if you pray for them, the hearing is canceled in your behalf. There will be no hearing. There is no indictment. There would be nothing brought before the judgment bar. That person will be held accountable for their own actions but not as they are related to you. What has taken place between them and you is now erased. And in a very real way, you have now saved a sinner from death because you advocated their cause. You became Christ-like in this situation, as it relates to you, and the person who seeks to accuse and condemn you. Comments?

Student 6: Mike? Will they be held accountable? You're saying that that person will be held accountable with God, but wouldn't be accountable toward you, or toward justice being obtained? Do you get what I'm saying? Do you get my question? They are held accountable for what they do, but it's a state of forgiveness for that person and not accountable, or whatever, then that means that they are not accountable?

Mike: Well, the interaction between you and them, changes dramatically. This doesn't mean that just because what took place between you two has been properly handled, that that will change their nature. In all likelihood, this one thing that's taken place between you and them isn't the only time they've done something like that. The person who is receiving the greater benefit from this is the advocate. **You're** the one that is receiving the greater benefit. Will this and can this have an effect on them and cause them to stop and consider which way they're going and come to Christ and have a mighty change of heart? It sure can! Will it? I don't know. But, the interaction between you two has been resolved in a Godly way, so that you are blessed for your Christ-like actions. Your nature is further transformed, and they, at least as it relates to you, will not be held accountable for their transgression against you, because you interceded on their behalf and pled their cause before the Father. And the Father will honor that because of your righteousness. Brothers and sisters, when you go to this level, it is beyond forgiveness. Forgiveness is marvelous, but **this** is beyond forgiveness! Let me read to you a statement by a person who understands this principle:

> *When we accuse others we interfere with **their** salvation.*

Now think about that a bit. Think about that for just a minute. If we are the one who was offended (we're the victim) and we make no accusation against them, then we become their savior. Ooooh, that is such a deeply profound principle! If we properly understood this, we would take our interactions with our fellow man to this deeper level, proving that we would take upon ourselves the nature of God the Father and the Son.

Student: That is Zion! That would be like a Zion people!

Mike: I think you're right. Going on with this comment by this person, listen to this,

> Satan's right to accuse is inferior to ours as the victim of the offense. We suffer in the flesh the wrong of others. If we make no claim for justice, surrender those claims, and seek instead for mercy on behalf others, [this is called intercession] then Satan's accusations have no claim on them. We mimic Christ, follow his example, and in our own limited way, also atone for the sins of others.

What do we do it? We suffer in the flesh the wrongs of others, and we make no claim for justice and no accusations against them. Now, go with me to 1 Nephi 19, we'll wrap up tonight's lesson.

Student 4: Can you send me that quote?

Mike: I can send you that quote, yes, but I won't give you a reference for it because the person who gave it to me does not want his identity made known.

Okay, 1 Nephi 19, and let's go to verses 7-9:

> [7]For the things which some men esteem to be of great worth, both to the body and soul, others set at naught and trample under their feet. Yea, even the very God of Israel do men trample under their feet; I say, trample under their feet, but I would speak in other words – they set him at naught, and hearken not to the voice of his counsels.

Now, tonight from the scriptures, we've heard the voice of the Lord give us some counsel on how we should properly interact with our fellow man, our husbands and wives, and with our children. In your interactions, brothers and sisters, whenever we have an interaction with each other, if one or both parties walk away feeling the other is an enemy, then your interaction was done wrong. Anytime that we interact with each other and if one or both parties feel that the other is an enemy, or in any way have any kind of animosity, then the way you interacted was wrong. You need to ponder that and do it differently. Now, we've learned some ways that we can do that tonight.

Go to the next verse:

> *[8]And behold he cometh, according to the words of the angel, in six hundred years from the time my father left Jerusalem.*

Pay attention to this part right here. Think about what we've talked about tonight. Think about advocacy, accusation, condemnation, and about intercession.

> *[9]And the world, because of their iniquity, shall judge him to be a thing of naught; wherefore they scourge him, and he suffereth it;*

The word *naught* means worthless, no value. Every time you see the phrase *"He suffereth it,"* it means that he does not make a claim. He does not accuse. He does not revile. He simply takes it. He does what I call, **absorbs the hit.** You absorb the hit. You take it in, and it stops with you. It goes no further than you. This is true. In the Sermon on the Mount it says:

> *Blessed are the peacemakers for they shall be called the children of God.*

A peacemaker is a person who is a victim, who takes the hit and does not pass it on. You take it and absorb it, and the whole condition stops with you. Usually, what do we do when and we take a hit? What do we do? Well, we hit back. And then that person hits back, and then you hit back, and that person hits back, and then you hit back, and there is no end. Somebody has to absorb the hit. So, in 1 Nephi 19:9, Jesus teaches us how to absorb the hit:

> *Wherefore they scourge him, and he suffereth it; and they smite him, and he suffereth it. Yea, they spit upon him, and he suffereth it,*

How can we do this? And here is the answer to how He was able to do it. And I testify to you tonight, if we will practice the principles taught and talked about tonight, from the scriptures, we can do this the same way Christ did:

> *because of his loving kindness and his long-suffering towards the children of men.*

When you advocate the cause of another person before God, it is impossible for you to **not** be transformed as a result of that process. You cannot do it. Do you want to know how to access the divine nature of the Father and the Son? Do you want to know how to take upon yourself the characteristics of God and become godly yourself? This is one of the primary ways. One of the ways is that you *forgive others their trespasses.* Do you want to really transform? Do you really want to access the flow of divine power and grace in your life and not only forgive them but pray for them? Can you see the Savior hanging on the cross, bleeding, and saying, *"Father forgive them"*? See, **we** need to do that. We need to take the people that hang us on our own crosses, spit on us, scourge us, revile us, and persecute us and we need to pray for them. If you will pray for them to the Father in the name of Christ, pray for mercy for your enemies; then you will see a transformation in your life to where you will become a son or daughter of Christ so much more rapidly that you could ever have conceived before.

The deeper and more significant ways that we can follow Christ will transform us quicker and more completely. That is really what we're trying to do, brothers and sisters. Aren't we trying to become Christ-like? 2 Nephi 31:17:

> *Wherefore, do the things which I have told you I have seen that your Lord and your Redeemer should do;*

Go and do those things. And as you go and do what you have seen and learned that He has done, then you will more quickly and more fully become like Him. Any thoughts? That's it for tonight.

Student 1: We bless them! We bless them.

Student 6: What a wonderful lesson! Thank you, Brother Stroud. We appreciate it so much.

Mike: Well, that was a great lesson the Lord taught us while we were in the mission field in New Jersey, and was one of the great lessons and concepts and principles that we've learned. I will tell you, though, that if you plug this into your awareness this week, it will be a great awakening for you to see how often we assume the role of an accuser. It is Satanic. We don't want to be that way. Now, here's a way where knowledge is power. Remember, Joseph Smith said, *"a man or a woman is saved no faster than they get knowledge."* We have studied the battle tactics of Lucifer and his followers tonight. We have also studied the grace and mercy of our Savior, and that we overcome the *accuser of the brethren* by the blood of the Lamb and the testimony of the brethren.

References:
Revelation 12:9
D&C 121:43
John8:1
D&C 64:8-11
Matthew 7:2
D&C 45:3-5
1Nephi 19:7-9
2 Nephi 31:17

Class Handout

Accusation

When we accuse others we <u>interfere with their salvation.</u> If we are the one who was offended, and we make no accusation against them, <u>then we become their savior.</u> <u>Satan's right to accuse is inferior to ours as victims of the offense.</u> We suffer in the flesh the wrongs of others. If we make no claim for justice, surrender those claims, <u>***and seek instead for mercy on behalf of others (intercession),***</u> then Satan's accusations can have no claim upon them. We mimic Christ, follow His example, and in our own limited way, <u>***also atone for the sins of others.***</u>

Intercession

Remember how often great souls have interceded for their fellow man. Intercession for your fellow man, including those who give offense to you, <u>***is one of the hallmarks of the saved soul.***</u> If an inspired condemnation is required at your hand, and by your voice, then immediately afterward you should make intercession with the Lord for those condemned. <u>***That is the way of those who know the Lord.***</u> Those who have been forgiven much, including those who have been forgiven everything, always love much in return. (Luke 7:47)

Chapter Seven
Podcast 007 Tokens and Signs

I would like to talk to you tonight about something I experienced this week. One of my grandsons came up and spent three days with me. He is 16 years old and is having some difficulty with his mother at home. It's the difficulties teenagers and moms have sometimes but times ten. It sometimes gets pretty heated and contentious, even to the point that the laying on of hands takes place, and this one grandson was pushed to the edge where he said he didn't know if he could restrain himself from hitting his mother. So, he came and I pulled him into my office. We have a good relationship and I talked to him a little bit. His father has forbidden him from doing that (hitting his mother) and has spent a considerable amount of time talking about the consequences if he were to give in to his anger and frustration and do that. And basically, the talks are about forbidding and threatening on what he had better not do, or else. So, I sat down and talked to him. And he did not need to hear about consequences one more time from grandpa. As I pondered what I was going to say to him, the following things developed in my mind. It was that saying by Boyd K. Packer that true doctrine, understood, changes behavior faster than a discussion of behavior will change behavior. And so, I took it upon myself to teach him some true doctrine. I was not going to threaten him. I was not going to talk about the dire consequences. I was not going to talk about forbidding him from doing something. I just went at it from a different angle. And so, I sat down and the Spirit began to unfold the following things. I don't know if I can tell it exactly right for you, but you'll get the gist of it. This story leads into what I want to share with you tonight. It has to do with tokens and signs. Now, these are two words that Latter-day Saints understand, but it will have very little meaning outside of the restoration doctrines restored through Joseph Smith. I want to talk to you a little bit about tokens and signs.

On with the story; I told him that there was something within every man that is a part of his core value, his nature. Every man comes into this life with the desire to protect women, and that desire is placed in us by Heavenly Father. The most opposite thing that a man can do, against his nature, is to harm a woman in any way, whether it be physical, verbal, emotional, or sexual. It goes against a man's nature. In a woman, there is also a part of her core nature that wants to be protected by a man. These are things that are placed within us by our Heavenly Father.

I told my 16-year-old grandson, "You may not understand this now, but you will later when you become a husband, and a father and these feelings begin to mature in you. Take my word for it, that you have something in you, given to you by God, which is designed to provide protection for women. The consequences of going against that are not what I want to talk to about. I want to talk about the damage that it will do to you because you have gone opposite of your nature. If you do that, it may be something that you will have a very difficult time getting over, or you may not get over it at all, in your life. It may be something that you will carry with you for the rest of your life. In this instance, physical violence goes against your very core nature given to you by your Heavenly Father." We chatted a little bit about that, and I asked him if he understood, and he said that he thought he did.

"But," I said, "Let's go a step further. What is the most precious, precious metal on earth?"

He quickly said, "Gold."

I said, "Yes, unless it is in nugget form because when you first find gold, it is usually in the form of gold ore. In gold ore, you will find a percentage of gold in the ore, mixed with other things, other metals, and other types of materials that have to be separated from the gold, otherwise, the gold remains valueless in its ore state. It cannot be used for jewelry. It cannot be used for coins. It cannot be used for anything until there is some kind of a process that separates the gold that is in the ore, from the other elements that are not as valuable as the gold." I said, "Do you know what the process is to separate the gold from the ore so that you get that precious metal out of there?"

And he immediately said, "Yes, it's heat and pressure."

I was impressed that he knew that. I said, "That is much like us in our natural state, in this fallen state that we find ourselves in, we are much like gold ore. There is something precious and valuable and divine inside of us, but it is mixed up in our natural man state, with things that are not godly, and we need to be able to separate those things out. Now, you're in a situation where you get angry at your mom, and she gets angry at you. Did you ever stop to consider that the situation you wish had never happened and that you'd never experienced is the very situation that God has allowed you to be? Allowed, so that under heat and pressure, the gold that is a part of your nature can be released from the other things and can become precious and valuable; and it can happen in no other way other than by heat and pressure?" I said, "Do you understand what I'm saying?"

And he said, "Yes."

Then I said, "The difference is not in what is happening. The difference is in how you view what is happening. And so, what I want you to do is to develop a different view of what is taking place in your life. Instead of something to forsake, escape, or physically react to, I want you to view it as perhaps one of the best laboratories you could ever be involved in to process the gold that is a part of you. Because there is gold in you, and it is a part of you that can only be released by heat and pressure. The greater the pressure, the greater the heat, the quicker the refinement."

He pondered these things, and we talked back and forth, and I said, "Your view now should be to see this as a blessing from your Heavenly Father. When you are asking to be delivered from it, you may be asking to be removed from the very thing that is the most important, valuable lesson, and laboratory that you could ever be in at this point in your life. So, rather than asking to be delivered from it, ask the Lord to strengthen you and change your view of it so that it can become a positive experience and refine the gold that is in your nature, and separate it from the dross that the natural man brings into the equation." I asked him if he understood that, and he said that he did.

I continued, "I want you to take the word GOLD, and I want you to use that as a **token**. In other words, when you get in a situation that's trying, and you feel like you're going to lose your temper, do things you know you shouldn't do and go against your very nature; I want you to think of the word GOLD and use that as a token. It's a token to remind you of the view you should take instead of the way you have looked at it in the past. So, if you're down there and you get into trouble, and a challenging situation arises, I want you to call me and as we talk I will say one thing. I'll say, 'Sammy!' And you'll say, 'What grandpa?' And I'll say, 'GOLD.' When you hear that one word you will understand what we're talking about. That becomes a token of something you can hang on to, to help you have a different view."

I also told him the story of when I was here in Eagar, attending the Assembly of God Church. A friend of mine, Dennis Weiskircher, who was the pastor, got up and gave a lesson. He said this, "The difference between life and death is 14 inches." I thought that it was awfully interesting and wondered what he meant. And then he did this: he pointed up to his head, and then he pointed to his heart, and the distance between the head and the heart is 14 inches. The difference between life and death is 14 inches. In other words, if we never let what's in our head, sink down into our heart, then we will never achieve what God wants us to do. In the LDS vernacular, up in the head, we have testimony, but down in the heart, we have conversion. As long as a Latter-day Saint remains with a testimony and is never converted, they will always be vulnerable to leaving the Church and being distracted and deceived by every wind of doctrine. Those who are truly converted never will fall away. And so, Brother Eyring has talked about from *head to heart*, and he makes this motion; finger at your head and then it moves down to your heart. That is a **sign**. And that sign is teaching us something. It is a key to unlock knowledge that changes the way we think and can eventually, change our very nature.

I once worked on a ranch down at Arivaca with a bunch of boys that were headed for prison, and one of them was a boy by the name of Josh Harris. He was Jewish, and we had *a good many talks* about the gospel, about Christ, about the *Old Testament*, and about the Jewish law when we were riding horses back out in that Sonora desert country. One of the things that I taught Josh was, "Unless you get what you know is truth from your head, down into your heart, you are never going to be the man that God wants you to be. You have to be **heart**-centered and **not head**-centered." So, Josh and I developed this relationship and every time we saw each other, and it was time to leave, he would touch his head, and then his heart and no words were spoken. And no words needed to be spoken because that became a **sign** of that doctrine; from head to heart. And until it gets to your heart, it really doesn't do the job it's supposed to in changing and transforming you. I told my grandson this same thing.

Right now, Josh is living in Israel. This month he is going into the Israeli Defense Force and will be an Israeli Commando. The other day he Skyped me from Jerusalem, and as we finished the conversation, I said, "Josh, it was so good to see you again."

He calls me big Mike because that's what they called me down there. He said, "Big Mike, I love you, and I'm thankful for our friendship," and then without saying a word he touched his head and then touched his heart. He said, "I love you" and that was all that was necessary. Nothing needed to be spoken because the message was there. We understood perfectly well the feelings, the doctrine, and the thoughts associated with that sign.

And so, I told that to my grandson. This is the sign. What you're doing here is you're in a laboratory, and if you will allow it, God will take something that is up here in your head and help you move it down into your heart. As you do that, all of these difficulties that you are experiencing in your home will take care of themselves, and you will be able to have a great experience and become the man that God wants you to be, because of the pressure and the heat involved in this learning laboratory. So, we gave him a **token** and a **sign**; the token is gold, and the sign is a move from head to heart. He now has a token and a sign to help him in this difficult, challenging situation that he is in.

Brothers and sisters, if you look in the topical guide, *token* is not a word that is used a whole lot. But I will tell you that all tokens are associated with covenants. All signs are associated with covenants. In the temple, we have five things. We have a law that is given to us first. Following the law, we are given a covenant. God gives us a covenant and invites us to enter into a covenant associated with the law. The law comes first and then an invitation to enter into a covenant. Remember, that man does not initiate covenants. Covenants always are initiated by the Father through His Son. When a covenant invitation is given, all man does is exercises his agency to accept the covenant, or reject it. Covenants with God never begin with man. Now, man can enter into vows and make vows and promises, but covenants come from God by invitation, you either accept or reject. Once you enter into a covenant, there is a token that is always involved with the covenant. And there is a sign. Then, the fifth thing is that there is a name.

Anciently, these five things were involved in all ancient societies that had any vestments of gospel truth within their framework; **law**, **covenant**, **token**, **sign**, and **name**. Now, these things were restored by the prophet Joseph Smith. Much of it was found within the Abraham papyrus. And Joseph received much of what he restored in the endowment ceremonies, in the Joseph Smith Red Brick Store, starting in May of 1842. Some of these ordinances were performed in the Mansion House and in the Red Brick Store. Some of them were performed out in the open nature. All of them had their beginnings through revelation, and much of what he found in the endowment came from the Abraham papyrus, and then further revelation.

Let's take an ordinance for just a minute and see what we've got. Let's take the first covenant that we enter into as members of the Church. What is the first covenant that we enter into? Is it church-centered or is it temple-centered? What is the first covenant that we enter into?

Student 6: Baptism.

Mike: Okay, it's baptism. The first covenant that you're invited to enter into is baptism. Is that correct?

Student 6: Yes.

Mike: And that is administered to by the Church of Jesus Christ of Latter-day Saints through the Aaronic Priesthood. That's an Aaronic Priesthood ordinance. Is that correct?

Student 6: Yes.

Mike: When John the Baptist restored the Aaronic Priesthood, he restored the gospel of repentance, baptism by immersion for the remission of sins, and the ministry of angels. That's all Aaronic Priesthood. Now, what is the token for the ordinance of baptism? You know what the law is. The law is if you're not baptized you cannot enter the celestial world. *"Except a man be born of the water and of the Spirit, he cannot enter into the kingdom of God."* That's the law. Now, let's look at the covenant. Mosiah 18, verses 8, 9 and 10 spells out the covenants that you are invited to enter into that are associated with baptism. Alma is speaking:

> *And it came to pass that he said unto them: Behold, here are the waters of Mormon (for thus were they called) and now, as ye are **desirous** to come into the fold of God, and to be **called his people**, and are willing to **bear one another's burdens**, that they may be light;*
>
> *[9] Yea, and are **willing to mourn with those that mourn**; yea, and **comfort those that stand in need of comfort**, and to **stand as witnesses of God** at all times and in all things, and in all places that ye may be in, even until death, that ye may be redeemed of God, and be numbered with those of the first resurrection, that ye may have eternal life –*
>
> *[10] Now I say unto you, if this be the desire of your hearts, what have you against being baptized in the name of the Lord, as a witness before him that ye have entered into a covenant with him, that ye will serve him and keep his commandments, that he may pour out his Spirit more abundantly upon?*

That is the baptismal covenant. You have to (1) be desirous; (2) be called his people; (3) bear one another's burdens; (4) mourn with those that mourn; (5) comfort those that stand in need of comfort; and (6) stand as a witness of God.

So what is the token? We now have the law, and we just read the covenant. What is the token? What is the token of baptism?

Student 1: You have to be dunked into the water.

Mike: That's right. The token is: you go down into the water, under the water, and are brought forth out of the water. That's the token of baptism. What is the sign?

Student 6: The arm being raised.

Mike: It is the arm raised to the square. That is the sign. What is the name?

Student 1: Jesus Christ.

Mike: It is. You now take upon yourself the name of Christ. Interesting. Let's take another ordinance that is performed. What is one of the most sacred ordinances performed in the Church of Jesus Christ of Latter-day Saints?

Student 6: The sacrament.

Mike: The sacrament, right? Let's look at the sacrament. There is a law there. The Lord issued that law, and he said, *"This do in remembrance of my body and of my blood."* What is the covenant? Think of the prayer. You take upon yourself the name of Christ, always remember Him, and keep His commandments. Is that right? Is that the covenant?

Student 6: Yes.

Mike: And if you do that, the other side of the covenant is: you have His Spirit to be with you. What's the token?

Student 6: The taking of the water and bread.

Mike: That's right, so the emblems of the token become the bread and water. Okay? You go through all of these different things, and you'll see that every ordinance has tokens and signs involved. What is the sign of the sacrament? When you look up there, every Sunday, what do you see up there? Before they speak the words of the covenant, what do you see up there? You see a table, don't you?

Student 3: Yeah.

Mike: Okay. And what does that table have on it? It has the emblems and the tokens, right? It has the bread and water and is covered with a white cloth. Have you ever wondered what that thing represents? What's the sign of the sacrament?

Student 6: The white cloth?

Mike: It is a funeral bier with a shrouded body. If you look up there, you will see that it becomes an altar with the body of Christ on it. And if it's covered with a white cloth, it resembles a body being covered with a burial shroud. It's an interesting sign, interesting symbols, interesting emblems, interesting tokens, all pointing towards what? It's all pointing to the death, ministry, resurrection, and Atonement of Christ.

Student 1: It **is** interesting! I never thought of that.

Mike: So, if you look, you will see every one of these things and some of them you have to search a little bit for. Let's go to the law of Moses. Okay? Because they rejected the higher law, they were given a schoolmaster law, but it still had laws and covenants. When you get down to the law of Moses, what was the token of the law of Moses? There were lots of laws, and there were covenants involved, but what was the token associated with the law of Moses? Did you know what it was? If you look up *token* in the topical guide, it will take you to Exodus, and it says that the blood of animals shed on those altars was the token of sacrifice. Blood was a token. When the destroying angel passes through the land of Goshen, what is the token of deliverance? How did the Israelites escape the death of the firstborn, which was the 10th plague? How did they do that? There was a token that was given for them to escape the destroying angel and Exodus tells us what was. What was it?

Students: The blood on the door.

Mike: Yes, it was the blood across the lintel and the posts of the door. If you had that token of sacrificial blood on your door, the destroying angel passed over you and did not destroy those within that house.

Student 6: That was quite a miracle!

Mike: You can have some fun with this, and I'm telling you this now so that you can take this into your temple worship because in the temple is where you really start to see where this comes alive. Let's look at another token; the Abrahamic covenant. There was a law given to Abraham. He was invited to enter into a covenant where certain promises were made by God, that if he were faithful, then he would enjoy such things as posterity, the blessings of the gospel, the blessings of the priesthood, and a land of inheritance. Abraham accepted that, and God said, "And here's the token of the covenant that you have made with me. I gave you this. I invited you to enter into it. You have accepted it. Now, here is the token of the Abrahamic covenant." What was it?

Student 3: Circumcision?

Mike: Yes! It was circumcision. Nobody had been circumcised at that time, young or older men had not been circumcised. Abraham was commanded to take all men who entered into and accepted that covenant, to be circumcised. Now, that circumcision is a token in your flesh, reminding you of something. There is a sign that accompanies that anciently and the sign anciently was upraised hands; ancient symbols that go all the way back to Adam. And there were also names associated with that. All through the scriptures, we can see tokens and signs that were used to help us successfully fulfill the covenants and reap the blessings associated with the covenants that God offers us. They become reminders. The tokens are in many cases physical reminders that point you toward and remind you of the covenant that you have entered into with God, to help you remain faithful and true to that covenant. The garment that we wear as a result of our temple experience is a token. The garment is a token of a covenant. Every time that you put that garment on, it is to remind you of the covenants that you made with God, in holy places, and to help you have the power to maintain faithfulness in your part of the covenant.

Let's go to the Book of Mormon and think of Captain Moroni. Can you see a token of the covenant that Captain Moroni used? Remember the covenant, "That we will remember in defense of our families, of our lands, of our religion, our...this that and the other?" Remember the covenant? What was the token?

Students: The flag. The Title of Liberty.

Mike: It was the Title of Liberty. If you read Alma 46, another one is when the people were invited to join Moroni. They came forth rending their clothes as a token of the covenant that they were entering into. Isn't that interesting?

Student 1: Yes.

Mike: Now, every token that we take upon ourselves as Latter-day Saints, has a superficial meaning followed by increasingly deeper meanings, as the Lord reveals them to you.

Tokens that we use are **gestures** that are designed to **teach** us something and to help us remember the promises, covenants, and obligations that we have entered into as we have accepted the covenant relationship when God has offered it to us. So, the token to my grandson is that he is to think of gold. I could have a gold piece. I could show him a gold ring, or anything that is made of gold, a gold coin. I could hold that up on Skype, without saying a word, and he would understand exactly what I am talking about. He would think of our discussion. I would not have to say anything. I could simply hold up this piece of gold, and not say a word and he would understand exactly what we are talking about. That is the same as tokens.

Student 4: Did you get him a gold nugget?

Mike: Ha-ha! I ought to find one. I should get something that I could use.

Student 4: Get a Krugerrand for him!

Mike: Geez, I can't afford that! Ha-ha! You're talking $1200 there. That's too expensive of a lesson.

Now, signs in the temple are used to identify, to discern, or as keys that unlock and open spiritual doors. Think of these tokens and signs around us all the time. I mean, we use them all the time, but we don't think of them. Then take that pattern and apply it to your spiritual devotion, especially as it pertains to temple worship. I think you're going to see a whole new world opened up to you that you haven't seen before.

Student 4: We never did get to Moroni. What did you want to show us in Moroni?

Mike: Captain Moroni had the Title of Liberty. That's over there in Alma 46. The Title of Liberty becomes a token of the covenant that there are willing to go into. They're willing to give their lives, in remembrance of their wives, their children, their lands, their God and everything else. So, you see, that becomes a token. And **rending** their garments is a sign accompanying that token that they are willing to enter into that relationship. They commit themselves. It became a sign that if you tore your garment and aligned yourself with that token, that Title of Liberty, that you, without speaking a word, no one had to say anything, it was understood that you would give your life for this cause.

In section 129 verse 7, in the *Doctrine and Covenants*, the Lord gives us a sign. If you have a messenger that comes to you, you are to ask him to shake hands with you. You are seeking for some kind of a sign that he is a true messenger. Okay? If you go to the temple, and I can't go into it any more than this, but in the temple, we talk about the tokens and the signs. The handshake is the token part, and then there is the sign that accompanies that, and you can determine whether or not the messenger is a true messenger, or it's a counterfeit from the devil.

Student 1: You're saying that the handshake is the sign?

Mike: No. The handshake is the token. And there is an accompanying sign that goes with it. When you go to the temple, you can look at that, and it's the token and sign given to Adam before he's cast out of the Garden of Eden. I find that interesting that he receives that before he goes into the lone and dreary world. In the lone and dreary world, he finds himself completely within the veil, forgets everything from the terrestrial Garden of Eden, and when Lucifer appears again in the telestial world, he says, "Who are you?" It's all forgotten. In the terrestrial world they can have a free discussion, both Adam and Eve, but in the telestial world they are within the veil, and so God gives him a token and a sign to detect evil from good. Look at verse 9 in section 129, and here is what the Lord says:

> These are three grand **keys** whereby you may
> know whether **any** administration is from God.

So, the tokens and signs that you receive in the temple are keys. Those are keys. I'm old enough to remember before there were some alterations made in the endowment ceremony, that they had a lecture at the veil. After you had gone through the endowment, there was a lecture at the veil where they repeated the whole endowment ceremony in a short form. And they referred to the signs and the tokens that you received in the endowment, as the keys of the priesthood. These are the *keys of the priesthood*. And they also referred to them as the *mysteries of godliness*.

Student 1: Now, can I ask you a question?

Mike: Yes.

Student: Okay, let's say tomorrow a messenger comes to you. You would really ask him to find out if he was a good one or a bad one?

Mike: Well, I would do this: If I received any kind of administration from behind the veil, the first thing I would say is, "Who are you?" That's the first thing I would say. And if he comes out and says, "I'm a messenger from God." I would say, "How do I know that you are a messenger from God?"

Student 1: Ok, so you would ask those questions.

Mike: Yes, and I would repeat what you are taught in the temple, word for word because he cannot give you the token and sign. He can't do that. He may try to deceive, he may try to give you a false sign, but what you received in the temple is Godly. So, I would say, "Who are you?" and then he would say who he is. And I would say, "How do I know that's who you are?" and I would wait for his response. If he is a true messenger, he would probably say something like this, "By me giving you the token and the sign that you've already received." If he doesn't do that, I would immediately have my radar up, and I'd be looking for an impersonator.

Student 1: I kind of thought so, but wasn't sure.

Mike: Now, section 129 talks about that. If it is the devil, he will stretch forth his hand, and you won't feel it and etc., etc. There is more to it than that. That's good, but I will just say that I would memorize what you learn in the temple, the whole dialogue that has to do with receiving messengers. And I'd make sure you understand that because that is a Godly, inspired dialogue and you need to be able to say and do it exactly. He may try to stretch forth his hand, you may not feel it, but the dialogue is what you want. You want to make sure that there is a token and a sign. See, in section 129, it's only talking about the token. In the temple, there is a token and a sign, and you want to do that. Okay?

Student 6: Does it matter what sign they give you?

Mike: It does. They need to give the sign that determines a true messenger from a false messenger. And you need to go back and listen in the temple. "How do I know that you are a true messenger?" Adam says. And you need to listen to that dialogue and memorize that dialogue. That dialogue cannot be duplicated and the token and sign that is given at that time cannot be impersonated or duplicated.

We had some people over here in this country that were doing some prayer circles out in the desert. A group of them got together, and they dressed in their temple clothes, and they built an altar, and they went out, and they offered up the signs of the priesthood, and Joseph Smith appeared to this group of men and women. One of them said, "Let me shake your hand." This person who was Joseph Smith said, "We don't need to do that. That is for less enlightened individuals. Obviously, you're out here practicing the *True Order of Prayer* and offering up the signs of the priesthood. You're more advanced, so we don't need to do that. That's for people who are less advanced." He didn't give his hand, and they accepted his administration. And a whole group of people left the Church and went to Manti, Utah and began that little church in Manti that's still up there. These were all endowed members. And I can only assume that this person who appeared took upon himself the appearance of Joseph Smith because that's who they thought he was. This person who appeared looked like Joseph Smith. These spirits can apparently do those kinds of things, so you have to be really careful.

Do you remember a few weeks ago when I read to you about Joseph telling us how you discern true from false spirits and he listed eight things? He said this:

> *No man can do this without the Priesthood, and having knowledge of the laws by which spirits are governed; for as "no man knows the things of God, but by the spirit of God," so no man knows the spirit of the devil, and his power and influence, but by possessing intelligence which is more than human, and having unfolded through the medium of the Priesthood the mysterious operations of his devices;*

And he lists eight things, listen to this:

> *Without knowing the angelic form, the sanctified look and gesture, the zeal which is frequently manifested him by the glory of God, together with the prophetic spirit, gracious influence, godly appearance, and the holy garb which are so characteristic of his proceedings and mysterious windings.*

He is describing Lucifer appearing as an Angel of Light. That all sounds godly, but it is not.

So, you need to have knowledge of tokens and signs in order to discern what is true and what is false. That is what the temple is teaching us. The temple wants us to be like Adam and Eve. The temple wants us to receive messengers. The temple wants you to have angelic ministration, either seen or unseen. The scriptures want you to do that. But, when you open the veil, you open it to both good and evil. That goes with veil piercing. When you pierce the veil, you open it to both the dark and the light. That should not scare you because you have been given the tools to discern the one from the other.

These angels and messengers, brothers and sisters, have information for you that you need and is reserved for you, that you can't get any other way. And yet, it comes also with a price. That price is the opposite of what God wants, so you have to be able to tell. And that little quote by Joseph Smith says, "It's the power of the priesthood that governs the laws pertaining to these ministering spirits, and the Lord will teach you." Do you have a comment?

Student 4: Where was that quote taken from, exactly? Was it *the Teachings of Joseph Smith*, or something?

Mike: What we will do is put it on the Dropbox if you like. Do you want me to do that?

Student 4: Sure.

Mike: It's in the *Teachings of the Prophet Joseph Smith*, and that was April 9, 1842. It's also in *Doctrinal History of the Church*, DHC, volume 4 page 587. I'll have Margie put that up for you. The name of this quote is *Discerning of Spirits by the Power of the Priesthood*.

Student 4: Thank you.

Mike: There's another part of this, it says this:

> A man must have the discerning of spirits before he can drag into daylight this hellish influence and unfolded it unto the world in all its soul-destroying, diabolical, and horrid colors; **for nothing is a greater injury to the children of men than to be under the influence of a false spirit when they think they have the spirit of God.**

Tricky stuff!

Student 6: Well, Brother Stroud, I remember you telling us that the adversary cannot duplicate the Spirit of peace and comfort; the peace that we know that comes with that. So, that's helpful to know.

Mike: That's another one, and that's such a valuable thing to know. That's another quote by the prophet Joseph Smith, and also from the words of Oliver Cowdery, that the things that accompany true manifestations of the Spirit of God are peace, and joy, and the whole desire that you will have to do good. Those are the three things. And you are right [student], it is those things that Lucifer cannot duplicate, but I will tell you that he will try to and you have to be on your toes. My feeling is, especially today, as we move closer and closer to the culmination of prophetic events, that he is going to become more and more devious, more and more cunning, and his impersonations are going to look more and more like the truth than ever before. And we have to take the knowledge and information that comes with the priesthood, its laws, its covenants, its tokens, its signs, and its names. We need to know that stuff so that we are not dragged off and find ourselves on strange roads because it's tricky. It's really tricky.

Student 6: But, Brother Stroud, it doesn't seem like it would be tricky. If the adversary can't duplicate joy and having the spirit of helpfulness, or the spirit of trying to do what is right, then that has to be a solid thing.

Mike: Do you know what? Did you know that it's not tricky to you because you've been taught true doctrine? You understand that. You have that in your mind. But, millions of Latter-day Saints are not familiar with that quote by the Prophet Joseph, and that he came back from the dead years after he had died, and told Brigham Young to teach the people this. See, you are in possession of that knowledge. And once you're in possession of that knowledge, then we can sit back and say, rightly so, "It doesn't seem like it would be too tricky to me." But if you are not in possession of that knowledge, which the majority of the Latter-day Saints are not, then it becomes a tricky, slippery slope. Does that make sense?

So, this is again an instance of where knowledge is power and where Joseph said a man cannot be saved without knowledge, "*A man is saved only as fast as he gets knowledge.*" Think about the keys that you are in possession of.

Now, in closing, I have a quote that I'm just going to refer to, and I am not going to get into it tonight. It was given in the Nauvoo Temple, it's in the Seventies book, and it teaches us about tokens and signs of the Priesthood. Go to section 124 in the *Doctrine and Covenants*, verse 94. When Oliver Cowdery apostatized from the Church, Hyrum Smith was called by revelation to take his place. What we're talking about here is what you receive in the temple. Okay, this is a reference to something that you have already received in the temple. Now, the date of section 124 is 1841, and the Lord is just beginning to open up the depth of the temple endowment. The first endowments were given in May of 1842. This was given in 1841, and the Lord is going to refer to something that Joseph and Hyrum have, that every Latter-day Saint can have access to as they go through the temple.

> *And from this time forth I appoint unto him* [Hyrum] *that he may be a prophet, and a seer, and a revelator unto my church, as well as my servant Joseph;*
>
> *[95] That he may act in concert also with my servant Joseph; and that he shall receive counsel from my servant Joseph, who shall show unto him the* **keys** *whereby he may* **ask and receive***, and be crowned with the same blessing, and glory, and honor, and priesthood, and gifts of the priesthood, that once were put upon him that was my servant Oliver Cowdery;*

Now, there's something here that is beyond prayer. Notice he says there are **keys** on how to **ask and receive** answers. Those keys are in the form of tokens and signs of the priesthood. You have already, through your endowment experience, received keys in the form of signs, which allow you to ask about things in the **past**, teach you how to ask about things in the **present**, and that teach you how to ask about things in the **future**. You have already received that in the endowment. Those are the kind of things the Lord is talking about. This is the voice of God speaking here in these verses. This is God speaking to Joseph, speaking to Hyrum through Joseph.

Student 1: When you say God, do you mean God the Father?

Mike: Ha-ha... That's another discussion. Let's just say this is being received from God. These are the words of God.

Now, look down at verse 97:

> *Let my servant William Law also receive the keys by which he may ask and receive blessings;*

William Law was a member of the First Presidency at this time. He became a conspirator and was one of the main reasons why Joseph Smith was shot to death in Carthage. These men were given very, very sacred **keys** that pertain to the past, present, and future, that are part of the temple endowment in the form of signs that the Lord wanted them to have, and the Lord wants **you** to have. What I am saying to you tonight, brothers and sisters, according to what we have in writing; we have received some very, very sacred keys that are designed to open up doors so that the Lord can give us knowledge that we can't get any other way. Take that now, and let it be a part of your temple worship, and ask the Lord to show you by revelation what's really going on, especially when you get to the prayer circle area before going *through the veil*. Ask the Lord to reveal to you. Tell Him that you want to understand it all.

Tonight's lesson is that with every law, you have a covenant, token, sign, and name. All of these things are ancient. They go back to the Garden of Eden. All of the ancient patriarchs, all of the great men and women of the time, in every dispensation when there has been a restoration of truth, have had these keys, and signs, and tokens. They are very sacred. They are only to be used as the Lord directs and as confirmed by the Spirit.

In summing up things here, the temple is teaching you things about how to communicate and establish a connection with the other side of the veil, and to do it while you are here. The Lord wants you to penetrate the veil. He wants us to receive information, by messengers either seen or unseen, that He has waiting for us there.

So, these are things that come from documents that are available to you. I can give you one such source. It is in the December 28, 1845, *Instructions of Brigham Young from the General Records of the Seventies*, book 3. Three other records concerning these instructions are *William Clayton Minutes, Heber C Kimball Diary, William Clayton and John D Lee Diaries*. They were all given by Brigham Young, in the Nauvoo period. What I've talked to you about tonight comes from those documents. We can't go into it any more than that because it's temple-bound and we have made covenants not to talk about that.

Student 4: Is that out of *The Home Sanctuary* document?

Mike: Yes. So, brothers and sisters, I hope that is helpful when we consider and talk about the tokens and signs and what they're designed to do. I'm sure that there is much more that I don't understand, but that much sure has helped me in my own personal devotion and in my "seeking the face of the Lord," which I'm commanded to do.

Go to section 101. As we close, here is the commandment in *Doctrine and Covenants*, section 101, verse 38:

*And seek the face of the Lord **always**,*
The Lord is on the other side of the veil:
> *that in patience ye may possess your souls, and ye*
> *shall have eternal life.*

There are three things here. As you seek for and obtain the face of the Lord, you will in patience possess your souls, and that will result in you obtaining eternal life. Interesting little statement. The commandment is *"Seek the face of the Lord always."* What the temple is doing is giving us keys and knowledge on how we can come to that point.

References:
Mosiah 18:3-9
Alma 46
D&C 129:9
Teachings of the Prophet Joseph Smith, April 9, 1842
Doctrinal History of the Church, DHC, volume 4 page 587
D&C 124:94-95

Discerning of Spirits
by the
Power of the Priesthood

Every one of these professes to be competent to try his neighbor's spirit, but no one can try his own, and what is the reason? Because they have not a key to unlock, no rule wherewith to measure, and no criterion whereby they can test it. Could any one tell the length, breadth or height of a building without a rule? test the quality of metals without a criterion, or point out the movements of the planetary systems, without a knowledge of astronomy? Certainly not; and if such ignorance as this is manifested about a spirit of this kind, who can describe an angel of light? If Satan should appear as one in glory, who can tell his color, his signs, his appearance, his glory?—or what is the manner of his manifestation? Who can detect the spirit of the French prophets with their revelations and their visions, and power of manifestations? Or who can point out the spirit of the Irvingites, with their apostles and prophets, and visions and tongues, and interpretations, &c., &c. Or who can drag into daylight and develop the hidden mysteries of the false spirits that so frequently are made manifest among the Latter-day Saints? We answer that no man can do this without the Priesthood, and having a knowledge of the laws by which spirits are governed; for as "no man knows the things of God, but by the Spirit of God," so no man knows the spirit of the devil, and his power and influence, but by possessing intelligence which is more than human, and having unfolded through the medium of the Priesthood the mysterious operations of his devices; without knowing _**the angelic form, the sanctified look and gesture, and the zeal that is frequently manifested by him for the glory of God, together with the prophetic spirit, the gracious influence, the godly appearance, and the holy garb**_, which are so characteristic of his proceedings and his mysterious windings.

A man must have the discerning of spirits before he can drag into daylight this hellish influence and unfold it unto the world in all its soul-destroying, diabolical, and horrid colors; for nothing is a greater injury to the children of men than to be under the influence of a false spirit when they think they have the Spirit of God. Thousands have felt the influence of its terrible power and baneful effects. Long pilgrimages have been undertaken, penances endured, and pain, misery and ruin have followed in their train; nations have been convulsed, kingdoms overthrown, provinces laid waste, and blood, carnage and desolation are habiliments in which it has been clothed.

Joseph Smith Jr.
Doctrinal History of the Church 4:587
April 9, 184

Chapter Eight

Podcast 008: Baptism of Fire and the Holy Ghost

An all mission training is given by Mike Stroud, in New
Jersey with Mission President Paul Taggart, 2015

Elder missionary: We'll proceed by hearing some opening
remarks by President and Sister Taggart. Then we'll move to Elder
Stroud's training.

Pres Taggart: Thank you, Elder. Thank you for the prayer. I pray
completely that the Spirit will be here, that we will be able to use
and receive revelation for ourselves and for our people that we
teach. Elders and sisters, that's really what this is all about today.
Sister Taggart and I went over to visit the Stroud's one morning.
We don't get to see the senior couples very often. And so, we had
one of those rare moments where we had a chance to connect with
them. As we started talking, Elder Stroud brought up a question of
a reality that there are a lot of people in the Church, who come to
the Church, receive a testimony of the gospel but then for one
reason or another, decide to leave. We've had about 21-22%
activity going on here in New Jersey. That means 78-79% of the
people who join the church no longer participate. So, we started
talking about that because it bothers us and it's not good. It's an
issue. It's kind of a problem. And Elder Stroud said, "Well, I know
what the problem is. It's in the scriptures…" And as we started
talking about it, he enlightened Sister Taggart and I on the
difference between being given the *gift of the Holy Ghost*, which is
something we get after we are baptized, and actually **receiving** the

gift of the Holy Ghost, receiving it in our hearts, and having what is called the *baptism of fire*. And if you think about it, it's pretty logical and scripturally backed. So, who is it that baptizes us? [Sister missionary], who baptized you?

Sister missionary 1: My dad.

Pres. Taggart: Your dad. For most of us, it was probably our dad or our brother, or **somebody** baptized us. Then who gave you the *gift of the Holy Ghost*? [Sister missionary], who laid their hands on your head and gave you the *gift of the Holy Ghost*?

Sister missionary 2: My bishop.

Pres. Taggart: Your bishop. Your dad is a man. Your bishop is also a man. Those are the people who give us the baptism, do the baptismal ordinance and give us the *gift of the Holy Ghost*. Well, elders and sisters, who gives us the *baptism of fire and the Holy Ghost*? Where does that come from?

Sister missionary 1: From God.

Pres. Taggart: From God. The *baptism by fire* comes from God, not from man. I testify to you that those people who receive, who actually receive the Holy Ghost, the *baptism of fire*, don't leave the church. If they continue to feel that Spirit, feel the Holy Ghost, which has sunk deep into their hearts, something they received from our Father in Heaven, they stay strong. Their testimony, their conversion, if you will, is solid, steadfast, unshakable, and immovable. **That** is why, elders and sisters, it's so important that we understand this doctrine, we know this doctrine, and are able to teach this doctrine: that it's not over when we are baptized. It's not over when we are **given** the *gift of the Holy Ghost*. It's like having a really nice Christmas present that's been under the tree for a week, and it's sitting there in this great box, and you're thinking, "Ah! What's in that box? That is a cool gift! Who gets that gift?" And instead, on Christmas morning they hand you the gift, and they say, "Here it is! It's yours." Then all of a sudden there's an emergency, and you all leave, and you have to get out of the house. And then a month has gone by, and you have that gift sitting there, and it's yours. You get it, but you never had a chance to open it. You never really had a chance to take the gift and celebrate what was inside that box. So, we need to open the box.

Let me just say that Elder Stroud is a very humble man and, I will say, that he's very qualified to teach this. He has a lot of experience, and he knows what he's talking about. He's had many years of experience doing this. But, I testify that as we listen today, as we are taught by the Spirit, and we allow the Holy Spirit to guide us, as we sang in the opening song: *"Let the Spirit heal our hearts through His quiet, gentle power. May we purify our lives to receive Him hour by hour."* I testify that as we do this, elders and sisters, our lives will change. We've told you this before, and we'll tell you again, Sister Taggart and I would say our main mission, our purpose here is you. It's you! We're not here to baptize our neighbors and the people who live next door, the people who we meet, which aren't very many. We spend most of our time with the members, or with you. **Our** purpose here is to help you receive the Holy Ghost, become truly, genuinely converted, and receive the *baptism of fire and the Holy Ghost* so that **you** will go home with a rock solid testimony of the Gospel of Jesus Christ. That is our purpose. That's why we're here today. So, please open your hearts. Open your souls to what we share today and allow the Holy Ghost to touch your heart. I testify that this is real. I testify that this is the Kingdom of God on the earth. And I say this in the name of Jesus Christ, amen.

We're going to turn the time over to Elder Stroud now, and let's be edified.

Mike: Brothers and sisters, I'm grateful to be here today.

You know this scripture because you use it in some of your teachings. John 15:16 says:

> Ye have not chosen me, but I have chosen you, and ordained you, that ye should go and bring forth fruit,

You're all familiar with that, aren't you? Aren't you in the business of bringing forth fruit? That's what we're doing, but we don't read the next part. The next part is sobering:

> and that your fruit should remain.

That's the part I want to talk to you about today. We've had a lot of discussion on bringing forth fruit. We want to talk about, *"That your fruit should remain,"* because, my young friends, **way** too many people are leaving the church; **way** too many. You heard the statistic given by President Taggart. We served a mission in Mongolia, and in Mongolia, the percentage of activity is about 27%. Then we served a mission in the Philippines, and this is a mission with 900,000 people that's been in existence for fifty years. It has twenty plus missions in it, 800,000 members, three temples, and have 12% activity. That means 88% of the membership of the Church in the Philippines don't come to church anymore. So, something is happening here, and this is not acceptable. There's not one of you in this room today that plan on going home and leaving the Church, not one of you. But if we don't do something about the statistics, how they currently are, a certain percentage of you, when you go home, will leave activity in the Church. That's the Church statistics. Every one of you here is probably familiar with a return missionary that doesn't attend church anymore. There's a reason for that, and it's subtle, and it's kind of slipped in on us, and that's what we want to address today.

Now, you're going to have questions. If you'll let me make a presentation and then at the end of the presentation, write down your questions, and we'll be glad to field those as best we can. A word of warning: I'm deaf. I have double hearing aids on. This comes from shooting guns all my life, and nobody ever warned me, "Cover your ears up!" Well, nobody ever warned me, and I'm popping 45's with nothing to protect my ears. So, I'm deafer than a cob up here. Now, ladies, I especially don't hear your voices. My wife says that's selective hearing, but I don't hear women's voices very well. So, when you respond will you just speak up. You notice I'm not using a microphone and you're not having any trouble hearing me are you, back there, brethren? You can hear me see, so respond to me like that.

On your worksheet, I want to refer to a statement made by President Packer years ago that I think is the key to what we are trying to do here. And I'd like to see this reinstated. It's in *Preach My Gospel*, but I don't think it's receiving the time and thought and pondering that it needs. Throughout the church, and later on in your families, you're going to counsel. And in the counsel, you're going to be discussing the behavior of people you love or people for whom you have responsibility. In almost all of our counsels, we spend an inordinate amount of time talking about unacceptable behavior. "Oh, we're not getting our home teaching statistics. The visiting teaching is not done. The tithes are not up. The people are not living the Word of Wisdom. How do we get people to attend the temple? How do we get more people to accept callings?" And we spend all this time talking about what needs to be done. Well, President Packer has a little clue for us. Let's go to his statement, right up at the top:

> True doctrine, understood, changes attitudes and behavior.

You ought to underline that because I testify to you that this is a true principle. Now, what I'm teaching you today, I've tried, I've done, and it works every time. This is tried and tested, and it's never failed. That's pretty good, isn't it? That's a pretty good record. *"True doctrine, understood..."* catch the *"understood"* part. Teach the true doctrine, make sure it's understood, and it changes behavior. The rest of the quote says:

> The study of the doctrines of the gospel will improve behavior quicker than a study of behavior will improve behavior. Preoccupation with unworthy behavior can lead to unworthy behavior.

It's a vicious cycle. So, what we do is, we spend all of our time in counsels in the church and in your families, as husbands and wives, mothers and fathers, in the future, talking about the behavior of your children. And the more you discuss inappropriate behavior, what does it do? It encourages inappropriate behavior. It's a vicious cycle. So, what's the answer?

> That is why we stress so forcefully the study of the doctrines of the gospel.

I think this is a key priesthood principle that you need to really take a look at. So, what do we do? Only discuss behavior to the degree that you can identify the behavior that's unacceptable and then, stop talking about it. Once you've identified it, whatever it is, then go to the word of God, go to the scriptures, find the doctrine that ties to that behavior, and teach it. The word of God that has power and virtue in it, according to Alma 31:5 there's virtue in the word of God. As you teach that doctrine, the Holy Ghost will carry the word of God, that doctrine, into the heart of the person and the **Holy Ghost** will change the behavior. Do you see that cycle right there? That's the take-off today. *"True doctrine, understood, changes...behavior."* I testify to you that that is true.

Now, let's go to the next part because we have something that's a little misunderstood. It's the baptismal ordinance of the Church. The baptismal ordinance of the Church has three parts to it. The first part is the baptism by water. You're all familiar with that. You've seen that. You've gone through it. The second part is confirmation by the laying on of hands. And the third part is the *baptism with fire and with the Holy Ghost.* Here's the problem. We're stuck right here (at the confirmation phase) as church members. We're stuck with the baptism of water and the confirmation by the laying on of hands. The wording and the verbiage of certain Articles of Faith and priesthood ordinances cause us to miss the point and, as President Taggart said, we never get to open up the present. We get stuck. Let me explain.

Baptism of water is the token of a covenant. It's a token. All covenants have tokens that go along with them. That token, you can study. It has to do with all kinds of things—a rebirth, a burial, a resurrection—all kinds of things, but it's a token. In the Church, however, we think that there is a remission of sins that takes place at the baptism of water. Let me ask you two questions and then think about this. As members of the Church, if I were to ask you these two questions, how would you answer them? Number one: Where does the remission of sins take place? And number two: When do you place your feet upon the *strait and narrow path?* Where does that take place? My experience is that most members of the Church, the majority of the Church, are going to answer that it takes place right here: when you're baptized by water and the following Sunday, somebody lays their hands on your head and says, "Receive the Holy Ghost." At that point, we think the ordinance is complete. We think the baptismal ordinance is complete. We think that when we say, "Receive the Holy Ghost," that the *baptism of fire and the Holy Ghost* takes place at that time.

Pres. Taggart: And it might.

Mike: It can.

Pres. Taggart: It might with some people.

Mike: It can, but generally speaking, the majority of the membership of the Church is going to have this part of the baptismal ordinance, the *baptism of fire and the Holy Ghost*, take place sometime in the future, after the water baptism and the confirmation. What's the confirmation then? What's going on there? You're laying your hands on their head, and you're saying, "Receive the Holy Ghost."

Let's see what President Uchtdorf says. Go down here on your worksheet. This is a talk given in 2012...

Sister Stroud: Bednar.

Mike: ...what did I say? Bednar! Uchtdorf? Bednar. Elder Bednar. Thank you. This is my damage control over here and boy; she's doing a dang good job! I pulled the excerpts out of this talk that pertains to what we're talking about. The Brethren, in particular, Elder Bednar, are trying to help us correct this misunderstanding, and it's church-wide. And again, I believe, the problem with people leaving the Church is that we are not getting to the last part of the baptismal ordinance. And yet people *think* they are. That's the challenge. **If you think you're already in possession of something, why would you seek for it?** Do you see that?

Let's look at Elder Bednar's quotes here:

> These four words—'Receive the Holy Ghost'—are not a passive pronouncement; rather, they constitute a priesthood injunction—an authoritative admonition to act and not be simply acted upon.

Do you know what that word injunction means? It's a command. A priesthood command.

When you do this, *"Receive the Holy Ghost,"* what you're doing is you're turning a key and pronouncing an injunction on that person, *"Now go, from this point, go and receive the gift of the Holy Ghost."* We think that it's happening right there... and it can but generally not.

Look what else he says:

> My message focuses on the importance of striving in our daily lives to **actually receive** the Holy Ghost.

We think that when we say those words, it does. He's saying it has to **actually** happen.

> The gift of the Holy Ghost is bestowed only after proper and authorized baptism and by the laying on of hands by those holding the Melchizedek Priesthood.

That's your confirmation. That's the key that opens the door for the *baptism of fire and the Holy Ghost.* The *baptism of fire and the Holy Ghost* is not going to come without these two other steps. Go on further down, and it says:

> *Baptism by immersion is the introductory ordinance of the gospel, and **must** be followed by baptism of the Spirit/Fire in order to be complete.*
> *The ordinance of confirming a new member of the Church and bestowing the gift of the Holy Ghost is both simple and profound.*

Now, watch this next statement because this next paragraph contains the heart of what we're talking about here:

> *The simplicity of this ordinance may cause us to overlook its significance. These four words— 'Receive the Holy Ghost'—are not a passive pronouncement; rather, they constitute a priesthood injunction—an authoritative admonition to act and not simply to be acted upon (see 2 Nephi 2:26). **The Holy Ghost does not become operative in our lives merely because hands are placed upon our heads, and those four important words are spoken.***

You ought to underline that because I think that's exactly what we think happens. I think that we think that when we say those words, it's almost like a command for the Holy Ghost to come in now and become the constant companion of that person who's being confirmed. Elder Bednar says that's not correct, and I testify to you that it's not correct, but we think that, and I'll show you why in just a minute:

> *As we receive this ordinance, each of us accepts a sacred and **ongoing** responsibility to desire, to seek, to work, and to so live that we indeed 'receive the Holy Ghost' and its attendant spiritual gifts.*

See! It's moving down the road. The key is turned, now go out, *"to desire, to seek, to work, and to so live that we indeed receive the Holy Ghost" and its attendant spiritual gifts."* Does this make sense? Do you see where we're going with this today? Can you see that we're just a little bit off in our thinking here, and we're just making a little course correction? I believe, and I believe that President Taggart believes that this little course correction is going to make all the difference in the world and you, like was said in the last general conference, will *"stay in the boat"* and not take a walk, okay?

*We more readily receive and recognize the Spirit of the Lord as we appropriately invite Him into our lives. We **cannot** compel, coerce, or command the Holy Ghost. Rather, **we should invite Him into our lives** with the same gentleness and tenderness by which He entreats us (see D&C 42:14).*

Praying, studying, gathering, worshipping, serving, and obeying are not isolated and independent items on a lengthy gospel checklist of things to do. Rather, each of these righteous practices is an important element in an overarching spiritual quest to fulfill the mandate to receive the Holy Ghost.

That's the pathway. He just outlined the pathway for you. Do you see that? Praying, studying, gathering; that's the pathway to the *baptism of fire.*

*I pray we will sincerely desire and appropriately invite the Holy Ghost into our daily lives. I also pray each of us will faithfully obey God's commandments **and in reality** receive the Holy Ghost.*

That's not being done.

So, generally speaking, here's the problem. Generally speaking, and not specifically, our brothers and sisters in the gospel, whose fruits are not remaining, are not remaining because we are not completing the baptismal ordinance. We're getting the first part of it, and we think we've got it all, and we don't. When the heat of the day comes up and when the adversities and the trials come, you guys are going to need to have this, or you won't be able to stand the heat of the day. If you think times in the past were hard, wait until you see what's coming! You need to have this conversion. Now, let me give you names that are different names for the *baptism of fire and the Holy Ghost.* They all mean the same thing. Here's one: the *gift of the Holy Ghost* is referring to the *baptism of fire.* So, when you use the term the *gift of the Holy Ghost,* this is what you're talking about. Here's another one: *a mighty change of heart.* Two more are: *born again,* and *sanctified by the Spirit.* Any of these terms we are talking about, refer to this completion of the baptismal ordinance. Does this make sense? Are you starting to get a feel for this?

Now, I'd like to say that this is a process. My hope is that you will ask yourself this question as a result of what we're doing: "Has this happened to me?" because first and foremost, like President Taggart says, you're his main stewardship. His main concern is you, young men and young women. You're going to be with him for 18 months to 2 years, and then you're going to go home. His concern is what could happen to you when you leave here. And I can tell you he's concerned about that, and we all are. So, what are you going to do to ensure that **you** remain? Because I'll tell you that there are forces at work that want to take you away. This is the key to remaining:

> I have a friend who's a pastor in the Assembly of God church back where I live, and I went to one of his meetings. He gave a talk and said, *"The difference between life and death is 14 inches."*
> I thought, *"What the heck are you talking about?"*
> He paused for effect, and then he said, *"It's the difference between here…"* and he pointed to his head, *"…and here,"* and he pointed to his heart: 14 inches. *"It's the difference between life and death."*

In the Church, we have what we call testimony. Testimony is a precursor to something deeper called **conversion.** Conversion is another word for the *baptism of fire and the Holy Ghost.* Testimony gets you to the point where you make the covenants, and you enter the water, and you're confirmed. That's testimony. You've received a message from God. He's spoken to you, and as a result of that, you're willing to enter into a covenant, which you do. But that's not enough.

Over on the back of this next sheet, the same sheet, go on the back, and you'll see the Joseph Smith quote. I love this quote:

> *You might as well baptize a bag of sand as a man, if not done in view of the remission of sins and getting of the Holy Ghost. Baptism by water is but half a baptism and is **good for nothing** without the other half—that is, the baptism of the Holy Ghost.*

Pretty bold words! President Taggart, would you like to add anything to this point?

Pres. Taggart: Well, and I think, elders and sisters, you may be thinking, "Wow! Has this happened to me? Have I actually received this?" Realize that this is a process. If you've received this, you would know. You would know it. You would feel it in your heart. You know, I'm three times as old as you. I've lived three of your lifetimes, and I'm still striving, still working to have this in my life. It's a continual process. It will always be there, and once you've received it and once it comes, you want to keep receiving it. You want to keep it coming, you know? And we all have ups and downs and challenges and problems. We have a lot of adversity that we face. Satan is the last person on the planet that wants you to have this, so know this and understand it. He is trying really hard to divert us and counterfeit. So, realize that it's a process that you go through. Purification or sanctification is that process that allows the Holy Ghost to touch us and is a process that even [Elder senior missionary] is still working on.

Missionaries: Ha-ha-ha!

Pres. Taggart: I'm working on it; we're all working on it. So, you know, don't be discouraged or dissuaded if you don't feel like, *"Wow! I have this fire in my belly, and I've received this miraculous revelation."* We're going to talk about **how** we receive the Holy Ghost as well, and how it speaks to us. And I think most of you've probably felt this or had this. Now, is it a matter of how strong and how converted we are? We're going to talk more about that, too, as we get into the scriptures.

*Transcript Note by Mike: It wasn't taught in this mission training because of the belief and circumstances at that time, but I testify that the baptism by fire and the Holy Ghost is a process that <u>ends in an event</u> All births are processes that end in an event. In the birth process, there is a 9-month process that ends in a baby's birth. That is the pattern.

Mike: Thank you. If you have a testimony, and I know you all do, or you wouldn't be here, but if your testimony has not moved into conversion, you're not going to make it. You're going to take a walk. It's that simple. Elder Eyring says this:

> We must take the pure gospel of Jesus Christ from our heads and sink it way down deep into our hearts.

That is what we're talking about here. 14 inches: the difference between life and death; activity and inactivity; fruits that remain and those that don't. That's the difference.

Now, let's take a look at some wording here in the 4th Article of Faith. Let me ask you a question. In the 4th Article of Faith, it's saying *baptism by immersion for the remission of sins.* So, according to that, when does the remission of sins take place? Right here (baptism of water). That's not correct, but our 4th Article of Faith, because we put the word *for* in there, makes us think that when we're baptized by immersion that our sins are remitted. You're going to see today from the scriptures, that that's not correct. We've got to twist our thinking a little bit. So, are we teaching false doctrine? No. We just do not quite understand it the way the Lord wants us to understand it. I talked to some sister missionaries the other day, and they said, *"Elder Stroud, are we teaching false doctrine?"* I said, *"No. Just go forth now and teach what you've learned. Don't worry about it."* Brothers and sisters, you can't teach above the level of your own individual conversion. We're always growing here, and as you grow, you're going to have an effect on people to a greater degree as you grow in the gospel and the Spirit takes place in your heart. Don't be worried about where you are right now. Don't be too concerned with that but be asking yourself some questions. I'm going to give you some keys from the *Book of Mormon* on how you can answer the question, "Has this happened to me today?" And you can measure where you are. It's not enough to tell you what needs to be done. We know in the Church where we **should** be. The big question is: **How** do we get there? Has it happened to me and how do we get there? Now, we're going to talk about that today so you can measure it.

Alright, let's go to section 20 in the *Doctrine and Covenants* and let's start looking at a scripture chain. This is where we'll get into the scriptures and remember the two questions: Where does the remission of sins come from? And when do I begin walking on the *"strait and narrow path?"* And it's my belief that the majority of us in the Church, believe that it takes place with the baptism of water and confirmation. Now, President Taggart mentioned something else that's interesting. Baptism by water and confirmation by the laying on of hands is performed by mortal hands. It's mortals who perform that, and the record of that part of that ordinance is kept in the Church of Jesus Christ of Latter-day Saints. It's your membership record number. There's a record there, right? When you get over to this part, the *baptism of fire and the Holy Ghost*, to complete the baptismal ordinance, this is not performed by mortals. This is done by immortals, and there is no earthly record that this has taken place. There is a record, and it's called the record of those who are *The Sanctified*. And you can read about it in the 2nd verse of section 88. And you can just write that up. There's a record kept of this when it happens to you, in heaven, but there's no person on Earth that's going to have an earthly record that you've received the *baptism of fire and the Holy Ghost.*

So, let's go to section 20, verse 41 and look at our first scripture. These are just a few. Once you're tuned into this; once you start to see this, you're going to see it everywhere. It's everywhere, but it's one of those things that you just have to have somebody show it to you like it was me. Can I tell you that I taught seminary for many, many years and I never taught this in seminary? I didn't know it. I didn't know it, and now that I've learned it, I want to pass it on to you, so you don't have to wait until you're 70 years old to figure this out, right? Let's go to verse 41:

> And to **confirm** those who are **baptized** into the church, by the laying on of hands **for** the baptism of fire and the Holy Ghost, according to the scriptures;

There are your first two steps; your **confirmation** and your **baptism** by water. And then to confirm those who are baptized you have the laying on of hands **for** the *baptism of fire and the Holy Ghost.* There are all three parts of the baptismal ordinance. There it is.

Let's go to section 33 for a minute. Let me just say that I made some places for notes on your handout. As the Spirit and the Holy Ghost speak to you and reveal things to you, you'll have thoughts that will come into your mind and feelings in your heart. I would encourage you to write those down because that's the Spirit talking to you about what you need to know concerning this ordinance and where you are at this point in your personal progression and journey back to the Father. So, write it down! This is a time to receive revelation. It will come to your mind, in the way of thoughts, and to your heart in the way of feelings. Write those down, okay? Section 33, let's go to verse 11:

> *Yea, repent and be baptized, every one of you, for a remission of your sins; yea, be baptized even by water, and* ***then*** *cometh the baptism by fire and of the Holy Ghost.*

There's your sequence again. See, you're going to see this everywhere. Look at the next verse:

> *[12]Behold, verily, verily, I say unto you,* ***this is my gospel;***

What you see on the board right here is the gospel of Jesus Christ. Want a definition of the gospel? There it is; repentance, baptism by water, confirmation by the laying on of hands, and *the baptism of fire and the Holy Ghost*. That is the gospel of Jesus Christ in its simplicity and its foundation. That's it. Look what else it says. Verse 13,

> *[13] And upon this rock I will build my church; yea, upon this rock ye are built, and* ***if ye continue****, the gates of hell shall not prevail against you.*

You ought to underline that, *"if ye continue,"* because we're not continuing. We're getting stuck. We're stuck at the confirmation, as a general church membership, so our fruit is not remaining and we're not continuing on to receive the *baptism of fire and the Holy Ghost*. If we keep our testimony in our heads and don't continue on to make it a conversion in our hearts, our fruit will not remain. But, if we continue on to real conversion, our fruit will remain and we will also.

> *[15]And whoso having faith you shall confirm in my church, by the laying on of the hands, and* ***I*** *will bestow the gift of the Holy Ghost upon them.*

You ought to circle that: *"**I** will bestow the gift of the Holy Ghost."* Now, you thought that the *gift of the Holy Ghost* was bestowed by whom?

Sister missionary: A mortal.

Mike: The person that said what?

Missionaries: "Receive the Holy Ghost."

Mike: "Receive the Holy Ghost." You thought that's when it took place. It's not. Who bestows it? Who's speaking here in section 33 that says, *"I will bestow the gift of the Holy Ghost?"* Who is this? It's **Christ**. So, now we're getting over here, like President Taggart said, into the part of the ordinance that is bestowed and performed by immortals. We'll see some more. Let's go to another one. Let's go over to 3 Nephi chapter 9. Now, the *Book of Mormon* teaches this doctrine in its plainness and its simplicity. If I were trying to teach what we're doing today, out of the *Bible*, it couldn't be done; I absolutely could not do it. You can't do this. You can teach it pretty well out of the *Doctrine and Covenants*, but if you want to *REALLY* find this doctrine, go to the *Book of Mormon* because this is *core foundation doctrine* of the *Book of Mormon*. So, let's go to 3 Nephi, chapter 9. The context for this: it's dark. In the chapter heading, *"In the darkness the voice of Christ proclaims..."* See? They hear the voice of Christ. Let's go to verse 18:

I am the light and the life of the world...

In verse 19, Christ discontinues 4,000 years of sacrifice by the shedding of blood.

And ye shall offer up unto me no more the shedding of blood;

Verse 20 is where we want to go. Watch –a new dispensation, a new sacrifice.

And ye shall offer for a sacrifice unto me a broken heart and a contrite spirit.

That is the key to the beginning of the *baptism of fire*. Do you want to know what you have to do to get this? Here's the key. And then look what the Lord says:

And whoso cometh unto me with a broken heart and a contrite spirit, him will I baptize with fire and with the Holy Ghost,

Pres. Taggart: You know, this is a very, very profound connection to everything that we do, elders and sisters. If you look at our "monthly scripture," it's interesting. This "monthly scripture" that we have today completely and totally ties into this. I don't think that was by coincidence. Listen to what it says in Helaman 3:35:

Nevertheless they did fast and pray oft, and did wax stronger and stronger in their humility, and firmer and firmer in the faith of Christ, unto the filling their souls with joy and consolation, yea, even to

*the purifying and sanctification of their hearts,
which sanctification cometh because of their
yielding their heart unto God.*

You wax **firmer** and firmer; **stronger** and stronger in your **humility**. How do you wax stronger and stronger? You perfect. You grow. You enlarge. You enlarge your humility. What does it do? It does exactly what Elder Stroud is talking about, what the scripture talks about: a broken heart and a contrite spirit. Are we willing to **yield** our will to the will of the Father? Are we willing to yield? Have we broken our pride, eliminated pride in our life? What we want versus what He wants? That is a key element here; Firmer and firmer in the **faith**. If we're humble, if we seek the Spirit, **then** the Holy Ghost can come to you; then, and only then. If we're proud and if what we want is more important than what He wants, we're blocking. We're blocking. We're damned. He can't help us. And when we do anything that blocks that Spirit, or that power, our forward progress is damned. I don't know about you, but I need all the forward progress I can get. I **need** to have a broken heart and contrite spirit.

Mike: Thank you. Helaman chapter 3, verse 35 **is** the *baptism of fire and the Holy Ghost.*

Pres. Taggart: Yeah, sanctification, joy, and consolation that comes only through the Holy Ghost.

Mike: How inspired you are to have that! Let's go to 3 Nephi, chapter 12, verses 1 and 2. We're not going to read the whole first verse. Go about half way, up at the top of page 431, and down one line where it says, "...Blessed are ye..." That's in verse 1, do you see that? This is the Savior now. This is not just His voice. This is a Second Comforter experience. He's there in person. 2,500 people have now gone up and seen and heard and **touched** something. This is not a vision; this is a **visitation**. And He's talking to them, and He says:

*Blessed are ye if ye give heed unto the words of
these twelve whom I have chosen from among you
to minister unto you, and to be your servants; and
unto them I have given power that they may baptize
you with water; and after that ye are baptized with
water, behold, I will baptize you with fire and with
the Holy Ghost;*

190

See? It's everywhere in here. Let's go down to verse 2:
> *And again, more blessed are they*

Now, He's talking about everybody that listens to and believes the words of the Twelve, which includes **us**! So, verse 2 is now talking to us in 2016:

> *And again, more blessed are they who shall believe in your words because that ye shall testify that ye have seen me, and that ye know that I am. Yea, blessed are they who shall believe in your words, and come down into the depths of humility and be baptized, for they shall be visited with fire and with the Holy Ghost, and shall receive a remission of sins.*

Now, here's a new addition, *"...and shall receive a **remission of sins."***

Remember the question I asked you at the beginning? When do we receive the *remission of sins*? The majority of the membership of the Church will tell you that it happens right here, in the waters of baptism, as though, when you come out of the water you can see the scum floating on the top. All your sins have been washed away, see? I know you have taught that and thought that. I know you have because I did and it's a common thought. That's the token of the covenant. Here's your key: **no remission of sin UNTIL the baptism of fire and the Holy Ghost** and that's the doctrine.

Now, there's a difference between *forgiveness of sin* and *remission of sin*. You can get a forgiveness of sin, and you can have that, but we won't go into that today. *A remission of sin* takes place right here, and it is a *HEALING* process. It not only justifies you so the law of justice has no demands on you, but it *HEALS* everything that's broken in you. If you're a victim, remission of sins heals that. If you're a perpetrator of a crime, it heals that. So, the *baptism of fire and the remission of sins* make everything WHOLE...W-H-O-L-E /slash/ HOL*Y*. That's what takes place with a remission.

Okay, let's think of a couple of other ones. Go over to Mosiah chapter 4 and let's talk about what we need to do to obtain this and how can we tell if we've got it? I would invite you to go home after today, sometime in the next few days, read again, in context with what we've talked about, Mosiah chapter 4 and 5. Read those two chapters because it contains the keys of How to obtain the *baptism of fire and the Holy Ghost* and RETAIN a remission of your sins, and how you can tell if it's happened to you; which is what we really want to know, right? You want to know where you are on the pathway back to the Father. You want to know, "Where am I at right now in March of 2015?" If you know where you are, you can move forward with power. Otherwise, if there's a question mark, there's no movement. Or if there is, it's backward. Let's go to Mosiah chapter 4, verse 2. Would somebody like to read verse 2 for me?

Elder missionary:

> *And they had viewed themselves in their own carnal state, even less than the dust of the earth. And they all cried aloud with one voice, saying: O have mercy, and apply the atoning blood of Christ that we may receive forgiveness of our sins, and our hearts may be purified; for we believe in Jesus Christ, the Son of God, who created heaven and earth, and all things; who shall come down among the children of men.*

Mike: So, what is it they want? They are asking for two things. What do you see that they're looking for here?

Elder missionary: Mercy.

Mike: Use the words of the scripture. What are they looking for?

Elder missionary: *"Have mercy and apply the atoning blood of Christ."*

Mike: That's the vehicle to get what they want. What is it they're looking for? Two things, what?

Sister missionary: A forgiveness of their sins.

Mike: A forgiveness of their sins and what?

Elder missionary: Purified heart.

Mike: Purified hearts. Now, there's a key: when you hear the word *heart*, you're starting to talk about things that pertain to the *baptism of fire*. Anything in the *Book of Mormon* that you see moving towards the *heart* means that you're now moving into the deeper parts of the gospel, where the Lord really wants you to be. Actually, brothers and sisters, the Lord only really wants one thing from you. After it's all said and done, He wants one thing from you. He wants your ***heart***! That's what He wants. And it's the hardest thing to give. Now, let's see if they got what they wanted. Go down to verse 3. Elder, please read verse 3 for us. Did they receive their desire?

Elder missionary:

> *And it came to pass that after they had spoken these words the Spirit of the Lord came upon them, and they were filled with joy, having received a remission of their sins, and having peace of conscience, because of the exceeding faith which they had in Jesus Christ who should come, according to the words which king Benjamin had spoken unto them.*

Mike: Did they receive the two things in verse 3 that they wanted in verse 2? Did they get it? They did. How did it come to them? Back up to verse 2. What was the vehicle? It was the atoning blood of Jesus Christ. Now, there's a law in heaven that God seldom answers questions that are unasked; seldom. I'm not going to tell Him what He can and cannot do, but it's my experience that if you don't ask a question, you're not going to get an answer when it comes to the Lord. How many times have you seen this? *"Ask and ye shall"*...what?

Missionaries: *"Receive."*

Mike: *"Receive." "Seek and ye shall"*...?

Missionaries: *"Find."*

Mike: *"Find."* Section 88 adds an interesting thing to it. The only place in the scriptures it says, *"Seek ME and ye shall find ME."* Interesting! What's the other one?

Missionaries: *"Knock."*

Mike: *Knock...?*

Missionaries: *"...and it shall be opened unto you."*

Mike: *"And it shall be opened unto you."* THAT has interesting temple implications. How many times have you seen these in the scriptures? They're everywhere, aren't they? It's the key! What do you think the Lord is trying to tell us? Is He trying to teach us something here? So, your first key to obtain is tonight, when you get on your knees and in the name of Christ, you approach the Father and say, "Heavenly Father..." and ask Him two questions. First: Have I received the *baptism of fire and the Holy Ghost?* And then wait until you receive a *feeling* or *thought* on that. If your feeling and your thought is that you have not received this completion of the baptismal ordinance, then ASK HIM to complete it for you. And He will. He will. It's not happening because we're not asking. There's your first key.

Now, let's look at a couple of things here. For the sake of time, if you'll read over Mosiah chapter 4 and look for these things: What kind of person do I need to be, according to King Benjamin's discourse that the angel gave to him? This is King Benjamin repeating what an angel gave him the night before. What kind of a person does he say I need to be to have this endowment of the *baptism of fire*? And you'll see it in chapter 4.

Now, go over to chapter 5 and let's look at a couple of things. How do you know it's happened to you? Let me give you five markers along the way. Chapter 5, verse 2. Do you want to read that for me? Elder, you're a great reader. You've got a good, loud voice. I hear you loud and clear. Go ahead; 5 verse 2:

Elder missionary:

> *And they all cried with one voice, saying: Yea, we believe all the words which thou hast spoken unto us; and also, we know of their surety and truth, because of the Spirit of the Lord Omnipotent, which has wrought a mighty change in us, or in our hearts, that we have **no more disposition to do evil, but to do good continually.***

Mike: So, was there a change wrought? Yes. Where does the change take place? In the heart. And what was the fruit of the change?

Elder missionary: *"No more disposition to do evil."*

Mike: *"**No more disposition to do evil, but to do good**."* How long? ***Continually***! Now, the word *disposition*, brothers and sisters, is interesting. It doesn't mean that you're not going to sin anymore. This doesn't mean that repentance is not going to play a role anymore. It just means that you're not disposed to do it. You're still going to make mistakes, but here's the difference; **you don't want to!** You just don't want to. Your disposition has changed because your *heart* has changed. This isn't up here, in the head. We're now talking down in the heart area, here. Ok. Let's look at the next verse. Look at verse 3. Elder.

Elder missionary:

*And we, ourselves, also, through the infinite goodness of God, and the manifestations of his Spirit, have **great views** of that which is to come; and were it expedient, we could prophesy of all things.*

Mike: Here's your second marker. *"**Great views**!"* You want to circle that. We have now, because of this, **great views** because your **view** of everything in this world changes. You do not **view** anything the same anymore. You don't see yourself the same. You don't see your relationship with God the same. Repentance takes on a different view. It's a joy! Service is not a duty; it's a privilege. I mean, everything changes because your *heart* has changed, the **views** change. President, you want to make a comment on that?

Pres. Taggart: Yeah, this principle that Elder Stroud is talking about, it's essential that we understand it. It's essential that our people understand it. It all has to come down to one thing and one thing only. What is our destiny? What is the purpose of life? What is your destiny? Where are you going? What do you want out of life? You're here in New Jersey for 18 months or 2 years, right? I promise you, and I've told you this before: This is your proving ground. This is your boot camp for the rest of your life. What you do here, what you establish here, the kind of person you become here will set the stage for the rest of your life; for eternity. For eternity! This is Heavenly Father's plan to prepare you for the rest of your life. You! You, individually: because every single one of you in this room will have a completely different experience than the person sitting next to you...totally. You'll have different companions. You'll have different people you teach. So, this is what this is about. They had a different *view* of life. Their hearts changed. They saw the big picture. Please, see the big picture! What you desire and what you want out of life changes. The kind of music you listen to; the kind of movies you'll watch; the kind of activities, or the jokes you listen to; the kind of conversations you have; the kind of language you use will change. **The study of the doctrines, the teachings of the doctrines will change behavior way more than the study of behavior will change behavior.** Please understand this. Put it to use in your own life. *That's* why we're having this meeting today. Please, please, please—I beg of you, focus on this! Let this sink into your *heart*. Ask yourself,

"What are the teachings that are here in the scriptures, trying to tell ME as an individual?" And apply that.

Mike: Let's go to chapter 5, verse 5. Here's another marker. This is the big one! Each one of these is building on each other. You see? It gets grander and more glorious. Verse 5; we know we've had the *baptism of fire* if:

> *We are willing to enter into a covenant **with our***
> ***God** to do his will, and to be obedient to his*
> *commandments in **all** things that he shall command*
> *us, **all** the remainder of our days, that we not bring*
> *upon ourselves a never-ending torment,*

If this happens to you, this mighty change of heart, with this *baptism of fire*, you're going to feel a desire to now **enter into a covenant with the Lord.** I testify to you that it's true. And you will. It'll make all the difference in your life. This is a marker along the way.

Let's look at another one. Go to verse 7. Something interesting happens through this process:

> *And now, because of the covenant which ye have*
> *made ye shall be called the children of Christ, his*
> *sons, and his daughters;*

Look who becomes your Father. Jesus Christ now becomes your Father. He's the Father of your spiritual rebirth. That's what the *baptism of fire and the Holy Ghost* is. That's what Christ was talking about with Nicodemus. *"Except a man be born of water and of the **spirit** he cannot enter into the kingdom of God."* This is a birth, and Christ is the Father of this magnificent change of heart. And, by the way, nothing is ever the same again. Nothing. Will you slip and go backward? Yes, but you're not the same. Here's another marker. Before you have the *baptism by fire*, you sin, and you repent, but there's a tendency to justify your sinning. There's a tendency to prolong your repentance. There's a tendency to hide it in the dark and just pray that it will go away. That disappears with this. When you commit sin, your repentance is NOW. There's also something else. Prior to this, you are the victim. Prior to this, you are the victim and what's going wrong in your life is everybody else's fault. When this happens to you, you readily and willingly accept full responsibility for your actions. You say, like in the

Book of Mormon, "My sins are mine and I know them." Oh yeah. And your repentance takes place when?

Elder missionary: Immediately.

Mike: NOW! There's no hiding, there's no justification, and there's no delay. These are the markers. So, where are you? As you look at these markers, how are you doing? If you're falling short on these, okay, that's alright. At least now you're being made aware so that you can **do** something about this. You know there's something grander and more glorious out there that you never conceived possible. Now, we go seek for that. Look what else it says in verse 7:

> *For behold, this day he hath spiritually begotten you; for ye say that your hearts are changed through faith in his name; **therefore**, ye are born of him and have become his sons and his daughters.*

That's where you want to be. I testify to you, when that happens to you, you will not go away. It is unlikely that you will leave.

Like the Savior, He preached some hard doctrine and a lot of people took a walk. You can read about this. And the Twelve turned to Him and said, *"This is a hard thing, who can bear it?"* And He looked at all the other people walking away, and He said to the Twelve, *"Will you go away also?"* And Peter spoke up and said, *"Where will we go? Thou hast the words of eternal life."* And that's you.

I'm going to testify to you that you're going to have stuff hit you that's going to try and drag you away, and it will unless you have this foundation. Your foundation isn't in the Church, brothers and sisters. Your foundation is in Christ. You know the scripture Helaman 5:12:

> *And now, my sons, **remember, remember,** that it's on the rock of our Redeemer, who is Christ, the Son of God, that ye must build your foundation; that when the devil shall send forth his mighty winds, yea, his shafts in the whirlwind, yea, when all his hail and his mighty storm shall beat upon you, it shall have **no power over you** to drag you down to the gulf of misery and endless wo, **because of the rock upon which ye are built**, which is a sure*

> *foundation, a foundation whereon if men build they*
> ***cannot fall***.

Now, that's what we're talking about. This is the foundation; the foundation whereon if men and women will build, they cannot fall, and your fruits remain.

Let's look at a couple of other things. Let's go to 2 Nephi as we wrap up, and let me show you my favorite of all on this. This has all been used right now to lead up to this point. 2 Nephi 31 and I remember when I saw this, I just rejoiced! I said, "How have I missed this?! I don't know how, after reading all of these things, I missed this." In verse 2, Nephi is an old man. He's in his 70's, and he's wrapping up his life. And this is a summation of his life and his doctrine and his teachings. You're getting here what he's spent a lifetime on. Now, think about what he's done and what he's accomplished. What he's going to give you in these next two verses is this, "I'm going to show you **how** I've accomplished what I've accomplished." This is what it is. This is a *How-To* booklet. Look at verse 2:

> *Wherefore, the things which I have written sufficeth*
> *me, save it be a few words which I must speak*
> *concerning the **doctrine of Christ**;*

Now go to your page, 2 Nephi 32:6 and it says:

> *Behold, this is the **doctrine of Christ**,*

Those 26 verses between 2 Nephi 31:2 and 2 Nephi 32:6, contain everything you need to go back to the Father and complete your journey. Only Nephi could have done this for us. Everything you need is in here. Let me show you some secrets. Go with me to 2 Nephi 31:13 and 14. Just kind of glance through 13 and 14 and just look and see if you can see the things we've talked about, thus far today. Just scan those two verses. Everything we've talked about is right there in those two verses. It is all there, isn't it? Now go down to verse 17:

> *Wherefore, do the things which I have told you I*
> *have seen that your Lord and your Redeemer should*
> *do; for, for this cause have they been shown unto*
> *me, that ye might know **the gate** by which ye should*
> *enter.*

Remember the two questions I asked you? When do you receive a remission of sins? And when do your feet begin to tread the *strait and narrow path?* Those are the questions we started out with today, right? We're going to answer those right now. He answers that question for us:

> *For the gate by which ye should enter is repentance and baptism by water;* **AND THEN cometh a remission of your sins by fire and by the Holy Ghost.**

There's the first part. You haven't even passed through the *gate* until you've received the *baptism of fire* and *the remission of sins.* That **IS** the gate. The baptismal ordinance we've been talking about is the gate.

Now, put your finger here and let's go back to 2 Nephi 9 and see something else about this gate. 2 Nephi 9:41. I know that most of us have thought that the gate was baptism. At least I did. Now, let's find out in verse 41:

> *O then, my beloved brethren, come unto the Lord, the Holy One. Remember that his paths are righteous. Behold, the way for man is narrow, but it lieth in a straight course before him, and the keeper of the gate is the Holy One of Israel; and he employeth no servant there; and there is none other way save it be by the gate; for he cannot be deceived, for the Lord God is his name.*

You can lie to your bishop and get away with it, as far as your bishop goes. You can lie to him, and he won't know it. You can lie to a stake president, and he may not know. You can lie to a general authority, and he may not catch it, but you cannot lie to the Holy Ghost, nor to the Holy One of Israel, who is the keeper of the gate. That's why He's the keeper because what's on the other side of the gate is so glorious and so fantastic that you have to have a broken heart and a contrite spirit, honor, and integrity to get to that point, to receive the present President Taggart is talking about.

Back over to 2 Nephi 31:18, *"And then..."* –see that? There's a sequence.

> ***And then*** *are ye in this strait and narrow path which leads to eternal life;*

When do you get on the *strait and narrow path?* When you complete the baptismal ordinance. When it's completed, both the mortal part and the immortal part, you receive a remission of your sins, and you're on the *strait and narrow.* Fantastic! How did we miss this? Maybe you didn't. I did—for years. 18, 19, and 20 tell you the things the Lord is going to give you. These are gifts and attributes and characteristics that come now, after the *baptism of fire* that leads up to the promise in verse 20. Just read those verses. See what you're going to have. Is it all finished? Have you all done it when you pass through the gate? No:

> *Wherefore, ye must press forward with a*
> *steadfastness in Christ, having a perfect brightness*
> *of hope, and a love of God and of all men.*

See, push forward, and He gives you gifts to do that. One of the gifts is that you speak with the tongue of angels. That comes with the *baptism of fire.* The ministry of angels now becomes personal and sometimes veil-less. That's what's on the other side. He's just waiting for us. Now, looking at verse 20. *"Ye must press forward with a steadfastness in Christ, having a perfect brightness of hope..."* –you can't do that; you cannot have any of these things in verse 20 without the *baptism of fire.* They are reserved for those people who are on the *strait and narrow.*

> *Wherefore, if ye shall press forward, feasting upon*
> *the word of Christ, and endure to the end, behold,*

–and this is one of the very few places in all of scripture where the Father's voice is recorded because the Father just doesn't do much in the telestial world. That's the realm of the Holy Ghost and angels, and Christ sometimes, but He's terrestrial:

> *Thus saith the Father: Ye shall have eternal life.*

That is something called *"calling and election made sure through the more sure word of prophecy."* At this point, according to 2 Peter, you cannot fall. Interesting, huh? You see the sequence? Build, build, build until you get to a point. The whole purpose of all this is to get you to where your fruit remains, and you don't walk away.

Pres. Taggart: There's an important principle here, too. It says, *press forward.* Press forward. What that means, elders and sisters, don't look to the past. Don't be weighed down by things, silly things, or stupid things you've done. We've ALL made mistakes. We are not perfect. We've all sinned, every one of us. Too many of us get bogged down by the things we've done in the past because we're not leaving them. They're haunting us. Press forward. Move forward. Don't be inhibited, or weighed down by that. Alright? That's really important. **Really** important. Look to the future and *know* that a remission of your sins alleviates you from those sins. *"I, the Lord, remember them no more."* Believe Him when he tells you that! Allow yourselves to move forward. Keep progressing. Don't look back. You know, we talk about being *normal*. When you go home, people are going to ask you, "How long before you become *normal*?" You know? "How long is it going to take for you to become a *normal human being* again?" You don't want to be a *normal human being*! The answer that you're going to give these people is, "I will never be *normal* again! I'm not *normal*! I went out on a mission to be *NOT normal*, as the world sees it. I don't ever want to be *normal* again." Don't apologize for that. Don't fall into the trap that, "Oh, it's uncool to be good. It's not cool to be good." I'm here to tell you, and I testify IT IS COOL TO BE GOOD! It is **REALLY** cool to be good! Really good, all the time. This is what the Lord wants. This is what He has in store for you. Take the shackles off of you and soar! Okay, I testify that that's true.

Mike: Let's end up in 2 Nephi 32 verse 6. Please look at these 26 verses. Please look at these 26 verses with **new** eyes and with **new** light:

> Behold, this is the doctrine of Christ, and there will be no more doctrine given until after he shall manifest himself unto you in the flesh.

This is talking about a *Second Comforter* experience. *The Second Comforter* is a visitation from the Savior. He wants to do that. That's what Nephi is talking about. He had it, and he wants you to have it:

> And when he shall manifest himself unto you in the flesh, the things which he shall say unto you shall ye observe to do.

He's got a message for you. There's an agenda. It's specific and intimate, and it's just for you.

Now look at verse 7:

> And now I, Nephi, cannot say more; the Spirit stoppeth mine utterance, and I am left to mourn.

"Now I, Nephi, cannot say more." He wants to, but he can't. *"The Spirit stoppeth mine utterance, and I am left to mourn."* He wanted

to put more down here, but the Lord said, "No, that's enough." This is for **you**. This is not for people outside the Church. People outside the Church aren't reading this. The *Book of Mormon* is for you! Nephi wanted to tell you something more, but the Spirit said, "No, that's enough. Let them work on what they've got, and when I come to them, I'll tell them more. This is enough until I come and manifest myself unto them in the flesh." Then he says:

> *And I am left to mourn because of the unbelief, and the wickedness, and the ignorance, and the stiffneckedness of men;*

That's an indictment against us if we're not moving towards this. Don't think for a minute that that's talking about gentile, non-Mormons. That's **YOU** that is being referred to:

> *For they will not search knowledge, nor understand great knowledge, when it is given unto them in plainness, even as plain as word can be.*

And I pray that this has been plain today. We prayed a lot about this because we know how critical this is for you.

I've got a cousin that struggles with activity. I've been teaching her the doctrine of Christ for the last year and her behavior has changed mightily. I taught her about the *baptism of fire and the Holy Ghost* and here's what she said. This email is just 48 hours old. I want to share it with you. She's a single mom in her late 40's, early 50's, living in Tooele, Utah. I had sent her a couple of recordings of this stuff:

> *I listened to the two sessions over and over. I had to give a talk in Sacrament last week. I prayed about topics and gave it on the baptism of fire. I worried how it would be received, but so interesting were the responses from the ward members. The Spirit guided me through my talk. I have a couple living next to me who, after 50 years, have decided to come back to church. The husband is an old cowboy with a heart of gold and has such a sweet wife. He said he was in tears and moved by what he heard. I'm so thankful the Lord used me for a vessel of this message. Another member said it was something he thought a bishop would tell his ward. I only hope I can leap into conversion. I know, like*

you Mike, I have been at my wit's end and cried, literally, to the Lord for help. Sometimes we as members don't feel worthy to ask: Can I really reach into this realm? What do I need to do after repentance and forgiveness?

When I read that I was so overjoyed! I was just thrilled for her. ***True doctrine understood changes behavior.***

We have WAY too many people leaving the Church. I believe this is the answer and I believe it's been in front of us all along. And I believe now, the Lord is coming to a point where we need to be awakened and *"...rise up, O men of Israel..."* and you sweetheart ladies. These men have understanding, but they have no wisdom. Can I tell you that? If you want to take the roles of men and women, here's what I've learned over my life: The number one attribute for men is *understanding*. The number one attribute for women is *wisdom*. That's why a man and a woman together are complete. One without the other is un-whole. I testify to you the truth of these things. I'm grateful for the Spirit of the Lord. I pray that you've been touched and this will begin a new study and a new adventure for you because truly the greatest things of the gospel of Christ are hidden. If you are bored in church and in the gospel, it's YOUR fault because this is flat exciting! I testify so, in the name of Jesus Christ, amen.

President, do you want to field some questions? President Taggart and I will field some questions here, and we wanted to take a little time for you to ask some questions.

Pres. Taggart: Yes, Elder?

Elder missionary 1: Obviously, after you've received the *baptism of fire* and after you've received the Holy Ghost, the Spirit is strong, but in the process, we're obviously going to make mistakes. So, would it be correct then to theorize that you have to receive the *baptism of fire* multiple times when you've messed up, and you have to receive it again or try to get back to that same level where you reached before?

Mike: It's possible to cycle in and out of this. You can lose it, but your way back is quicker because your repentance is quicker. It is possible for you to slack out and lose some of these gifts. Just persevere. Each time you have this spiritual experience, it changes

203

you so that you're not ever the same. Will you still make mistakes and slip back? Yes, but the recovery is quicker and more complete.

Pres. Taggart: Just look at it like this: It's a process, and it's a ladder. I've drawn this for a lot of missionaries. I'm going to say this is your missionary life. You start out down here, and maybe this is the 2-year mark, up here. You start out; you have ups and downs, peaks and valleys. And some of them are bigger than others. You have times when you feel the Spirit. You have times when you're being guided and directed. And you have times when you think, "I don't feel anything. I'm as low as a whale turd at the bottom of the ocean."

Missionaries: Ha-ha-ha!

Pres. Taggart: You're not happy. So, elder, the point is, you're going to have these peaks and valleys the rest of your life. Some of them get real big and some not so big. That's just the way life is. You have 3 or 4 kids, and you have a kid go haywire, you're going to have a pretty big dip. Trust me, the challenges in your life you're having right now are nothing compared to what they're going to be and what they can be. So, recognize that once you've had this *baptism by fire*, you KNOW! You **know** the path, and you're **on** the path. So, you've just got to get back to the path. And climbing out of all of these pits is just getting back on the path. Elder?

Elder missionary 2: So, our goal now is that *baptism of fire*. The next step is the Second Comforter? Is there something in between that?

Mike: Now, that's a whole other lesson that we won't go into today. The next steps are interesting things called *calling and election made sure, more sure word of prophecy, translation, Second Comforter*, I mean on and on and on. But, let's just stay right here for a minute!

Missionaries: Ha-ha-ha!

Pres. Taggart: There are people that that happens to. They used to publish those names in the Church News, way back in the day. It happens, and it CAN happen. I think the important thing to know is that it's not impossible. And if you seek that and you want that and you're worthy for that, that can happen. It is absolutely within your reach, within our reach, to have that happen. People become sanctified enough that they receive the *Second Comforter*, which is an actual ordinance given by the Savior.

Mike: Let me give you a reference really quick. Go to your Joseph Smith Translation. Look at Genesis 14, not now; later. Look at Genesis 14, and it will tell you what's available to you when you come to this level in your progression. JST Genesis 14 lays it out. That's who you can and should be.

Pres. Taggart: Elder, here's the thing. Look at what's going on here. It's your trajectory. It's your trajectory that matters. It's not where you are on these dips and these peaks and valleys. It's the understanding that every single minute, every single hour, every single day of your life is designed for you to grow, to learn, to overcome adversity, to overcome challenges that this earth gives you, and to overcome evil and Satan so that someday you can return to our Heavenly Father. It's your perspective, and the vision Elder Stroud talked about. You have a new vision. Your vision changes. What you want, what's important to you changes. We talk about obedience in the mission. You want to be obedient because you want to be up here. That's your goal. That's your vision. You don't want to do whacky things here that prevent you from getting there. You, in your heart, have changed.

Senior missionary: This has been a wonderful presentation! Don't you wish that when we were missionaries in England, we would have gotten this at this age?

Pres. Taggart: Yep!

Senior missionary: Instead of, like you said, at three times their age and we've had to learn along the way. You've gotten some great stuff here today. You know, modern theology today teaches that being *born again* is an event. "I've been *born again!*" President Taggart repeatedly said today, that it is a process. The scriptures teach us; the Brethren teach us that we have drops put in our lamps day by day, as we are studying the gospel, as we are testifying and praying, attending church, and all of these things. These are adding drops to our lamp, and they don't stay there. When you go home, you are going to have to rely on some of those drops that you've put into your reservoir. And when you hit some of these low spots, like President Taggart said, you've got to have the reserve there. And if you use the reserve and you don't continually, by enduring to the end, keep putting drops in, pretty soon your lamp is going to be empty. And you will have forgotten all that you had in that spiritual reservoir. So, this is enduring to the end, to keep going, not giving up. You've got to keep replenishing the drops in the lamp.

Pres. Taggart: Well, remember 2 Nephi chapter 2: opposition in all things. The opposition in all things is the eternal law. We cannot experience the joy, the happiness, the highs unless we experience these dips. They come together. You think about Joseph Smith and Jesus Christ, you know, their dips were like this: they had the highest of highs and the lowest of lows. Why? That's part of the gospel doctrine: opposition in all things. The more severe your trials, the more intense your trials, probably the more intense your joy. That's just an eternal law. When you're having these times that many of you have on your mission, realize and recognize what they're for, why you have them, and celebrate the day that the sun will come up in the morning. It will come up. Any other questions?

Elder missionary 4: So, with the *gift of the Holy Ghost*, we teach about the companionship of the Holy Ghost and how as long as they stay worthy they will have the constant companionship of the Holy Ghost to guide and protect them spiritually and physically. Does that fall under the same category with...

Mike: The term *gift of the Holy Ghost,* which means the constant companionship of that member of the Godhead, is the *baptism of fire and the Holy Ghost*. Those are synonymous terms. There is something in section 109. I put it down here if you look at the bottom of the page under *conclusion*. Section 109, verse 15 mentions something called *the fullness of the Holy Ghost.* You want to write down two scriptural references I'll give to you with that, where you can see the culminating experience of what we're talking about here. Look in Helaman 5. Nephi and Lehi are in the Lamanite prison in Middoni, remember that? And look at 3 Nephi 19, which I believe is the Holy of Holies of the *Book of Mormon.*

Pres. Taggart: But Elder, in answer to your question, let me ask you this: Have any of you in this room, any of you—I'm talking about Elder Stroud and even [other senior missionaries]—have any of you received or felt the Holy Ghost continually, constantly? I haven't. We're entitled to that. That could happen at some point in our lives, but very rarely is that a reality. You know, it just doesn't happen, so recognize that. Try not to be disappointed when you're not feeling inspired every minute of every day; it comes, and it goes. And the more we can feel it the better off we are. And the way we feel it is how? Through what? How can we feel it?

Elder missionary 5: The fundamentals.

Pres. Taggart: The basic fundamentals. One particular thing is determining whether we feel the Holy Ghost or not. What is it?

Elder missionary 6: Repentance.

Pres. Taggart: Perfection? No. I'm not perfect. No one's perfect.

Elder missionary 6: I said REPENTANCE.

Pres. Taggart: Oh! Repentance! I thought you said perfection. What do we have to be in order to receive the Holy Ghost?

Sister missionary 3: Obedient.

Elder missionary 7: Worthy.

Pres. Taggart: Worthy! We need to be righteous. Worthiness and righteousness are what allow us to become sanctified, or pure. That means obedience. That means following the Savior and doing what He does. And that business, that 14 inches between the head and the heart? Our hearts need to become pure and clean so that the Spirit of the Holy Ghost can actually dwell in us. Elder?

Elder missionary 8: So, what is something that would keep us out of the routine of just being like some of our converts? You know, just coming to church, taking the sacrament, because that's what we're *supposed* to do. What is something we can do to stay out of that?

Pres. Taggart: Wow! That is a great question. Let's answer that. What is it? What is the answer to his question? That's a great question!

Elder: Somebody asked me, "How do I know if I'm really active? How do you know if your activity is good or not? How do you gauge that?" What you're thinking about during the Sacrament is a pretty good answer.

Pres. Taggart: What you're thinking about when you're taking the Sacrament. That's very good. What you think about day to day. What you do day to day. That's very important. What are some things you can actually do? That's what he is asking. What are some things you can actually do on a day to day basis when you go back to the real world, you're in college, or you get married, you've got kids, and you're in the real world? Well, what do you do? What are the things you do to stay active and not just go to church as a habit?

Sister missionary 4: [comments unintelligible]

Pres. Taggart: She just said a couple of really good things, and I don't know if she knows how significant they are. She said three things. Teach ourselves the doctrine. Keep studying! Now, I don't' know about you, but you can ask Sister Taggart; I'd get up at 5:30 in the morning because that was MY time. I would feast on the scriptures. I'd find manuals, and they came out with these new subtitled scriptures in 1978, where they had all the cross references. I ate that up! It was like, "Oh! This is so exciting!" And I just feasted on the scriptures. Teach yourself the scriptures. Keep studying.

She also said to help others. Help others to study the scriptures. Do that.

And then keep the Sabbath day holy. I will tell you right now, elders and sisters, the Sabbath day and honoring the Sabbath day, and the **doctrine** of the Sabbath day, we don't understand. That could be a whole other topic. We could spend an hour on the Sabbath day and the blessings that are inherent and accompany Sabbath day observance. There are promises, **unbelievable** promises that come with Sabbath day observance! You know, and we have the church of the NFL in this country, which is really… if you think about Satan and… well, I'm not going to get into this. But Sabbath day observance; understand what it means! Understand what Sabbath day observance means. And if you obey the Sabbath day, unbelievable blessings come, and part of those blessings are that you are close to the Spirit. So, that's another one.

My advice and we don't have a lot of time left, but in answer to your question; stay connected to your Heavenly Father. Now, how do you do that? Pray, use real, true, genuine, connecting prayers. You have to make time for that. It may take time. Prayer is work. It takes time. You can't just kneel down and in 3 minutes go, "mumble, mumble, mumble, in the name of Jesus Christ, amen," and be edified by that prayer. It doesn't work!

Sister Taggart: It's a wrestle.

Pres. Taggart: It's a wrestle! Wrestle with the Lord. Make time for it. If you don't make time for it, I'm telling you right now, if you don't do it in the morning when you wake up, you probably won't do it. You probably won't do it, that's why you need to get up early. That's why in the mission they teach you to get up early and get going. Those are things you can do. Make sure you have real connecting prayers, good ones. Make sure you study. Feast upon the scriptures. Serve others. She also said that. Serve people. Forget yourself and go do things for other people. Be engaged, anxiously engaged. And when you have a calling, magnify your calling. Talk to Elder [senior missionary] about home teaching. How many people go *home teaching*? Actually *home teach*, or *visit teach* the way the Savior would do it, by ministering. Be a great minister in your calling. If you do those things, you won't just be going to church to go to church. You'll be progressing on that scale. I testify to that.

Mike: So, can we put our money where our mouth is for a minute here? This is all good, but you asked a question that addresses behavior. See that? What have we been talking about here today? Are we going to endlessly talk about the behavior, or are we going to find the doctrine that addresses the behavior? The questions are; how are you going to stay in the church, how are you going to maintain, how are you going to keep from falling away? Let's go to 1 Nephi 15:23 and find the doctrine. Otherwise, we end up counseling endlessly again, and what does it do? Preoccupation with behavior encourages what? Unworthy behavior. These are two unworthy men asking a question, Laman and Lemuel. Rather than seek, they go to Nephi. They don't ask questions. 1 Nephi 15:23, they asked:

> *What meaneth the rod of iron which our father saw, that led to the tree?*

Watch, here's the answer. Here's the answer to your question in verse 24:

> *And I said unto them that it was the word of God; and whoso would hearken unto the word of God, and would hold fast unto it, they would never perish; neither could the temptations and the fiery darts of the adversary overpower them unto blindness, to lead them away to destruction.*

See, the promise first promise is, if you will hearken to, hold fast to, the word of God, you will *"never perish"* meaning, you won't take a walk. And promise number 2, the temptations of the devil have no power over you. How about that one?

Let's go to one more: Moroni 6. Moroni struggled with this problem. It was the same among the Nephites. They didn't have good home teachers. Okay? Now look for the answer. When you find the answer that addresses the problem, what do you do with it? You teach it. You're teachers. Teach it. And when you teach the word of God that has virtue and power, it changes behavior. Verse 4:

> *And after **they** had been received unto baptism, and were wrought upon and cleansed by the power of the Holy Ghost, they were numbered among the people of the church of Christ; and their names were taken, that they might be remembered and nourished by the good word of God, to keep them in the right way, to keep them continually watchful unto prayer, relying alone upon the merits of Christ, who was the author and the finisher of their faith.*

"They" means all of us. They were baptized, cleansed and their names were taken. See, they've got membership records that they might be remembered and nourished. They're not letting them drop. Throughout the world, President Hinckley gave three things that every member needs in order to keep our fruits from going away. What were they? Tell me. Number 1?

Missionaries: A friend.

Mike: Okay, you need a friend. Number 2?

Missionaries: A calling.

Mike: You need a calling, number 2. Number 3?

Missionaries: Nourishment by the good word of God.

Mike: I've asked that on three continents, and I've only had one or two people who could tell me what that 3rd thing was. And that's the reason we have problems. That's the missing link. We all know about the friend. We all know about the calling. It's the nourishment by the good word of God that's lacking. Now, look at the promise. If they're nourished, look at the three promises: number 1, *"To keep them in the right way,"* number 2, *"To keep them continually watchful unto prayer,"* and number 3, *"Relying wholly upon the merits of Christ, who is the author and the finisher of their faith."* These are people who don't walk away. And by the way, how do you finish faith? When is faith finished? If He's the author and finisher of your faith, when is faith finished? When it's replaced with what?

Missionaries: Knowledge.

Mike: What kind of knowledge?

Missionaries: Perfect knowledge.

Mike: Perfect knowledge. And that happens when you stand in His presence. Your faith is done. It's a process.

Pres. Taggart: That's what Elder Packer was talking about.

Mike: There's the answer to your question. It's in the scriptures. So, teach it and live it and you won't walk away.

Pres. Taggart: Elders and sisters, we pray that each one of you will feel the Spirit that is here, present, right now. It's here in this room, very strong. We hope that you comprehend: that you understand what you've been given today, that you allow this to sink deep into your heart and that you become different from this day forward. Being given this information, that you now seek and have a clear vision, a clear picture of what you, as an individual, as a son or daughter of Heavenly Father, must do to get back into His presence. Take this information. Embrace it! Celebrate it! And watch what happens to your life. Watch how your heart changes. Your motives change. How you address and attack adversity and opposition will change because you trust that the Savior has your back and that He knows what He's doing. He knows your path. He knows your heart, and he knows where you're going. And you believe Him, and you know that no matter what it is, no matter how bad it can get, that you can get through it and you'll be stronger as a result of it. You are entitled to receive and feel the *gift of the Holy Ghost*. I promise you, I testify to you in the name of Jesus Christ, that if you comprehend and do this, you will find joy and happiness; here, now, in New Jersey, and for the rest of your life. And that this will be the foundation of your faith: the foundation of how you live, the foundation for your children, your wife or your husband, as you progress throughout life. I'm grateful for Elder Stroud. I'm grateful for him revealing this to us, for sharing this with us. I testify of these things in the name of Jesus Christ, Amen.

The Baptismal Ordinance

"True doctrine, understood, changes attitudes and behavior."

"The study of the doctrines of the gospel will improve behavior quicker than a study of behavior will improve behavior. Preoccupation with unworthy behavior can lead to unworthy behavior. That is why we stress so forcefully the study of the doctrines of the gospel." *Boyd K. Packer of the Quorum of the Twelve Apostles. ("Little Children," Ensign, Nov. 1986, 17).*

"Receive the Holy Ghost"

by David A. Bednar

These four words— "Receive the Holy Ghost"—are not a passive pronouncement; rather, they constitute a priesthood injunction—an authoritative admonition to act and not simply to be acted upon.

My message focuses on the importance of striving in our daily lives to actually receive the Holy Ghost.

The gift of the Holy Ghost is bestowed only after proper and authorized baptism and by the laying on of hands by those holding the Melchizedek Priesthood.

Baptism by immersion is "the introductory ordinance of the gospel, and must be followed by baptism of the Spirit in order to be complete" (*Bible* Dictionary, "Baptism").

The ordinance of confirming a new member of the Church and bestowing the gift of the Holy Ghost is both simple and profound

The simplicity of this ordinance may cause us to overlook its significance. These four words— "Receive the Holy Ghost"—are not a passive pronouncement; rather, they constitute a priesthood injunction—an authoritative admonition to act and not simply to be acted upon (see 2 Nephi 2:26). The Holy Ghost does not become operative in our lives merely because hands are placed upon our heads and those four important words are spoken. As we receive this ordinance, each of us accepts a sacred and ongoing responsibility to desire, to seek, to work, and to so live that we indeed "receive the Holy Ghost" and its attendant spiritual gifts.

We more readily receive and recognize the Spirit of the Lord as we appropriately invite Him into our lives. We cannot compel, coerce, or command the Holy Ghost. Rather, we should invite Him into our lives with the same gentleness and tenderness by which He entreats us (see D&C 42:14).

Praying, studying, gathering, worshipping, serving, and obeying are not isolated and independent items on a lengthy gospel checklist of things to do. Rather, each of these righteous practices is an important element in an overarching spiritual quest to fulfill the mandate to receive the Holy Ghost.

I pray we will sincerely desire and appropriately invite the Holy Ghost into our daily lives. I also pray each of us will faithfully obey God's commandments and in reality receive the Holy Ghost. *(David A. Bednar, "Receive the Holy Ghost," Ensign, Oct. 2012)*

Baptism with Fire and with the Holy Ghost

"You might as well baptize a bag of sand as a man, if not done in view of the remission of sins and getting of the Holy Ghost. Baptism by water is but half a baptism, and is good for nothing without the other half—that is, the baptism of the Holy Ghost."
Teachings of the Prophet Joseph Smith, sel. Joseph Fielding Smith (1976), 314.

(Make notes below as The Spirit directs)

2 Nephi 31:4-5, 7, 11-17	Baptism with water.
2 Nephi 31:13-14, 17-18	Baptism with fire and with The Holy Ghost.
2 Nephi 31:9-18	The gate and the strait and narrow path.
2 Nephi 32:4, 7	Why we don't receive the Baptism with Fire and with the Holy Ghost.
2 Nephi 31:19-20	The fruits of the Baptism with Fire and with the Holy Ghost.
2 Nephi 31:13-14, 32:2-3	Speak with the tongue of angels.
2 Nephi 31:15	Calling and Election made Sure by the more sure word of prophecy.
2 Nephi 32:6	The Second Comforter.

_____

_____

_____

_____

_____

_____

_____

The Doctrine of Christ
2 Nephi 31:2 through 2 Nephi 32:6

D&C 20:41   Baptism with Water - Confirmation - Baptism with Fire and with the Holy
Ghost
3 Nephi 9:20   Baptism with Fire and with the Holy Ghost
3 Nephi 11:32-35   Baptism with Water and with Fire and with the Holy Ghost
3 Nephi 12:1-2   Baptism with Water and with Fire and with the Holy Ghost for a
Remission of Sins
Mosiah 4 & 5   How to obtain and retain a Remission of Sins

_____
_____
_____
_____
_____
_____
_____
_____
_____
_____

Conclusion
Moroni 6:1-4   D&C 109:15   3 Nephi 19

Chapter Nine
Podcast 009 Claim the Blessing

Today in church we had a discussion in the High Priest Group. I'll just share this story as we start out. I won't go into what the topic was, but it was again an emphasis from the scriptures, from the brethren, and from the gospel, on what kind of people we should be and what we should be doing in life, to be successful spiritually, and prosper temporally. The thought came to my mind again, and we hear this over and over, that we have no problem, as members of the Church, knowing where we should be, what we should be doing, or what kind of people we should be. We hear that, and it's very successfully taught. The impression to me was that we never talk about the "how." It seems that *how* we become that kind of person is, at least in my experience, sadly lacking when we get together as members. I discovered something a few years back that's just a simple little experience. Let's go to 2 Nephi 32, and I'll share with you what I think was one of the big break-through doctrinal moments in my life. It's the *how*. *How* do we accomplish these things? *How* do we become a man or woman of Christ? We know that we should be humble. We know that we should be meek. We know that we should be lowly in heart. We know that we should have a broken heart and a contrite spirit. We know all of these things. And all of these characteristics and attributes are the criteria for us to rend the veil, be redeemed from *The Fall*, and have an encounter with that society that dwells on the other side of the veil. The problem is that we never discuss the *how*. I think this is one of the great mysteries, and the Lord hides it in simplicity in the scriptures. So, by way of context, when you're reading the last chapters of 2 Nephi, chapters 28-31, it is the summary of Nephi's life and what he's learned throughout his life. He's now, we guess, somewhere in his 70's, and a few pages later in the *Book of Mormon*, we'll see that Nephi dies. So, this is a summary and he's teaching us *how* he became a *favorite of heaven*, and what we need to do to become one of *heaven's favorites*. That term, a *favorite of heaven*, is not found anywhere in the scriptures, but it is found in *The Sixth Lecture on Faith*, and that's where that comes from. The formula is simply: **ask**, **seek**, and **knock**. If we want to obtain and have these endowments or spiritual gifts in our lives, the secret is to ask. This is a three-part formula: what is it we ask for, what should we seek for, where do we knock, and on what do we knock? Usually, we knock on doors, so, what's the door that we should knock on? If we start to ponder that simple formula— ask, seek and knock—then it opens up a whole vista on *how* we can become the kinds of people that the scriptures abundantly tell us that we need to be. Verse 4 is a summary. Keep in mind; this is Nephi's summary of his lifetime and what he's learned. He says:

> *Wherefore, now after I have spoken these words, if ye cannot understand them it will be because ye **ask** not, neither do ye **knock**; wherefore, ye are not brought into the light, but must perish in the dark.*

I remember when I read that, the Spirit impressed me. That was a great day for me because that answered my question; the key of **how-to** in every gospel subject and topic. Do you want to have the gift of charity in your life? You have to **ask** for it. Do you want to be more humble; do you want to be meek and lowly in heart, which are the three criteria to parting the veil? You have to **ask** for it. Then look at what else he says, *"Wherefore, ye are not brought into the light, but must perish in the dark."*

Now, look at verse five:

> *For behold, again I say unto you that if ye will enter in by the way, and receive the Holy Ghost, it will **show** unto you all things what ye should do.*

So, there is the formula. It is so simple and hidden in plain sight. Many of us will go our whole lives and miss that. Margie was showing me one in Matthew 21:22, that says:

> *And all things, whatsoever ye shall ask in prayer, believing, ye shall receive.*

Margie: Ask in prayer!

Mike: It's a real simple formula, but it's the one that we skip over, and we miss. Now, go over to Moroni 7, and I'll show you another place. Charity is one of those gifts of the Spirit. In fact, it is the ultimate gift of the Spirit that we need to have in order to obtain anything worthwhile in this life. In Moroni 7:48, the Lord talks about charity. I want to concentrate on one word:

> *Wherefore, my beloved brethren, pray unto the Father with all the energy of heart, that ye may be filled with his love, which he hath **bestowed** upon all who are true followers of His Son, Jesus Christ;*

Now, remember that charity is the ultimate gift of the Spirit. It's the pure love of Christ. Moroni points out that if you're in possession of charity, by nature of that attribute, you're in possession of all other gifts. It circumscribes all of the gifts of God. Charity is the greatest of all the gifts. He says in verse 46 that you may have some of the other gifts, but they will fail. But, *"charity never faileth."* Then we are admonished to, *"cleave unto charity, which is the greatest of all, **for all things must fail—**"*

The keyword there, brothers and sisters, is ***bestowed***. If we are asking in faith, with real intent, having a sincere heart, reasoning with the Lord, He will bestow this gift upon you. It's a *bestowal*. It's an endowment. It's not something you can develop by any criteria on your own. It's something you have to have faith for, and when the timing is right, or it's the will of the Lord, He bestows this gift upon you. It resides in the Father and the Son because all of these gifts of the Spirit can be found in their fullness in the Father and the Son. We can't have it in fullness, but we can have a portion of it.

Section 88 says that if you're in possession of a portion of any of these gifts, the day will come when you'll be bestowed with a fullness, but before you can ever have a fullness, you have to have a portion. The portion of these gifts, come as a *Bestowal or Endowment* when you ask in faith, nothing doubting, and ask not amiss. Then He *bestows* these things on you. That's the **how**. That's **how** you become a man or a woman of Christ. He bestows Christ-like attributes and characteristics upon you. Any comments on that? That was just a great eye-opener for me. That forever changed the way I pray, and **how** I seek for the gifts of the Spirit, and to become Christ-like. Thoughts or impressions? Does that make sense?

Student 1: Yeah. You are right! I believe we are lacking in knowing the **how-to**. That's why I like your lessons so much because you teach us **how**.

Mike: That's been my observation. I'm not trying to find fault in any way, it's just that it seems like we do well in discussing *the what* and *the who*, but we could do a whole lot better on **the how**. So, I give that to you for your consideration.

Now, tonight I want to talk to you about a title. The title of this podcast will be *Claim the Blessing*. Before we start on it, I'd like to go to 2 Nephi 2 and look at something that Lehi talks about. Again, these are Lehi's closing messages because over in chapter 4, Lehi dies. So, here we have the benefit of this great prophet's last words and life experiences on **how** he was able to pierce the veil, have an encounter with God, and enter into the *Rest of the Lord*, which is what we want to do. The whole purpose of the *Book of Mormon* is to give us examples of what men and women have done before us so that we can do the same. Since God is no respecter of persons, then everything we read in the scriptures that have taken place with others, must be available to us now, in order for God to be no respecter of persons. We just need to find out what the formulas are, what the patterns are, what the keys are, and the doctrinal truths so we can apply those same truths in our lives and have the same results that all these great men and women in the *Book of Mormon* had.

Let's go to 2 Nephi 2:13. In verse 11, Lehi is talking about the great principle of opposition. We talked about that, and we'll probably talk about it in the future. Going along with this law of opposition, that there has to be opposition in all things, in verse 13 we're at the end of that opposition doctrinal statement, and he says:

> *And if ye shall say there is no law, ye shall also say there is no sin. If ye shall say there is no sin, ye shall also say there is no righteousness. And if there*

be no righteousness there be no happiness. And if
there be no righteousness nor happiness there be no
punishment nor misery. And if these things are not
there is no God. And if there is no God we are not,
neither the earth;

Now, this part is what I want you to be aware of for tonight's discussion, and notice the semicolon after earth. You know the purpose of a semicolon. It means that you now have a statement following the semicolon that is going to substantiate the rest of verse 13:

for there could have been no creation of things,
*neither **to act nor to be acted upon**; wherefore, all*
things must have vanished away.

The whole purpose of the creation of the telestial world is to place men and woman in a place where they can choose to *act or be acted upon*. We'll come back to that in a minute:

[14] And now, my sons, I speak unto you these
things for your profit and learning; for there is a
God, and he hath created all things, both the
heavens and the earth, and all things that in them
*are, **both things to act and things to be acted upon**.*

Now, in the Garden of Eden, he points out two great objects that stand in opposition one to the other.

[15] And to bring about his eternal purposes in the
end of man, after he had created our first parents,
and the beasts of the field and the fowls of the air,
and in fine, all things which are created, it must
needs be that there was an opposition; even the
forbidden fruit in opposition to the tree of life;
[there are the 2 opposites—one brings death, and
the other which sustains life] *the one being sweet*
and the other bitter.

If you take the sequence of how that's written, the forbidden fruit is the one that's sweet, and the tree of life is the one that's bitter. That's a lesson in and of itself. Now, the last verse:

[16] Wherefore, the Lord God gave unto man that
he should act for himself. Wherefore, man could not
act for himself save it should be that he was enticed
by the one or the other.

220

The principle here is that everything in creation, whether it's in the telestial world, or the terrestrial world, or I would venture to say, in the celestial world, or anywhere in the eternities, there are always things that act and things that are acted upon. To be acted upon is to forfeit your eternal life. Ultimately, if you remain in a state of being acted upon, you forfeit eternal life. Those who act, in the environment where *acting or being acted upon* is present, are exercising the seeds of Godhood. So, you always need to be in a place, where you're doing things without being asked to do them. You need to be able to be in a state of revelation and prophecy so that you know by the Spirit beforehand, without being instructed what you should do, or should not do, and then act.

Remember that verse we just read over there in 2 Nephi 32:5 that says:

> *For behold, again I say unto you that if ye will*
> *enter in by the way, and receive the Holy Ghost, it*
> *will show unto you all things what ye should do.*

If you have to wait in this life, to receive instructions from another mortal being on what you should do on your pathway to godhood, you place yourself in a very serious position of vulnerability, because all men are subject to error, and are prone to sin and transgression. Now, that's not to say that there isn't a time in our progression, where we need to be acted upon. I'm not saying that at all because we learn step-by-step, line upon line, precept upon precept.

The Prophet Joseph Smith, who was also the mayor of Nauvoo, was visited by the mayor of Boston. The mayor was impressed with the industry, and the order and beauty of the Nauvoo society. He asked Joseph, "How is it that your people are so well ordered? How is it that you have such an industrious people and such a beautiful city?"

The prophet made this great statement:

> *I teach them correct principles, and they govern*
> *themselves.*

Now, that's a wonderful concept. Notice that Joseph teaches them correct principles, and they **act** on the truth that he taught them.

If you were to take the pattern of the Three Degrees of Glory: the telestial, the terrestrial, and the celestial, you can see this principle of acting, or being acted upon, in all three of those places.

Telestial individuals, by nature, are rebellious and place themselves in a place, more or less, to be acted upon. If you were to take a concept like what the Church is teaching now, to *"Honor the Sabbath day to keep it holy"* and apply it to a telestial person, that telestial person might say this concerning the Sabbath Day, "Don't tell me what to do. Sunday is my only day off. I'm going to do what I want, and you're not going to tell me what to do. Go away." So, telestial people are by nature rebels. That's all of us in the natural man, unredeemed state.

The terrestrial person is a step above. The person would say in regards to the Sabbath Day, "I want to keep the Sabbath day, but I'm not sure what that means. Can you tell me, what should I do on the Sabbath day, and what shouldn't I do on the Sabbath day?" So, terrestrial people rely on lists, but it's a step above.

A celestial person will say, "What's the principle? Tell me what the principle is, and I will govern myself by revelation from the Holy Spirit and the Holy Ghost." You don't need to tell them what to do. They learn the principal, which is to *honor the Sabbath Day and keep it holy,* and then God reveals to them how to live the principal. So, that's the difference between acting and being acted upon.

I'd like to read to you a David A. Bednar quote. When it is all said and done, I believe that he will be known in his ministry, as the general authority that pointed our minds towards this doctrine of *acting and being acted upon.* It's so important! Eduardo Zanatta sent this to me in New Jersey. I'm thankful for that. It's called *In a State of Happiness,* given at a BYU-Idaho devotional January 6, 2004. Let me read it to you:

> It is one thing to perform the **outward actions** of obedience; it is quite a different thing to **become inwardly** what the commandments are intended to help us become. It is one thing to obey the **institutional** [the Church], **public,** and shared commandments associated with the Lord's kingdom on earth—commandments such as the law of chastity, the law of tithing, and the Word of Wisdom;

Now, Brother Bednar takes these commandments: chastity, tithing, and Word of Wisdom, and puts those in the **outward** action of obedience category in the institutional, public, and shared environment of The Church of Jesus Christ of Latter-day Saints. Isn't that interesting? Now, semicolon here's the rest of it:

> *It is an **even greater** thing to receive and respond to the **individual, private** and **personally revealed commandments** that result from continual and faithful obedience.*

So, we're looking at two ways that you live your life, and I believe that the one leads to the other. We all come into the Church, and we perform the outward acts of obedience, such as the law of chastity, the law of tithing, the Word of Wisdom, and all of the questions on the temple recommend interview. But now, he takes us into something deeper, something that is inward, not outward, and he calls it *"the individual, private and personally revealed commandments that result from continual and faithful obedience."* Listen to the last sentence; think of *act or be acted upon*:

> *Such instruction, the individual private and personally revealed, typically are **proactive** and **anticipatory** in nature.*

I looked up the definition of "proactive" in the dictionary and here's what it says:

> *Creating, controlling a situation by **causing** something to happen rather than responding to it after it has happened.*

Do you see the tie-in?

I want to tell you a little story of something that's happened in the last month. Margie is going to participate and share this because it's her experience. I'll just start out by saying that for some reason she developed some pain in her neck and the base of her skull. She'll describe that, and then I'll tell you what we did and then she'll pick it up from there.

Margie: Well, I had spent three weeks, going on the fourth week with just intense pain in my neck. I couldn't turn my head left or right more than an inch without excruciating pain, so I finally went to the doctor. The doctor didn't have much to say, gave me some muscle relaxers, and that didn't work. I went back and said, "This is not working." I went to the emergency room one night with our daughter who works there, and they gave me some steroid shots in the base of my skull and said, "That will take care of it." Well, it didn't do anything. So, in the meantime, I had a blessing from Mike. Then on a Sunday, Mike went to his High Priest Quorum, and I'll let him tell you that part.

Mike: Well, we were fasting, and I had the impression that I should get two of the brethren from the High Priest Quorum, to join me and give Margie a blessing. I believe in the power of quorums, and the smallest priesthood quorum is three members. You can't have a priesthood quorum unless you have at least three members. So, I sat in that High Priest group, and I looked around the room and tried to have the Spirit direct me on which brethren I could ask to come out after church to give this blessing. I picked two men, went up to them after church and said, "Would you come over to the house at 5 o'clock today?" I gave them a little short explanation as to what was going on, and they said, "Sure." So, at 5 o'clock we came together, and one of them anointed Margie with oil, and then the three of us, a priesthood quorum, stood around, laid our hands upon her head, and gave her a blessing. We rebuked this sickness, this pain, which with 10 being the maximum; she described it as being up in the 12 range. I could see that it was just wearing on her after three weeks, and I was really quite concerned. The doctors had not been able to do anything, so I said, "We will rely on the priesthood." So, we gave her that blessing and the Spirit of the Lord was there, we felt good about it, and the men left. At that point, we didn't notice anything had happened. Go ahead, Margie.

Margie: Well, the intensity level of the pain, dropped probably to an 8 or 9, but I was still very uncomfortable. I went back to the doctor and asked for stronger pain medicine. I never take anything. I don't even take anything for headaches, but I was to the point where I just couldn't handle the pain anymore. So, they gave me some Indocin, which seemed to take the edge off, and the pain level dropped down to maybe 5 or 6. When I take this medicine I have to take food, so I took that for three or four days, and then we were coming up on Sunday. It was Saturday night, and I was thinking, "Okay, tomorrow is fast Sunday. I want to fast, but I can't fast because I have to take food with the medicine." I thought, "Well, I'll just eat a little tiny bit, just enough to get by so I don't get an upset stomach." I woke up the next morning, and the pain was there. I thought, "Okay, what do I do? Do I go to church in pain, and not take this medicine, and be fasting? Or, do I just go ahead and take the medicine and eat a little bit?" Immediately the words came to my mind, ***"Claim the Blessing."*** I was having this thought process as I was lying in bed before getting up because I didn't want to get up and face even more pain with movement. So, as I sat there and pondered that, I felt this overwhelming feeling of power and strength. I thought, "You know what? I'm going to claim the priesthood blessing that I was given the week prior." All I had done was allow them to give me a blessing, and I sat back, and nothing happened. I was a little bit frustrated wondering, "Why didn't the Lord heal me?" And with these words, *claim the blessing*, I just thought, "By golly, I'm not going to take the Indocin, I'm not going to eat, I'm going to fast, and I'm going to get well!" So, I went to church, and the pain level was just almost more than I could handle. In fact, after Sacrament Meeting, I was tempted to leave, and I thought, "No, I'm going to stay. I'm going to claim this blessing." As the three-hour block was over and we went home, I noticed that the pain was lessening and lessening. Over a period of the next 2 or 3 days, the pain continued to drop as my excitement continued to rise. And I kept hearing over and over in my mind, "*Claim the Blessing*."

Mike: And we are now to the point where the pain went completely away, and it's just a miraculous thing! After one month in just terrible pain, no sleep, you could just see it in her eyes and her countenance that it was wearing on her. She would tell me, "I'm just so tired, I'm being worn out." I was very concerned because we didn't have any idea what was going on. She had an MRI and had gone through all kinds of things. This concept of the Spirit whispering to her, *"Claim the blessing,"* was something that we hadn't considered before. It's very much in line with *acting or being acted upon*. When we receive a blessing from the Lord, we expect that when we have exercised the faith to have someone lay their hands upon our head, and a blessing is pronounced, that all we should have to do, is sit back at that point, and wait for the desired results. But, this revelation has taught us both that after you have exercised the faith, and received the blessing, you need to now go out and show the Lord through your actions, that you have a right to ***claim the blessings*** that are promised in that administration.

Margie: It's like the Holy Ghost.

Mike: Yes, it's like when you are confirmed a member of the Church and they lay their hands upon your head, and say, "Receive the Holy Ghost." What most people think, at that point, is that the Holy Ghost is now obligated because of that ordinance, to now come in, and become a companion. When in reality, a key has been turned, and a door opened, through that confirmation ordinance, for you to now go out and "**Claim** the companionship of the Holy Ghost" that's promised to you.

Margie: By exercising your agency.

Mike: See? There's that whole principle of agency that ties in with Lehi, and everything that we're talking about here tonight.

Student 1: Let me ask you, *claiming the blessing* by Margie, was going to church and enduring, no matter how difficult it was, right?

Margie: Part of it was just my attitude. I started to add my faith to it. Since I had the blessing, I just expected it like a magic wand to wave over me, and I was going to be well. I had even forgotten about the blessing until that morning when the thought came to me, "*Claim the blessing.*" I'm thinking, "What blessing?" And then I remembered I had had this priesthood blessing and nothing had happened, and I thought, "Well, **I** haven't done anything." **I** hadn't exercised **my** faith, and **I** hadn't said, "Hey, I have a *right* to have this blessing." I had not *claimed* it. It had just been pronounced, but I had not done anything to have it become active, in **my** life for **me**.

Mike: I want you to notice the words she said. "I have a *right* to that blessing." Asking in faith is a form of sacrifice. If you exercise faith to ask for the administration in the first place, that's the faith and sacrifice required for that blessing to be pronounced, and you have a *right* now. If you come up through faith, and you've sacrificed to *claim that blessing*, in order to receive the blessing, you have a *right* to claim it. Let me see if I can give you another scripture that seems to fit in with this principle. Let's go to Ether 12, and then we'll talk about a couple more experiences. This has been a very powerful principle. One of the things that she did to receive that blessing, was to forego taking any more of the medicine that Sunday morning, in spite of the fact that her pain was up to 8, 9, and 10 plus. She still went to church. How easy would it have been to stay in bed moving less? Just getting up, the pain accelerates with the extra movement, so now, not only getting out of bed but going to church? Think about acting and making a conscious decision to not take those medicines. So, that morning when she went to church she didn't take any of them. We have some high-powered narcotics here, which are designed to cut major pain, and she decided to just not take any of it. So, she was **acting** upon the revelation given to her to *claim the blessing*.

Margie: But that was what I felt impressed to do. That's not to say, "Everybody go out and ditch your medicine!" That was just my own personal revelation for this particular circumstance in my life; because there is a place for medicine.

Mike: Absolutely! In any situation where we want to exercise this *right to claim the blessing*, you'll be guided by the Spirit to know what you need to do on your part to act, and not simply sit back and be acted upon. Revelation plays a part in this whole process. Let's look at Ether 12:

> *[17]And it was by **faith** that the three disciples obtained a promise that they should not taste of death; and they obtained not the promise **until after their faith**.*

See, faith is an action principle, brothers and sisters. Faith can be divided into two groups: one is an **action** principle of faith, and the other one is a **power** principle. The action principle of faith **precedes** the power principle. Most of what we talk about in the Church is the action side of faith. The action side of faith is that every action that is done, every decision that you make, every action made, is a part of faith in some desired result. If you didn't have in your mind some end result of this action, there would be no need for you to act at all. Faith is an acting principle, and it moves from the action principle of faith, into power. It's the same difference as being ordained to the priesthood and having power in the priesthood. Those are two different concepts. Just like faith, the action principle is completely different than faith as a power principle. The one precedes the other. Now, look at verse 18:

> *[18]And neither at any time hath any wrought miracles until after their faith; wherefore they first believed in the Son of God.*

Now, on this next part think about the experience that Margie had, and then think about verse 19:

> *[19]And there were many whose faith was so exceedingly strong, even before Christ came, who could not be kept from within the veil, but truly saw with their eyes the things which **they had beheld with an eye of faith**, and they were glad.*

Now, people who physically see miracles happen in their lives are more likely to physically see those miracles take place in the telestial world, within the veil, if they first **visualize those results in their mind**. Or, in other words, **see with the eye of faith**. So, seeing something happen with the eye of faith precedes the actual physical fulfillment of that. That fits in again, with the question: what are we doing when we are expecting blessings and miracles in our lives? Are we actually going the extra mile and seeing the desired results of those miracles in our mind? The *Book of Mormon* seems to teach that until you can see it in your mind, you're never going to see it physically. Until you can conceive of that in your mind, then you're never going to have the physical occurrence.

I'd like Margie to tell you another story that I think is just a marvelous story. She's told this story on three continents, on our missions, and it's blessed the lives of many, especially young women. It has to do with an experience she had, and I'd like to turn the time over to her for a few minutes and tell you a little bit about the background from which she comes, and what led up to this wonderful experience. Now, think about what we have talked about tonight: *"Claiming the blessing"* and acting instead of being acted upon.

Margie: We've been married 13 years now, but prior to meeting Mike, I was living in Snowflake, Arizona teaching school. I was single, and I had several people that were concerned that I was getting to be older in age, and not having been married. At first, it was no big deal when I was younger but then as I got older; it was harder and harder to attend church because it's a family-oriented church. I sat there on the bench, and looked around and watched how everybody had their families and I just sat there all alone. I would often throw a little pity party for myself thinking, "Poor me!" because I didn't have any companionship at home, no family around, or anything. I remember several times, lots of ups and downs. I was at this point 46 years old, still not married. It almost became an embarrassment, and I started thinking, "What's wrong with me that I'm not married? Surely, I'm a nice person; at least I think I'm a nice person." Satan has a way of twisting everything that's true and making it into our own self-destructive action. I remember one Sunday evening in June when I was 46 years old. Now, I had had lots of dates. Oh, my gosh! Everyone in Snowflake liked to set me up with blind dates, with this, that, and the other person. I went on lots of double dates! In fact, I could probably apply for the *Guinness Book of World Records* for blind dates. Anyway, I had been fasting and feeling really down on this particular evening. Kneeling beside my bed, pouring my heart out to the Lord, I finally was just so tired I said, "You know, I've been praying all my life that I would be married and for the first time in my life I decided, you know what? I'll tell you what: I have a **right** to be married. I'm doing everything. You've told me to do. I go to church. I serve. I do all the things I should." I knelt there at the side of my bed, reasoning with the Lord, with tears streaming down my face. I can still see the picture and remember the feelings that I had. And I had often said that prayer, but my prayer had been, "Help me get married, help me get married, help me to get married, I want to be married!" But for the first time, I reasoned with the Lord. I told him why I wanted to be married. I told him why I felt I had merited the right to be married and have an eternal companion, but then at the end, I said this, "You know, however, if I can be a better influence forpeople as a single person, I'm going to be the best dang single person you've ever met! And I will never, ever again bring up the subject of being married. I will just do whatever You want me to do." That was a Sunday night in June.

Two or three weeks later, I was supposed to be the guest speaker at a regional singles conference. I started telling my friends, "I want to be married by the end of this year." They're all looking at me like, "Yeah right." I said, "I'm going to the singles conference, and I'm going to see all these single people." In my mind, I had it all set up that when I went to the singles conference, I'm going to be up talking in front of everybody, and I'm going to have an opportunity for all these guys to look at me and say, "Wow! Cool lady here! Let's go ask her out on a date!" And I get up there, and I give my talk, and it was great, it was fine and dandy, and then the conference was over, and I hadn't met one guy, really. Ha-ha-ha! In the meantime, prior to that, I told all my friends, "I'm getting married, and I'm going to find my guy at the singles conference."

A couple of weeks before that conference, a friend said, "I can make your wedding cake," and someone else said, "Oh, my husband is a professional photographer. He'll take your pictures." And another person said, "I'll plan your wedding, and I'll do your reception." Everybody had everything planned, and they said, "Alright!" And when the singles conference came and went, I remember a particular friend said, "Are you disappointed you didn't find your guy?"

I said, "Nope. I told the Lord that I wanted to get married by the end of this year, and it's only August now, so it's no big deal! Look, I've got everything planned: I've got the cake, and I've got the wedding and reception all planned." I even knew what my friends were going to serve at the reception.

They said, "Don't you think you need to find a guy first?"

Mike: Ha!

Margie: And I said, "No, we've got it all planned. We're all organized and ready to go. It'll happen if it's supposed to. If not, I'm not going to worry about it. I'm just going to go out and live my life."

Well, three weeks later I met Mike. Long story short, within two months we were married. We did get married before the end of that year, on December 13, at 3:33, because three is my favorite number! The Lord provided what I had wanted all along. I had just **asked** all my life, "I want to be married, I want to be married, I want to be married. Wah-wah-wah! I want to be married." But, the time was right. I think it was through personal revelation that I felt like I could qualify. One other thing, as I was praying that night, I said, "If I'm to be married, I want options, I want choices. Everybody in the world gets choices. I'm at a point in my life, that when I have a date, I go out once and decide if he's a dim bulb, or if he's marrying potential. And all I was finding was packages of dim bulbs!

Mike: Ha!

Margie: I had quite a collection of those! I decided that I had a right to have choices. Sure enough, as soon as I met Mike, several other guys also came into play. So, I now found myself talking to, dating, and juggling these guys and I remember, Mike wasn't too happy about that. I told him one weekend that I was leaving for the weekend to meet this guy in Mesa, to see if he was marrying potential. Anyway, long story short, we got married, and it was definitely the right thing. It was directed, but the whole perspective and my whole life changed when I changed my attitude. Number one, I tried to *claim the blessing* that I felt was rightfully mine, because my patriarchal blessing said that I **would** be married in the temple, in the own due time of the Lord. I just kept thinking, "When is it going to be time?" So, I knew that I was going to get married; it was just that I wasn't expecting it to be that long. I wasn't expecting to be that advanced in age, prior to that. So, I reasoned with the Lord, which we see in the scriptures all of the time, especially in the *Book of Mormon*. You reason with the Lord; you explain your situation, you explain your solutions, you explain why you need it, and then, "*Claim the blessing.*" I had done everything but "*reason*" and "*claim the blessing.*" When I finally did that, then things fell into place, and here we are living happily ever after!

Mike: Amen to that!! I say that happily with a double exclamation point. She's the best thing that ever happened to me! Thanks, Margie. I never tire of hearing that story.

Let me share another thought on that. We are a generation now, as members of the Church that must do something different than we've done before. We can't continue to do the same things that we've done up to this point. Satan's chain has been lengthened in the wisdom of the Lord. Satan has been given a longer chain and a broader base from which to operate among the children of men. With that, we now need to do things much differently than we've ever done before. It's not going to be enough to do what we've done in the past, in order to meet the challenges that are here now. I believe that when we talk about *a marvelous work and wonder*, we always, in my life, attribute the *marvelous work and a wonder*, which is Isaiah 29, to the restoration of the Church. And, certainly, the Church restoration and everything that goes along with it, is *a marvelous work and a wonder*. But I believe that the ultimate *marvelous work and a wonder* has not happened yet. From out of the society of the Latter-day Saints, there will be a small group of people who will hear the call and answer the call, to become a Zion people, a society prepared to meet the King of Kings, and the Lord of Lords. That society doesn't become a society all at once. It starts here and there, by one man and one woman hearing the voice of the Spirit call them to step up, to awake and arise, and be and do something different than they've been doing up to this point, in order to claim blessings that are reserved for the Latter-day Saints in the days that are here. And that is to establish a Zion society that will endure from this point forth, through the Second Coming, and during the Millennium, to fill the whole earth. That has never been done. It's our privilege and blessing and responsibility to do that. Priesthood brethren, we need to do more now, than we've done, way beyond just being ordained to the priesthood. We now need to move up and have *power in the priesthood*. The only place we hear this statement is in the temple. At the most sacred place in the temple, you'll hear the words *"power in the priesthood,"* not, "power **of** the priesthood," but *"power **in** the priesthood."* Ordination comes first and must precede *"power in the priesthood."* And now with *"power in the priesthood"* here in the telestial world, we can do things and become people that we otherwise could not become.

Can I share with you just a personal experience about how I feel that I've done this in one way? I say this just to share it with you as an example. I've lived in Eagar now for almost 25 years. When I first came here, I planted fruit trees. We put them in, and I now have 42 mature trees that are anywhere between 15 and 25 years of age. Some that were already on the property are much older than that. They might be 40 to 50 years old. They're all mature, and they're all producing trees. The problem with Eagar is, in the spring we have terrific winds that come in, anywhere from 50 to 70 miles-per-hour, and we have late frosts. We have an early spring and the trees warm up. They come out beautiful with blossoms and everything. Then these winds and frost come along and just destroy everything. So, out of the 25 years that I've been here, we've only seen our fruit trees produce maybe only 5 or 6 times. All the other times they were wiped out. Up to this point, I've said, "It doesn't matter. When the time comes that we need this fruit to live off of, in a day of devastation and a day of challenge, of geopolitical and worldwide turmoil that the scriptures seem to indicate are coming; if I've had the faith to plant the trees, then, at the time we need them, God will provide and we will have a harvest." That's been my prayer. The missing part is, what am I doing to help that process, besides just planting the trees? I thought that just planting the trees was enough. What more can I do now to act, rather than simply ask for a blessing, ask God to do it all, and come August, September, October, go out and pick the fruit and bottle it and have a great harvest laid up in store in the season thereof?

I've been thinking differently for the last two years about these things. So, this year, for the first time in seven years, I really pruned back our trees. I took them all back a good third, and maybe a little bit more. I've got two great big brush piles out in front of the house, that will take two truckloads to haul them off, or it will make one-heck-of-a bonfire! The thought came to me that these trees are living entities. I thought about the temple where the Lord creates all the vegetation on the earth, the grasses, shrubs, trees, every herb and tree bearing seed in itself after its own kind, to bring forth fruit in the season thereof, to fulfill the measure of its creation, **and have joy therein**. And I thought, "The measure of the creation of all of these fruit trees is to give me fruit. If the fruit tree that I've planted doesn't give me fruit, it's not fulfilling the measure of its creation. Its whole purpose is to provide fruit for me. My job is to take good care of those trees and do all that I can to ensure that they fulfill the measure of their creation, and have joy therein." So, my thinking now is going beyond what I have thought in the past, which was to just pray for the Lord to protect them, and wait for the fruit to come on. So, I'm thinking now, "What more can I do? How can I act in this area, to help bring to pass the purpose of the Lord, in the creation of fruit trees, and to gladden the heart and please the eye of Mike and Margie Stroud?" The Lord says that they are to fulfill the measure of their creation and **have joy therein.** These trees are living souls! All in the vegetation kingdom are living souls. They are intelligent spirits accompanied by physical bodies. That, by the definition in section 88, is a living soul. And the temple ceremony tells me that they have **joy** in the fulfillment of their creation. So, what I did this year after pondering and pruning these trees was different. One afternoon when it was quiet, and no one was looking, I went out and placed my hands upon them, and by the power of the

Melchizedek Priesthood, I gave each one of these trees a priesthood blessing. I blessed them that if they had been wounded in the pruning process, that they would heal quickly. I blessed them they would be healthy and strong and that they would have the power to withstand the elements so that they might bring forth fruit in the season thereof, and fulfill the measure of their creation. I closed those blessings in the name of Jesus Christ, and I blessed each one of our fruit trees. The temperatures up here in Eagar at 7,000 feet have gotten down into the low 20's in the last few days, so each night when the frost comes in, I walk out privately, I stand in the orchard, I petition the Lord and ask for His blessings upon these fruit trees. Here's something else I've learned, brothers and sisters: if you want specific blessings, you cannot ask for vague promises. So, in my prayers, I name each, "Please bless the peach trees, the apple trees, the cherry trees, the plum trees, the apricot trees, and the pear trees." I have faith that we will have a bounteous harvest this year as a result of the power of the priesthood, and exercising this power on behalf of all living things, and not just human. Let me read a scripture to you from Alma 34 that got me thinking about this. Starting in verse 17:

> Therefore may God grant unto you, my brethren, that ye may begin to exercise your faith unto repentance, that ye begin to call upon his holy name, that he would have mercy upon you;
>
> [18]Yea, cry unto him for mercy; for he is mighty to save.
>
> [19] Yea, humble yourselves, and continue in prayer unto him.
>
> [20] Cry unto him when ye are in your fields, yea, over all your flocks.
>
> [21] Cry unto him in your houses, yea, over all your household, both morning, mid-day, and evening.

President Benson said we need to associate ourselves with men like Daniel, who prayed three times a day to God.

> [22] Yea, cry unto him against the power of your enemies.
>
> [23] Yea, cry unto him against the devil, who is an enemy to all righteousness.

[24] Cry unto him over the crops of your fields, that ye may prosper in them.

[25] Cry over the flocks of your fields, that they may increase.

[26] But this is not all; ye must pour out your souls in your closets, and your secret places, and in your wilderness.

[27] Yea, and when you do not cry unto the Lord, let your hearts be full, drawn out in prayer unto him continually for your welfare, and also for the welfare of those who are around you.

In summary, brothers and sisters, it's time for us to do something different than what we've been doing up to this point. It's time for us to awake and arise. It's time for us to *claim the blessings* that are ours by foreordination; to be here at this time and in this place and under these circumstances. There is no chance in all of this. It's an exact plan foreordained for you. It's time for us now, to have revealed to us, by the Holy Spirit, what our foreordained purpose is and to rise up and to **claim those blessings**. I testify to you of these things and do so in the name of Jesus Christ, The Holy Messiah, amen.

Student 1: Can I share something with you?

Mike: Yes, please do!

Student 1: I don't know what year it was, maybe 2010 or 11? Somewhere in there. We too had the same problem that you guys had because of the late frost and the strong winds. I had a good friend, and she had older fruit trees that were planted before she moved there. There was a time when her mother asked her, "Are you praying for your fruit trees?"

My friend said, "Yeah, yeah, yeah…" and dismissed it.

So, every time she would call her mother, her mother would ask her, "Are you praying for your fruit trees?" We had a late frost, and her mother wondered what happened to the trees. She asked, "Are the blossoms frozen?"

She answered, "Yes."

And her mother said, "Remember, I told you to pray for them because you need this blessing?"

So, she did, and they started re-blooming! I went by there later on, and they had some apples and some pears. Her husband was not a member, but he said, "Wow! This is a miracle!" So, you see, even if they are frozen, they can re-bloom a second time. That's my story. They were frozen and they re-bloomed. There was not a lot but enough for the miracle to appear to them.

Mike: Wonderful story! We have chickens here that we're raising and we are going to have some rabbits. We have a garden. We have strawberries, raspberries, blackberries, and multiple grapevines. I will be pronouncing a blessing on each one of them. All of these things, brothers and sisters, whether it's a vegetable, or a plant, or an animal, rely on me in order to exist. If I didn't take care of them, they would all die. I have a stewardship over each one of them, and a responsibility to do all that I can to make sure that they are healthy, and then the Lord provides the harvest as a result of our faith and our acting on behalf of those things we have a stewardship over. We do all that we can and then through the grace of the Lord; He will provide a bounty. So,this is the first time we have done this, and we are really excited this year. This whole thing came about as a result of this concept of *claim the blessing*.

*On the comments below the podcast, someone later asked, "Did you get any fruit?"
Mike replied; "Yes, everything except apricots and plums. We harvested apples, peaches, cherries, and pears. We also had a bumper crop of grapes, raspberries, and blackberries. This year's garden was the best I've grown in 40 years. Eight-foot corn!"

Chapter Ten
Podcast 010 Channels of Light and Truth

Let's start out by saying I hope the Holy Ghost is with us tonight because nothing really gets done unless we do it that way and have that influence to help us out.

A few weeks ago I was sitting in a Gospel Essentials class, and they were discussing the *gifts of the Spirit*. Now, the first question we would ask if we were scriptural detectives, seekers after truth, and we had more than a basic understanding of gospel doctrine, would be, "What is the Spirit that we're talking about when it says *gifts of the Spirit?*" The first question before we even discussed the gifts, should be, "Who or what is the Spirit?" There are three places in the scriptures, where you can find a list of the *gifts of the Spirit*. One of them is 1 Corinthians 12, verses 8 through 11, and another one is in Section 46 of the *Doctrine and Covenants*. Let's go to Section 46 for just a minute. I will kind of set the stage for the discussion that took place in the Gospel Essentials class a week ago. Look at verse 7, and you can ask a couple of questions in discussing the *gifts of the Spirit,* and verse 7 gives you a scriptural answer to the question, "Why are these gifts necessary and to what end are they given?" So, there's one question we could answer, "Why does God give these gifts?" We also talked about how these gifts are missing among way too many of God's children, simply because they are not asking for them. We are assuming that if God wants me to have it, He will give it to me. When in reality, He

237

wants you to have more than you can possibly comprehend, but He is bound by some principles and laws, that questions unasked are infrequently answered. Look at verse 7:

> *But ye are commanded in all things **to ask of God**, who giveth liberally; and that which the Spirit testifies unto you even so I would that ye should do in all holiness of heart, walking uprightly before me, considering the end of your salvation, doing all things with prayer and thanksgiving,*

If I were to double underline anything in the first verse, it would be *to ask of God*. You're commanded in all things *to ask of God*. Now, these verses are talking about the *gifts of the Spirit, who giveth liberally;* notice that? I don't know if you can even put a number on the how many of the *gifts of the Spirit* there are. I don't remember who it was but a few years back a General Authority, possibly Sterling W. Sill, said that "There are innumerable *gifts of the Spirit.* For every challenge, or situation in immortality, there is a gift that God has prepared to help you successfully handle that challenge."

There are three things there in verse 7 that you should do with holiness of heart; **walk uprightly, considering the end of your salvation**, and **doing all things with prayer and thanksgiving**. And here's the purpose of the *gifts of the spirit;* this is your double under liner:

> **That ye may not be seduced by evil spirits, or doctrines of devils, or the commandments of men; for some are of men, and others of devils.**

So, if you had a question as to why God has these gifts so abundantly available, that he wants to give liberally, it is because you live in a world of deception, and it is becoming more so. If there was ever a time when we needed these gifts it is now, and between now and the coming of our Lord, the deception is only going to increase. So, according to section 46, verse 7, the need for the gifts increases dramatically. Now, look at verse 8:

> *Wherefore, beware lest ye are deceived; and that ye may not be deceived **seek ye earnestly** the best gifts, always remembering for what they are given;*

And what are they given for? To keep you from being deceived. Isn't that great?

[9]For verily I say unto you, they [the gifts] *are given for the benefit of those who love me and keep all my commandments, and him that seeketh so to do; that all may be benefited that seek or that ask of me, that ask and not for a sign that they may consume it upon their lusts.*

That was the verse that was quoted today in general conference. Okay? I think that was Brother Holland who quoted that. And then it goes on through to first 26, to list some of these gifts. You just scan down there and take a look at those. From verse 10 all the way through 26, you can see those; especially from 17 to 26. Now, look at 26. So, here's the question: Who has access to these gifts? I've been a missionary long enough to have many people come up to me and say, "That minister down the street is practicing the laying on of hands in his congregation, and it appears that he's healing people from some pretty serious illnesses. What do you think about that Brother Stroud?"

I used to say, "Well, the devil is a counterfeiter," and I immediately went to the dark side anytime that would come up. Now, even though it was subconscious, the thinking behind that was that these gifts are only truly available to Latter-day Saints, those who have made a covenant with the Lord. And notice what He says in verse 26:

And all these gifts come from God, **for the benefit of the children of God.**

Now, who is that?

Student 6: Everybody.

Mike: See, that's everybody isn't it? So, we're not limiting. As I participated in this discussion, the first question that came up was, "Who is qualified to access these gifts?" And the feeling was kind of, that you needed to be a Latter-day Saint to tap into these resources. And that people outside of the Church can do some things by faith, and yes, it's possible, I guess, that you could have a healing that comes by faith; but Latter-day Saints are really hesitant to allow anybody outside of Church membership, to have **all** of these gifts. And if you look at those you will see what it says:

[19] faith to be healed.
[20] to have faith to heal.
[21] to some is given the working of miracles;

[22] to prophesy;

[23] the discerning of spirits.

[24] to speak with tongues;

[25] the interpretation of tongues.

on and on. And what the *Doctrine and Covenants* is telling us is that these gifts are all available **to every one of God's children** that seek them, and have the faith to access the power of these gifts.

Sister Stroud, make a comment here. Sister Stroud brought her scriptures, and I want her to comment.

Sister Stroud: [Student] brought it up. She says that in *Doctrine and Covenants* 46:16, it says it also:

> *And again, it is given by the Holy Ghost to some to know the diversities of operations, whether they be of God, that the manifestations of the Spirit, may be given to **every man** to profit withal.*

Mike: Thank you, [student]. Excellent point. That's good. Again, evidence that this is available to **all**!

In Moroni chapter 10, is another list of the *gifts of the spirit*, and these are duplicated over in Galatians. You can find them. Let's go over to Moroni chapter 10, and verse 8 is where it starts. So, here's another list. And as the *Book of Mormon* is known to do, it makes it even **more** plain. It is stated that the *Book of Mormon* is **plain** to the understanding of men. You'll see here that there is no question that all of these gifts are available to **every man and woman**, who has the faith. Moroni chapter 7 says that if these gifts disappear, it is because of unbelief, and that's not limited to just the Latter-day Saints. Look at Moroni 10, verse 8:

> *And again, I exhort you, my brethren, that ye deny not the gifts of God, for they are many; and they come from the same God. And there are different ways that these gifts are administered; but it is the same God who worketh all in all; and they are given by the manifestations of the Spirit of God unto **men**, to profit them.*

Now, it's my feeling, and from my experience, that because it says *men*, this is one of those places where *men* refers to *mankind*. That includes women also because I've personally seen many of these gifts operating in a major way, among women, sisters.

Look at verse 17, the summary scripture:

And all of these gifts come by the Spirit of Christ;

Now, that's a key that we didn't get in the other two scripture lists. We call them the *gifts of the Spirit,* and the *Book of Mormon* now tells us what that Spirit is: it is the *Spirit of Christ*; **not** the Holy Ghost. Continuing on:

*and they come unto **every** man severally, according as he will.*

[18]And I would exhort you, my beloved brother, that every good gift cometh of Christ.

So, we just answered some things there. Now, look at some of the things in this list that are available to everybody:

[11]And to another, exceedingly great faith; and to another, the gifts of healing by the same Spirit;

[12] And again, to another, that he may work mighty miracles;

...and so on. Look at verse 14. Verse 14 is available to anybody:

And again, to another, the beholding of angels and ministering of spirits;

You see? Angels can appear to our Baptist friends, brothers and sisters. They can have dreams and visions. The Lord can show Himself to them in dreams and visions. That is not just something that is available to Latter-day Saints.

So, there again, we have this list, and the *Book of Mormon* tells us that they come through the Holy Spirit, the light of Christ, the Spirit of Christ, the Spirit of truth, the light of truth, man's conscience. This is the beginning step in every man and woman to lay hold upon these gifts. Here's how it works, and we heard a little bit about it in general conference from President Monson, when he talked about making choices. Every choice that you make either adds or detracts light. I'll put in a few other words that are synonymous with light: truth, glory, and intelligence. All four of those words mean the same thing. So, every decision you make either adds to your store of light and truth, or you're losing it. That's kind of new doctrine to Latter-day Saints. And I venture to say that some of you have felt that these kinds of things were only available to members of the Church, in good standing, that make covenants with the Lord. Any questions or comments on that before we go any further?

Student 4: The 10th chapter of Moroni, is the last chapter of the *Book of Mormon*, and you'll notice that about every third or fourth verse, he says, "I exhort you." In the 3rd verse, "I exhort you to read these things." He exhorts to all do these things. "I exhort you, my beloved brethren..." The whole thing is exhortation. He put about fifteen of them in there. I think he's trying to tell us something! We need to be awake. We need to read, hear, and see.

Mike: That's a good point [student] because it starts right over there with the most famous scripture of all, Moroni 10:3-5. And that starts out *"I would exhort you."* I happen to have those underlined, and I can count eight times where he says *"I exhort you."*

Now, before we leave this, I'd like to go to verse 19 and see what the stumbling blocks to the gifts are. What is it that denies us access to these gifts? [student] would you read verses 19 and 24 for us?

Student 4: Sure:

> *And I would exhort you, my beloved brethren, that*
> *ye remember that he is the same yesterday, today,*
> *and forever, and that all these gifts of which I have*
> *spoken, which are spiritual, never will be done*
> *away, even as long as the world shall stand, only*
> *according to the unbelief of the children of men.*
> *[24] And now I speak unto all the ends of the earth*
> *– that if the day cometh that the power and gifts of*
> *God shall be done away among you, it shall be*
> *because of unbelief.*

Mike: Okay, then what is the great stumbling block that keeps us from having these gifts? And remember in section 46, the purpose of the gifts are so that we avoid what?

Student 4: To avoid deception.

Mike: To avoid deception. So, to the degree that we are not getting these gifts to be functional in our lives is the degree to which we are vulnerable to the deception of the telestial world.

What is unbelief?

Student 4: The lack of faith.

Mike: That is what we think. Can you be more specific than that? Why don't we just say faithlessness? Why is it called unbelief? Why don't they just say faith-less-ness if it is the lack of faith?

Student 6: We're not willing to believe? Maybe our hearts aren't willing to believe?

Mike: Okay. I have a friend, a mentor of mine that taught me this definition. What you said is right, but the real core of unbelief is that whatever we're talking about that God has for us, we have no problem accepting that **others** can enjoy these gifts. And where we fail is when we think about **us** enjoying that gift. For example, unbelief would come into play when you read of the brother of Jared, Mahonri Moriancumr, seeing the Lord. And you say, "Yeah, I believe that. I believe that. I believe that Moses saw. I believe Joseph Smith saw the Father and the Son in open vision. I believe that." Well, do you believe that the 15 men who are Prophets, Seers and Revelators have that experience? And most members of the Church would say, "Yeah, I believe that. I believe that." Do you believe that your stake president can have that experience? And here they might hesitate but say, "My stake president is a spiritual man. He probably could." What about your Bishop? Do you see what we're doing here? You get down to your Bishop they may say yes or no. Then you come down to it and say, "Well, if any of these people can have these experiences, and you believe that then how about you?" And then you look in the mirror and say, "Me, having a personal encounter with the Lord Jesus Christ, like in Ether chapter 3?" And we look at that and say, "No way!" And that's unbelief. I like that definition.

Student 4: It's self-imposed.

Mike: Yeah, it is self-imposed on you. So, we got to this point in class, and then I asked this question: I said, "If all of these gifts are available to all of God's children severally, as He will, according to their faith, and they don't consume it upon their lusts, what is the advantage of being a Latter-day Saint? If all of this is available to anybody in the world, then what's the advantage of being a member of the Church?"

Student 4: You get baptized and are given the opportunity to receive the Holy Ghost, if we put forth the effort to hear Him, and to follow Him, and do the things that are important for us to move up.

Mike: That's good [student]. When I look at this list of the gifts, and I ask, "If I'm in possession of these gifts and enjoying those, why would I even be concerned about the Holy Ghost?"

Student 4: That's where they come from. They come from Christ.

Mike: Okay, but tell me what advantage is the Holy Ghost, or the gift of the Holy Ghost, or anything past the reception of the Holy Ghost, to a person who has access to, and is enjoying these other gifts. The point is; what is the advantage of being a Latter-day Saint if you have access to all of these wonderful gifts?

Student 6: Wouldn't it be for protection? I'm not sure what you're looking for. Is it the protection it gives us from the deception if we have Him as a constant companion? Can we have Him as a constant companion?

Mike: Okay, that's a good comment. When I asked that in the Gospel Essentials class it was kind of dead and nobody went anywhere. I didn't answer the question. I just left it there, and they were all looking at me. I said, "Just think about it. You're all Latter-day Saints, and I just told you that all of the things that we previously thought belonged to us and our culture are now available to everybody in the world, so what is the advantage of being a Latter-day Saint? What more can you have? What's available to you through membership that you can't get in this list of gifts?"

Student: It gets you a recommend to the temple, where you can learn how to come into the presence of the Father...

Mike: All right.

Student 4: ...and be invited through the veil. If you're not a Latter-day Saint, you don't have the covenants; you don't have all the blessings that come with the things that are given to you in the temple, and that they seal upon you, and the anointings, and these different things. That gives us our pass, our membership, and temple recommend gives us our pass to get to the place where we can learn these things.

Mike: Very good. So, you brought up the temple. Let's go to the temple for just a minute. When the Father and Son are speaking to Adam and Eve in the Garden, they say two things. *We will provide a way for them to come back into our presence, and with us partake of eternal life and exaltation.* Remember that phrase?

Student 6: Yeah.

Mike: Notice it didn't say immortality. It says eternal life and exaltation. The two things are **the resurrection of the dead**, and **the redemption of man**. Now, you don't have to be a member of the Church to be resurrected from the dead, but you do need to be a member of the Church and have made covenants, to get **a more desirable resurrection**. In other words, not all resurrections are the same. Everybody who has ever been born, and has had a birth in mortality, and has experienced a physical death, at some time in their journey back to the Father, will resurrect, but not all resurrections are to be desired. For example, sons of perdition, who sin against light to the degree that they become sons of perdition; they will resurrect from the dead. They'll have a resurrection, and that resurrection comes to even them, because of the resurrection of Jesus Christ. Then you've got the majority of God's children who find themselves in a state of rebellion, ostracized from God, because of their choices, who will resurrect into the Telestial Kingdom. They will resurrect and so will the Terrestrial and the Celestial. Not all of these are to be desired. So, even the resurrection, when we say that it's a free gift given to everybody is only true in a broad way. For you to inherit the **best resurrection**, it's going to require something more than just living in a telestial world and dying there. Even when we say that the gift of the resurrection is a free gift to everybody, it's not doctrinally, completely correct. But now, the redemption is something else. To be redeemed from the Fall and brought back into the presence of God and inherit with Them eternal life and exaltation, as the Father says to Adam and Eve, will require a covenant relationship with Them. You cannot obtain that redemption outside of membership of His earthly church, in our day. You can't do it.

Student 4: Instead of saying *best*, wouldn't it become part of a fullness? Wouldn't it be a complete fullness? As we go through the various steps to belong to *The Church of the Firstborn*, we have to have a fullness.

Mike: Well, now you're hitting on something! So, what it boils down to is this: people outside the Church who enjoy all these gifts, can only go to a certain point in their progress, and then they hit a wall. If they're not able to progress past that wall, then all of the blessings of redemption in the celestial world, with exaltation and eternal life in a resurrected celestial, spiritual body, are denied them. They will not get it. You can enjoy all the gifts of the Spirit that will keep you from being deceived, but if you get to the point where the restoration is presented to you, and because of unbelief and the precepts of man, you reject that invitation; you can only go so far. And that's where covenants enter in. I liken it to a channel, through which light and truth can flow. Every one of God's children comes into this earth with a gift. We are all born with the Light of Christ, and the basic function of the Light of Christ is to teach us right from wrong, good from evil. When Christ speaks to you, we could liken it unto a channel, or for a visual, we could liken it unto a straw. There is only so much water or so much liquid that can pass through a straw. If you want more liquid to pass through that channel, you have to increase the size of the channel. You have to expand that channel. So, you have a straw/channel, and then you progress up to where you have a river channel, called the Mississippi. It's interesting that they call where the river flows, *the river channel*. The width of the channel determines how much you can get through it. Here is a simple way to understand this. Every time you are obedient when light and truth is sent to you, as a gift from God through the Spirit of Christ, your obedience to that light increases the size of the channel and increases your ability to assume and collect more. You open up the channel. Without making covenants, that channel can still widen a good amount, considering all the gifts available in these lists, but that channel will only expand so far. You're bumping up against a wall unless you enter into a covenant. When you enter into a covenant, that channel expands. When you have hands laid upon you, and you have the confirmation ordinance performed, and the gift of the Holy Ghost is made available to you, it expands. When a man is ordained to the priesthood, it expands more. When a man and a woman go to the temple and participate in those covenants, it expands even more. So, every covenant that you make, beginning with baptism, expands the channel of light and truth, intelligence and glory, until eventually, the channel opens, and you find yourself standing in the very presence of God, in the world of glory, in which case, there would be no more channel.

That's the place that the brother of Jared finds himself in Ether chapter 3. He finds himself redeemed. Let's go to Ether chapter 3, and I will show you a little secret in the scriptures. The question is: What does it mean to be redeemed from the Fall? What does that mean? If you were to ask that in a class, you would get a lot of discussion on it. Well, here in Ether 3 verse 13, Moroni answers that for us, from the records of the Jaredites. You know the story. The Brother of Jared has seen the finger of the Lord. The Lord said:

> [9]Sawest thou more than this?
> [10]And he answered: Nay; Lord, show thyself unto me.
> [11] And the Lord said unto him: Believest thou the words which I shall speak?
> [12] And he answered: Yea, Lord, I know that thou speakest the truth, for thou art a God of truth, and canst not lie.

Our question is about the definition of redemption from the Fall:

> [13]And when he had said these words, behold, the Lord **showed himself** unto him, and said: Because thou knowest these things ye are **redeemed from the fall;** therefore, ye are brought back into my presence; therefore, I show myself unto you.

Now, this was a personal encounter with Jesus Christ. And then there's a definition of redemption from the Fall. It has been my experience that most people in the Latter-day Saint community, believe that the redemption from the Fall will take place after death, in the resurrection, when we stand before God at the final judgment, and every knee bow and every tongue confess. Here, the brother of Jared says that redemption from the Fall is a personal encounter with God in this life, and to be brought back into His presence while you're still a mortal. Now, can you be redeemed in any other way? Sure. Is this the most desirable form of redemption from the Fall? And the answer is...

Student 6: What are the other ways?

Mike: Another way is that this takes place after you die. Your spirit spends a sojourn in the spirit world; you're called forth out of paradise, found worthy, and redeemed. So, redemption from the Fall can take place after death. Redemption from the Fall is being brought back into God's presence. Remember that is the definition of it, right?

Student 6: Yes.

Mike: This is going to happen before the final judgment. You're going to resurrect from the dead, which comes first, and then you're going to be brought back into the presence of Christ to be judged. So, resurrection precedes judgment according to the *Book of Mormon*; and that's redemption from the Fall. But the one here, while in mortality is to be desired. Why would it be desirable to be redeemed from the Fall in mortality, rather than waiting for it to happen after death, resurrection, etc.? What do you think?

Student 1: Didn't you say once that it is because we would have certain privileges that way?

Mike: What would be some privileges? What would be some advantages? You're still a mortal. You're still living in a fallen world, but you have been redeemed from the Fall. You have been brought back, you have had that encounter with God, and all of the things that take place in that encounter, have now taken place with you. You're still living in Arizona; you've still got to make a living, you've still got your taxes, etc., etc. So, what's the advantage?

Student 1: Well, isn't Alma the great example, when he prays for his son, Alma the Younger, that he would change?

Mike: The advantage is that you can now ask things from God because you're now what Lecture Six in *The Lectures on Faith* calls "A Favorite of Heaven." He will grant them to you. The *Book of Mormon* uses the term *highly favored of the Lord*; these are the same things. You can read that in 1 Nephi chapter 1, verse 1. Nephi is telling you he had an encounter with God and is redeemed from the Fall. So, it has happened. When he's writing those words in 1 Nephi chapter 1, verse 1, all of these things that we are talking about, have taken place with him.

Student 6: Wouldn't it be true that someone who has been redeemed from the Fall, would not have the pull of the world like they did before?

Mike: You would think so. You would think so.

Student 6: Yeah, I think that's true.

Mike: Go with me to 2 Nephi 4. You would think that when you get to that point, that you would be immune from the tugs and pulls of a fallen world wouldn't you? You would think, "Boy, I've got it made now!"

Student 6: Well, I don't think he was free from all of it. But wouldn't he have *rest in the Lord* to a certain point there?

Mike: Let's take a look at these things. Look at 2 Nephi 4, verse 15. Now, when Nephi is writing this, he is an old man, and he has already had many, many encounters with the Lord. Angels are a common occurrence. He has experienced all the blessings of the gospel, and the rights of the priesthood are fully active in Nephi's life. We can read about them being fully active in Jacob's life. We don't read about them being fully active in Laman and Lemuel's life. Look what he says. He's talking about the small plates:

> *[15]And upon these* [plates] *I write the things of my* **soul**, *and many of the scriptures which are engraven upon the plates of brass. For my* **soul** *delighteth in the scriptures, and my heart pondereth them, and writeth them for the learning and the profit of my children.*
> *[16]Behold, my* **soul** *delighteth in the things of the Lord; and my heart pondereth continually upon the things which I have* **seen and heard**.

And I would add **touched**. Now, look at the next word in verse 17. What's the next word? *"Nevertheless."* What does that word mean in the *Book of Mormon*? Put that into other words, so we can understand it. He just said, "Oh, I have enjoyed all these things, I've had these great blessings, nevertheless," or, in *spite of all of this*. *In spite of all this*, then look at what he says:

> *[17] Nevertheless, notwithstanding the great goodness of the Lord, in showing me his great and marvelous works, my heart exclaimeth: O wretched man that I am!*

And then you read on, and he mourns because he's living in a fallen world, and cannot completely escape the tugs and pulls of this world, and won't as long as he is in it. Now, this is a man who has had all of these things. This is a man who, over in chapter 1 verse 1, Nephi says was, *"Having been highly favored of the Lord."* Do you know who else that terminology is used for? You want to tune into this phrase *highly favored* over in Ether. Jared goes to his brother, and he says, "You go and approach the Lord because I know you are *highly favored of the Lord*." Ether 1:34:

> *And the brother of Jared being a large and mighty man, and a man* **highly favored of the Lord**, *Jared, his brother, said unto him: Cry unto the Lord, that*

he will not confound us that we may not understand our words.

Did you ever wonder why Jared always went to his brother? You ever wonder why Jared didn't go himself? He always went to his brother. Do you ever wonder why Nephi, who had mighty experiences, went to his father? It is because these patriarchs had obtained something that put them in the category of being *highly favored*. They had been redeemed from the Fall and had entered into the *rest of the Lord,* which is, according to section 84, the fullness of the glory of the Lord. They had been in his presence, in a world of glory, and had seen and heard and touched things, and then came back into this telestial school room, and experienced the tugs and pulls. Isn't that interesting? Any thoughts and comments on that?

Student 4: Jacob went to Nephi. Enos even mentioned that about his father. Moroni communicated with his father. It seems like everybody in the *Book of Mormon,* who was writing and talking about the spiritual things, every one of them used their fathers, in most cases.

Mike: Exactly. I want to go back to what [student 1] said a minute ago. One of the advantages of obtaining this redemption, obtaining this status of favorability with the Lord, is that you now can ask for certain things, and because of your standing with the Lord, the Lord will honor you in those requests, as long as they're not asked *to consume it upon your lusts.* And you probably won't do that because you're beyond that point. So, when you're requesting things from the Lord, it is probably given to you by the Spirit, before you verbalize the request, therefore, the request is always granted. So, here we have Lehi, who is highly favored of the Lord, and even though it doesn't say it, if we had the rest of the record, I'm sure it would say that he prays for Laman and Lemuel. And the Lord sends an angel in that case, and they see that angel face to face. They not only see the angel, but they also hear the voice of God, and yet they're a couple of knot-heads. You have to ask the question, "How did these two characters have these experiences?" Well, it isn't because of them. It's because their dad is *highly favored.* Go over to 1 Nephi chapter 1, let's look at verse 1. So, yeah [student], you're right. If I'm a father, and I have a child that is struggling, and I have obtained this favorable status with the

Lord, I can ask the Lord and receive from Him, and He will honor me because of the status I have before Him. Having been tried and proven in all things, and proven worthy and trustworthy, He will answer those prayers, because, in these prayers, I will not ask amiss. They will be asked in the Spirit because I'm in that spiritual flow now. We always read the first part of verse 1, but to me, the second half is the greatest part:

> I, Nephi, having been born of goodly parents, therefore I was taught somewhat in all the learning of my father;

Now stop. If we apply what we're talking about here, Lehi has knowledge of things that he's obtained directly from God, through a personal encounter with Christ. He has obtained an ordination to a higher order of the priesthood, and a ministry that you get in no other way. Lehi is going to teach that to his **obedient** boys. He is not going to throw those pearls before Laman and Lemuel, but Nephi is going to be taught:

> somewhat in all the learning of my father; and having seen many afflictions the course of my days,

This is a prerequisite for being redeemed in the flesh, in the telestial world. There is no way you're going to make it until you have gone through hell. Joseph Smith said that the Lord *would* *"wrench your very heartstrings"* to see what you're made of and to see if He can trust you in all things. Once you are redeemed from the Fall, if you fall from this place, perdition is the reward. I can promise you the Lord is not in the business of consigning his sons to the state of perdition. He wants you to be exalted, but the only way He can know if you're worthy of this is to put you through the ringer. Then Nephi goes on, he says:

> Nevertheless, [meaning: in spite of all of these things] having been **highly favored of the Lord** in all my days;

You're never going to open the doors on these things, until you get your mind and spirit to a point where you stop and say, "Whoa, wait a minute. What does this mean to be *highly favored of the Lord*? What does that mean?" Because the word *highly* indicates there are degrees. It's like bad, good, better, best. All right? There are degrees. To get to this *highly favored* place, he is going to have adversity and afflictions, all the days that he's in this world. Then look what he says:

> *Yea, having had a great **knowledge** of the goodness and the mysteries of God,*

And that's what you get when you have these encounters with the powers of heaven that reside on the other side of the veil. When they come to you and when you pierce that veil, and you start to knock on that, and they start to communicate with you, that's what you get. You get a great knowledge of the goodness of God, and His mysteries. And do you know what the greatest of all mysteries of God is? The *Doctrine and Covenants* calls it *the mystery of godliness*. Do you know what it is? The key is in the term, *the mystery of godliness*? The mystery is: how does a fallen man in this world, a natural man who's an enemy unto God, become god-ly? That's the greatest of all mysteries. And Nephi had access to that. We want to seek for these things.

So, your advantage then, through the covenants in the temple, is that you are given fast-track information through ordinances and covenants on **how** to be redeemed from the Fall. Even in the allegory itself, you're taken right up through ordinances, signs, tokens, covenants and laws, and names, to where you are presented at the veil and invited to enter in. When you pass through the veil in the temple, what you're doing is being symbolically redeemed from the Fall. That is redemption! Are we okay with that? Does that make sense?

Student 4: Yes.

Mike: Any comments or thoughts?

Student 4: Regarding Joseph Smith, with all the readings that you've done, or in the *Doctrine and Covenants*, was he highly favored?

Mike: Yeah, you can read it. Go over to section 132 in the *Doctrine and Covenants*, and you can see where that takes place. There has to be an encounter with God. Remember we talked about the importance of visions versus visitations? Joseph Smith said that visions are where you see and hear things, but visitations are where you see, hear, and **touch** (handle) something. Joseph is giving us keys here, and he said that you have not been redeemed until you touch something. You need to touch. Touch is a very important process in the redemption from the Fall. There is a recognition ceremony that goes on when you enter into the presence of the Lord. There is a recognition ceremony; it's an exact ceremony. You can see it hinted at in Luke 24 and in 3 Nephi chapter 11. In Luke 24, the Savior comes as a resurrected being, with a body of flesh and bone, and appears in that room without going through the door. And He stands there, the ten are there, and He says, "Handle Me and see." So, what's happening? They are seeing, hearing His voice, and He invites them: "Come and touch Me." And the recognition ceremony starts out with them touching the wounds in His hands, in His wrists, the feet, and the last part is thrust their hands into His side. That's a recognition ceremony. It's my opinion that when you have this encounter, you will be invited to do that.

Go to section 132, and look at the date. Take a glance at that quickly. What is the date?

Students: 1843

Mike: Okay, if you read on down there, the information given in this was as early as 1831. Do you see that?

Students: Yes.

Mike: Go over to verse 49:

> For I am the Lord thy God, and will be with thee even unto the end of the world, and through all eternity; for verily **I seal upon you your exaltation**, and prepare a throne for you in the kingdom of my Father, with Abraham your father.
>
> [50]Behold, I have seen your sacrifices, and will forgive all your sins; I have seen your sacrifices in obedience to that which I have told you. Go, therefore, and I make a way for your escape, as I accepted the offering of Abraham of his son Isaac.

This is Joseph's calling and election made sure. That's where that happens.

Now, the question comes up about these dates: did that happened in Nauvoo in 1843, or did it happen as the Kirtland area in 1831? And it really doesn't matter. The point is, Joseph Smith had these blessings and was *highly favored of the Lord.* Now, he is a little different character than the rest of us, because of a foreordained mission. But nonetheless, he had to go through all of the vicissitudes and trials and tests that we do. What did he say, "Deep water is what I am wont to swim in all the days of my life."

The greater the blessings, then the greater the trials, the adversity, and the opposition. That's just the way it is. Now, the brethren talked about that today when they talked about adversity. There were a number of things that were in general conference, which had to do with these more significant doctrines of the gospel that we don't generally discuss. If you are aware of these things, and you listened to general conference today, you kind of perked up and you said, "Ah-ha!" If you listened to Elder Holland close his testimony, you know that Elder Holland has had this encounter. You know that Elder Holland has been redeemed from the Fall. You pick that up from some of the brethren when you hear them refer to sacred things in really public places. But nonetheless, they talk about it. Thoughts and comments?

Student 3: Yeah, I'm wondering if you said this before. It kind of sounds like those who are *highly favored* are not necessarily terrestrial beings.

Mike: I believe that they are terrestrial beings living in a telestial world.

Student 3: So, you said they can still feel sorrow and pain.

Mike: Right. And there are some things that they won't eventually see. For example, some of these people are not translated, terrestrial beings. The doctrine of translation is the doctrine of a terrestrial world, and there are some keys to that. One of them is that they have no more sorrow, except for the sins of the world. Nephi sorrowed because of the sins of his own flesh, because of his weaknesses. It's up to you to decide where they are, but they certainly have reached a lofty place, someplace to be desired. One of the things that also take place when you have this encounter is that the Lord asks you a question. After your interview with Him, after you have obtained from Him what He has reserved for you, He will ask you if you have any requests before He leaves and goes to the Father. He'll say, "What can I do for you before I go to the Father?" Now, in the temple, this is alluded to by the statement, "What is wanted?" So, you are allowed, in this encounter, to make a request from Him. You can see in of all those people who have achieved this status, the request that they've made. For Peter, James, and John; Peter and James requested, "We want to come into thy kingdom as soon as our ministry on this earth is finished." If you take that literally, they wanted to bypass their spirit world sojourn, and go right from mortality and pass through the process of death, be resurrected, and come into the presence of the Lord. John, however, had a different request. The Lord, by the way, grants Peter and James' request. This is the same request that the nine disciples had in 3rd Nephi, "We want to finish our ministry, and when our ministry is over we want to come to You." He touches each one of them, and when they reach the age of 72, the request is granted. The important thing is, He gives them all an opportunity to make a divinely inspired request. Now, these requests are always going to be granted at this point. You know why they're always going to be granted?

Student 3: It's through the Spirit.

Mike: Yeah, because the request is given to them beforehand, through revelation, by the Holy Ghost. You're going to know what to ask, and you need to know that before the encounter takes place. You don't get into His presence, and He says, "What do you want?" And you say something, and He says, "Oh gee, I can't really do that. Sorry." You're going to get that request because it is revealed to you what the Father and the Son want you to request. For John, it was, "I want to stay on the earth as long as the earth remains, and bring souls to Christ." For the three Nephites, it was the same. Now, Moses had this encounter; Joseph had this encounter, Adam had this encounter; I mean **all** of the great patriarchs had this experience. You may want to look at their stories and their lives and ask yourself the question, what is it that Moses would have requested? What is it that Joseph would have requested? When they had this encounter with the Lord, and He said, "What can I do for you before I leave?" because they all had this opportunity; and if you ask that question, and you look into the lives of these patriarchs, you will find what it is they asked for and received.

So, brothers and sisters, we started out tonight talking about the *gifts of the Spirit* and what's available to everybody. Can you see that these things that we're talking about here cannot be given to people that have not had the experience in the temple? The experience in the temple; the endowment, the allegory, the signs and tokens, the keywords, the names, and laws and covenants, are absolutely necessary knowledge for you to have, and ordinances to participate in, in order to achieve redemption from the Fall while in this life. See? *While IN this life*. Does that make sense?

You could ask the question; why is priesthood so important? And why is it so important? Why is temple endowment so important? Why is the gift of the Holy Ghost necessary? Why? It has to do with each one of these things increasing the channel between you and God, you in a fallen world, and He in a world of glory. It increases the channel so that more light and truth can flow to you, until you get to a certain point that the Lord can say, "That's enough," and He steps through the veil and says, "I redeem you from the Fall." To the brother of Jared, the Lord said, *"Because you know these things you are redeemed from the fall."* See, he knew something that redeemed him and that the reward for that knowledge was that the veil disappears and you stand in the presence of the Savior. You've got to ask yourself, what knowledge? *"Because you know these things you are redeemed from the fall."* There are all kinds of things to ask. If we just take a cursory reading of the scriptures, we're going to miss so much. We ought to train ourselves to go slowly. Comments or thoughts? We've been at it over an hour.

Student 4: This was really good!

Mike: Thank you. There are advantages to being a member of The Church of Jesus Christ of Latter-day Saints in our day, or the Church of Jesus Christ in the Meridian day, or belonging to the Patriarchal Order of the Priesthood from Adam up to Jesus Christ. There are advantages for those who enter into covenants through ordinances. Did you notice in conference, that one of the brethren said that you are born again **through the ordinances**? Remember that? You can't obtain the *mighty change of heart* that Alma talks about without ordinances that are offered in the Church of Jesus Christ of Latter-day Saints. You can do other miracles, have dreams and visions, but you can't get that which Alma experienced, and the sons of Mosiah experienced, and what you read about in the scriptures, outside of a covenant relationship with Christ.

References:

D&C 46: 7 – 9
D&C 46: 26
D&C 46: 19:25
D&C 46: 16
Moroni 10
Ether 3:9-13
2 Nephi 4:15-17
Ether 1:34
1 Nephi 1:1
D&C 132:49-50

Chapter Eleven
Podcast 011 Being Made Perfect in Christ

Well, I hope we have the Holy Ghost with us tonight. I want to talk about one of the great mysteries of the gospel, and it has to do with what I call an *indwelling principle of the Father and the Son.* Let's introduce it this way: in your *Bible*, go to John chapter 17. This has been a great mystery in the Christian world, and this is what has caused the Trinitarian doctrine and the Nicene Council in 325 A.D. They just could not understand what the Savior was talking about in John chapter 17. I want to start at verse 20, and this is what they call the intercessory prayer, the great intercessory prayer. Jesus is interceding and advocating for man, fallen man before the Father. Here's the prayer that the Savior is uttering just before they leave the upper room at what we call the Last Supper, and go to Gethsemane. He says:

> *Neither pray I for these alone, but for them also*
> *which shall believe on me through their word;*

He's not just praying for those apostles that are with him in the room but for all of us that believe in Him. That's everybody else. That's us. Verse 21 is where it starts, and we want to look at the word "**in**:"

> *That they all may be one; as thou, Father, art **in** me,*
> *and I **in** thee, that they also may be one **in** us: that*
> *the world may believe that thou hast sent me.*

> *[22] And the glory which thou gavest me I have given them; that they may be one, even as we are one:*
>
> *[23] I **in** them, and thou **in** me, that they may be made **perfect** in one; and that the world may know that thou hast sent me, and has loved them, as thou hast loved me.*

Now, the word "**perfect**" is the one we want to concentrate on tonight. There are two mysteries that I want to talk a little bit about. One is this *indwelling;* where Christ is **in** the Father; and the Father **in** Christ; and the Father and the Son **in** us; and we **in** Them. All of this being "**in**" is a great mystery. And the other mystery is this *perfection* that verse 23 is talking about, *"That they may be made **perfect** in one."*

> *[25]O righteous Father, the world hath not known thee: but I have known thee, and these have known that thou hast sent me.*
>
> *[26]And I have declared unto them thy name, and will declare it: that the love wherewith thou hast loved me may be **in** them, and I **in** them.*

Now, Eastern thinking doesn't have as much difficulty with this as Western thinking, because as Westerners, we see two people; one here and one there. And we see separate and distinct persons and we can't easily comprehend how one person can be **in** another person. So, what we do is we want to wrest that, change that, switch it, and manipulate it so that we can somehow make Christ's words fit into our Western mind way-of-thinking.

And so, what I want to do tonight is present this as more literal than symbolic, because we're always wanting to make this symbolic for us to understand it. I want to make it more literal and use the scriptures to show that. Now, what I would like to present to us tonight, is that in a very literal and real way, Jesus Christ is **in** each one of us. And we, each one of us, are **in** Him. There is a real connection between the Savior and each of God's children, which we have a tendency to overlook. Now, obviously, that can't be physical. When we talk about the Savior being **in** us and us **in** Him, we're not talking about a physical *indwelling*. There has to be another way to look at this, for us to understand what the scriptures are saying. I want you to know that there is no way that any of us can be *perfected*, without Christ being **in** us; without this *indwelling* principle. To get a feel for this, we have to go and look at a couple of other scriptures. Let's go to your *New Testament* for just a minute and look at 1 Corinthians chapter 3, verse 16. This is Paul speaking to the members of the Church who were living in Corinth. This is a letter to the Corinthian members of the *New Testament* Church:

> *Know ye not that ye are the temple of God, and that the Spirit of God dwelleth **in** you?*

There is our first key. Now, keep your finger here and go over to 1 Corinthians 6, verse 17:

> *But he that is joined unto the Lord is one spirit.*

That's an interesting little statement. Now, go down to verse 19:

> *What? know ye not that your **body** is the temple of the Holy Ghost which is **in** you, which ye have of God, and ye are not your own?*
> *[20]For ye are bought with a price: therefore glorify God **in your body**, and **in your spirit**, which are God's.*

Now, here are some clues! Paul is teaching the members of the Church in Corinth, that the physical body (your body and my body) is a temple of God, *"And that the Spirit of God dwelleth in you."* Notice in one place he says the Holy Ghost, and in the other one, he says the Spirit of God.

Now, we know there is a difference between the Holy Ghost and the Holy Spirit. The one is a person, and the other is not. The one I want to talk to you about is the Holy Spirit, not the Holy Ghost. The Holy Spirit, which has other names, and one of the other names of the Holy Spirit is the Spirit of Christ. Today in our sacrament prayers, we entered into those prayers *"That they are willing to take upon them the name of thy Son, and always remember him and keep his commandments which he has given them."* Who? Christ, right? *In the name of thy Son;* keep Christ's commandments. Always remember Christ that *they may always have His Spirit*, Christ's Spirit, *to be with them.* We are not talking about the Holy Ghost here. The sacramental prayers are not referring to the Holy Ghost. They are referring to the Spirit of Christ, the Light of Christ, the Holy Spirit, and the Spirit of God. Every one of us that comes into this world has this Holy Spirit inside us. We call it conscience. We can call it the Light of Truth, the Spirit of Truth, the Light of Christ, the Spirit of Christ. It's an ever-present connection, a part of God that is **in** us all the time.

Now, what you can do through your knowledge, and through your progress, is that you can increase that channel we talked about last week. You have a small portion of that as we come into this life, and then it can increase from a portion to a fullness. Now, I want to look at another verse. Let's go back to 1 Corinthians chapter 2 verse 7:

> But we speak the wisdom of God in a mystery, even the hidden wisdom, which God ordained before the world unto our glory:

Skip to verse 9:

> But as it is written, Eye hath not seen, nor ear heard, neither have entered into the heart of man, the things which God hath prepared for them that love him.
>
> [10]But God hath revealed them unto us by his Spirit: for the Spirit searcheth all things, yea, the deep things of God.

Now, go to verse 16. And here's the kicker that we skip over in our studies:

> For who hath known the mind of the Lord, that he may instruct him? **But we have the mind of Christ.**

The mind of Christ; do you know what that is? This is something that Paul says is desirable to have; to have something called the mind of Christ. To figure out what that is, we have to go to the Fifth Lecture on Faith, which is the lecture on the Godhead; the Father, Son, and Holy Spirit. I'm just going to read part of this, listen to this. In describing the Godhead, Joseph said:

> He being the only begotten of the Father, full of grace and truth, and having overcome, received a fullness of the glory of the Father – possessing the same **mind** with the Father; which **Mind** is the Holy Spirit.

Do you know what the **mind** of Christ is? It is the Spirit of Christ, the Light of Truth, the Light of Christ, and the Holy Spirit. Another name for that is the Mind of Christ. Now, just kind of hang on to that for just a minute. And it goes on and says:

> *These three constitute the Godhead and are one: the Father and the Son possessing the **same mind**, the same wisdom, glory, power, fullness; filling all in all—the Son being filled with the fullness of the **Mind**, glory, and power; **or in other words** the **Spirit**, glory, and power of the Father.*

So now, we are putting together a puzzle piece. There is in each one of us, as we come into this life, a connecting link with the Father and with the Son. To the degree that you have that **in** you, is the degree that you become like Them. This last general conference, what we heard—and I've heard it over and over, and you hear it over and over also—is that no one is perfect, nor can we be perfect in this life. Have you ever heard that? It's not possible for us to be perfect in this life. And I would like to just spend a few minutes on that tonight. Now, I've presented the idea that in each one of us is something sacred, something holy, and to completely extinguish that, you have to sin the unforgivable, unpardonable sin and be completely cut off from God. Otherwise, you have inside you, what the *Fifth Lecture on Faith* says: the mind, glory, and power of God that is **in** us and it is **in** us all of the time. And the reason that it's **in** us all of the time is that our physical bodies in this life, are temples. Now, back in 1 Corinthians, the Lord said that if any man defiles that temple, God will destroy him. So, our physical bodies are designed, brothers and sisters, to be holy temples wherein the Spirit of God can dwell. Now, we can defile that temple, and we do. By the natural man, it is defiled just by being in a telestial world. But understanding this doctrine, what we need to do is take this temple and during our sojourn here in the telestial world, make it holy. No small thing. No small thing.

Student 1: I thought that only Christ could make us holy.

Mike: That's correct, and we're coming to that. He can't do anything unless you choose to allow Him to. You see, He never ever overrides your choice. If you choose to remain in a defiled state, He will honor that agency. Let's stop for just a minute, and see if there are any questions or comments because this is a little difficult for us to understand. No comments? All right, let's pick it up and go from there.

Now, this perfection thing; go to Matthew chapter 5, verse 48, and it says:

> *Be ye therefore perfect, even as your Father*
> *which is in heaven is perfect.*

Verse 48 is the last statement out of the first chapter of the Sermon on the Mount. It comes after the Beatitudes. In the temple, the third covenant that we enter into is called the *law of the gospel*. Now, the *law of the gospel* is entered into in the telestial world. The first two covenants we entered into in the temple are the *laws of obedience and sacrifice*. Those are entered into in the pre-mortal, or in the paradisiacal world before Adam and Eve are cast out of the Garden. In this world, in the lone and dreary world, we enter into a covenant to obey the *law of the gospel*, and a charge that goes with it. I don't know if you ever wondered about what the *law of the gospel* is. I've pondered that, studied it, prayed about it, and had shown to me that the *law of the gospel* is the Beatitudes that you find in the *New Testament*, and in 3 Nephi. In the *New Testament*, it is called the Sermon on the Mount. In 3 Nephi, it is the Sermon at the Temple. Again, the first chapters of both of these sermons end with the 48th verse; 3 Nephi chapter 12, verse 48 and Matthew chapter 5, verse 48. Now, there is a difference. In Matthew 5:48 Christ says, *"Be ye therefore **perfect**, even as your **Father which is in heaven** is perfect."* Christ **does not** refer to Himself in Matthew, as a perfected being. Interesting!

Student 1: Well, because he hadn't been resurrected yet.

Mike: Okay, the resurrection certainly was a part of that. Now, over in 3 Nephi 12:48, he says:

> *Therefore I would that ye should be **perfect** even as*
> *I, or your Father who is in heaven is perfect.*

So, something took place between Matthew 5 and 3 Nephi 12. Didn't it? Something we call perfection.

Student 1: He got the *fullness*, right?

Mike: Yes, so there's something going on. You're hitting on that *fullness*. Now, let's go over to *The Pearl of Great Price*, and let's look at something else. I'm going to give you a couple of scriptures to consider here. This is talking about Noah. And you can find the counterpart of this in Genesis chapter 6, verse 9, but we are going to look at Moses 8:27. This is before the flood:

> *And thus Noah found grace in the eyes of the Lord;*
> *for Noah was a **just** man, and **perfect** in his*
> *generation; and he walked with God, as did also his*
> *three sons, Shem, Ham, and Japheth.*

Now, there's a mortal man, a natural man who has been *justified*. There's a process here. The first step is: find grace with God. Do you see that? There is a little list here. I want to know how it is that Noah became perfect. The first step was: he finds **grace** and uses of the grace of Christ's Atonement. The next step is he now becomes a **just** man, not perfect, not yet, but a **just** man. I was teaching the gospel doctrine class today, and it came out that Enos said of his father Jacob, that *"he was a **just** man—and taught me...in the nurture and admonition of the Lord."* I asked a member of the class, "What does it mean to be a **just** man?" I think we just read that end we don't give it any thought. It comes from the word to be *justified*. Now, *justified* is a precursor to *sanctified*. And *justified* and *sanctified* are related to *perfection*. The end result of *justification*, *sanctification*, and *perfection*, is *glorification*. **Just** means that if you've been *justified* through the Atonement of Christ, that the Atonement finds you blameless and guiltless before the divine demands of justice. Justice has no claim on you anymore, because you have accessed the Atonement of Christ, repented of your sins, and Christ now picks up the burden and punishment for unresolved sin and transgression. If you were to die in the state of justification, *the law of divine justice* has no claim on you. Christ pays the price for your sinning. The keywords for justified are **blameless** and **guiltless**. Those are your keywords. So, when it says that *"Noah found grace in the eyes of the Lord; for Noah was a **just** man,"* it means that he has applied the blood of Christ. This is 2000 years before Gethsemane, and he had applied the blood of Christ, the future sacrifice, and Atonement of Christ, to the degree that his sins are forgiven him through faith in the Atonement of Christ, Who is yet to come. And now he's guiltless and blameless. Then look what follows it, *"And perfect in his generation."* Then what follows that is what? *"And he walked with God."* You see that sequence?

Let's look at another one. Let's go to *Doctrine and Covenants* Section 107, and we want to look at verse 43. Now, this is talking about Adam's son Seth, who fulfills the role, or the place in the priesthood patriarchal order of Abel, who was killed by Cain:

*Because he (Seth) was a **perfect** man,*

Now, here again, we have a man, a mortal man, who is referred to as **perfect**. And yet we hear in the church all the time that the only perfect man who ever walked the earth was who?

Student 1: Christ.

Mike: Christ. So, we can see from the scriptures we are missing something here. If we just make a blanket statement and say that the only perfect man who ever walked the earth was Christ, then we are not scripturally correct. Therefore we need to look at this *perfection* differently. We have to look at this a little bit differently, in order for us to understand the scriptures. Let's go to section 67 in the *Doctrine and Covenants*. So, here we have Christ commanding us to become perfect like His Father, like He Himself is. Because we teach in the one place that it's impossible for any man to be perfect, when we read the scriptures we, therefore, have to push becoming perfect forward somewhere into eternity, and we completely deny that it has anything to do with mortality, while we're still in the flesh. I submit that we just need to look at it a little differently. So, let's go to let go to section 67. Here's another one. Now, this was given in 1831, the church is just a year old and already in verse 10, the Lord is promising the people:

> *And again, verily I say unto you that it is your privilege and a promise I give unto you... [that if you] humble yourselves before me... the veil shall be rent and you shall see me and know that I am—*

And then in verse 12, He says:

> *Neither can any natural man abide the presence of God, neither after the carnal mind.*
> *[13]Ye are not able to abide the presence of God now, neither the ministering of angels; wherefore, continue in patience until ye are **perfected**.*

Now, if you look at verse 10, He says this is a *privilege and a promise I give unto you [that if you]...strip yourselves from jealousies and fears, and humble yourselves... the veil shall be rent and you shall see me and know that I am."* Now, that's not a promise into the millennium. That's a mortal promise. Then in verse 13, He says that you're not able to do this right now, you can't do this right now, and you're not ready for it, so *continue in patience until ye are **perfected***. Now, that's every Latter-day Saint that reads these verses. So, there we go again. There's a promise to see the face of the Lord, which is the Second Comforter, but you can't do it now until you are perfected.

Let's take a look at another one. Go to *Doctrine and Covenants* section 88:34. I'm just presenting a little case here from the scriptures, some things to think about. Now, where it says "that," you could make it a <u>who</u> by putting, "he," or "she."

> *And again, verily I say unto you, **that** which is governed by law is also preserved by law and **perfected** and sanctified by the same.*

Here is this perfection again. Now we're learning that this takes place by law. There is a law involved in this. This isn't something arbitrary that you just hope will happen there is a formula involved here. If we want to fulfill the commandment to *"be ye therefore perfect,"* there are laws involved that we need to find out about and then align ourselves with these laws. Look at verse 35:

> *That which breaketh a law, and abideth not by law, but seeketh to become a law unto itself, and willeth to abide in sin, and altogether abideth in sin, cannot be sanctified by law, neither by mercy, justice, nor judgment. Therefore, they must remain filthy still.*

Now, here is the Lord is drawing a comparison that law can sanctify and perfect you and that violation of the law will cause you to remain filthy. Obedience to law sanctifies and perfects you. Disobedience to the law will cause you to remain in your sins and remain filthy, as though there had been no redemption made. Interesting stuff!

So now, the huge kicker comes at the end of the *Book of Mormon*. And this is to where all this is going. Go to the end of the *Book of Mormon*, Moroni chapter 10. Now, keep in mind that these are the last verses, of the last chapter, of a thousand years of history and the son of the chronicler, the abridger, is deciding, "What is the most important message I can leave with you, as we close this thousand years of Nephi history?" Turn to verse 32, and there it is:

> *Yea, come unto Christ, and be perfected **in him**,*

How can we look at all of these verses, and there are more on this subject of perfection, and push this into some future estate, after the spirit world sojourn, after death, and after the resurrection? How can we do that? It doesn't fit. And if you also look at verse 33, after you have been perfected, and I want to emphasize the word "**in**" here:

> *And again, if ye by the grace of God are perfect **in** Christ, and deny not his power, then are ye **sanctified in** Christ by the grace of God.*

So, what comes first; perfection or sanctification? Perfection comes first; perfection in verse 32; sanctification in verse 33. Notice that he says in verse 33, there is no *sanctification* unless you're *perfect* in Christ first. It has to come first. Obviously, brothers and sisters, the terminology **perfect in Christ** does not mean the same as **perfect like Christ**. When we talk about the perfection of Christ as we read about Him in His *New Testament* ministry, in His atoning sacrifices, His resurrection from the grave, His ascension to the Father, and now, as He sits enthroned in glory on the right hand of the Father, we're not talking about the same perfection that Moroni is telling us to accomplish and to desire. It's something different. [Student 1] is absolutely right. This perfection, whatever it is, that we're commanded to obtain while we're mortals, cannot be obtained in any other way, except **in and through Christ**. You can't do it.

So, here's a thought for you as we kind of wrap this up a little bit. First, in this lesson, we went into this **indwelling** principle. Christ is **in** the Father, and the Father is **in** Christ, and the Father and the Son are **in** us, and we are **in** Them. There is a connection link with something already perfected that we have a connection with **in**side of us. When Paul says we have the *mind of Christ*, (talking about himself and the *New Testament* members of the Church in Corinth) and the *Fifth Lecture on Faith* tells us the *mind of Christ* is *the spirit of God*; it's the Holy Spirit. Another name for it is the *light of Christ*.

Student 1: That's substance, right?

Mike: It's inside us. It's always inside us. Now, you can increase its influence and power and revelatory process. You can increase that as you grow in knowledge and righteousness in keeping the commandments and being obedient to what the Lord gives you. It increases. As it increases, the influence of God the Father and His Son, Jesus Christ have a refining, cleansing, sanctifying, purifying, and transforming effect on you.

Student 1: Isn't it true that if we don't listen to that voice, to that Holy Spirit, that eventually we won't have it?

Mike: This is Mike Stroud's opinion: I don't believe that you can totally extinguish that connection unless you sin against the Holy Ghost. Now, I believe that it can become so dim as not to have an effect in your life. I believe that's the point where the Lord says, through Mormon and Moroni speaking about the Nephites in their terrible degeneracy, *"I fear lest the spirit of the Lord hath ceased striving with them."* We come to a point where its influence in you is not negligible. And this is my personal opinion, I don't believe that you are completely cut off unless you sin against the Holy Ghost, and you have to obtain a lot of light and a lot of knowledge and a lot of truth and then turn against it. The point is, it doesn't do you any good, it does not expand, and it does not increase its sanctifying power in you unless you are obedient to the covenants and commandments of the Lord. And then that channel we talked about continues to grow. So, what does it mean to be perfect in Christ? How can we become perfect in Christ? Jesus Christ possesses a fullness of all the attributes of godliness. He possesses a fullness of it. Take the attribute of patience; right now, the Savior possesses a fullness of godly patience. You and I can have some of that in us. You and I can experience a portion of that godly patience in us. And we do it because Christ is **in** us. His Spirit is **in** us. His **mind** is **in** us. We're connected with Him. As we allow that to expand and become fuller, then those characteristics also increase.

A friend of mine, John Pontius, taught me this and I'd like to present it to you tonight. Some of you know him. I was chatting with Brother John while I was on a mission in the Philippines. And I was talking to him about how we have a misunderstanding of this "being perfect," and how it's impossible and nobody can ever do it. And yet, the scriptures clearly command us to be perfect in this life. So, it has to be something different than what we think, and here's what Brother Pontius said to me, and it's been a blessing in my life:

*To the degree that you do not offend the light of Christ that is **in** you, to the degree that you do not offend the Holy Spirit, to that degree you are perfect.*

For example: if I can go for one hour, on any given day, without offending the Holy Spirit, based on my progression and the knowledge and truth that I have at this point in my life, to that degree, I have been perfect in Christ for one hour. The Holy Spirit is what? It is Christ. *The Book of Mormon* says, *"Come unto Christ and be perfected **in** Him."* Notice it doesn't say, "Be perfect in him." It says, *"...be **perfected,"*** which alludes to a process, doesn't it? To be perfected alludes to a process. It's not something that happens all at once. It's something that you attain line upon line, here a little, there a little, in the way the Lord dispenses light and truth. Christ possesses a fullness of perfection. He is the epitome, the perfect description of a perfect, saved man. To the degree that I can have his influence **in** me, i.e., His spirit, His mind, the Spirit of truth, the Holy Spirit; and the degree that that finds a residence in me, and my physical body begins to be a temple wherein the Holy Spirit dwells; to that degree I'm *perfected* **in** Christ. Now, with that in mind, you can look at any hour, any six hours, any day, any number of days, any week, that you can go and not offend that Spirit, for that period of time you are perfect **in** Christ. When you don't offend the Spirit, it increases its influence **in** you. Look at the bottom of verse 33 in Moroni 10:

That ye become holy, without spot.

That's the definition of sanctification and of being sanctified; holy, without spot.

Now, guess what follows, according to the little formula we read over there in Moses 8 verse 27? Remember what it was? You access the grace of God. You see, none of this is possible without the grace of God. The grace of God is only available because of the Atonement of Christ. Without Christ's Atonement, there is no grace. And without Christ's Atonement, there is no repentance. You can't repent. Without Christ's Atonement, there is no mercy. All there would be is violated law with its accompanying penalties and demands. That's all there is without the Atonement. So, what you and I really merit, by the natural man status in the telestial world, without the Atonement of Christ, is going to hell, with no hope of redemption or rescue. None! *Grace* comes first, followed by becoming a *just man*, followed by *perfection*, followed by *walking and talking with God*. There's a little formula from the *Pearl of Great Price*.

Student 1: Say that again... Grace... Perfection...

Mike: *Grace*; then comes *just*, where you're *justified*. That means you're held guiltless, and the law of justice has no demands on you. That happens through the Atonement, through the grace of Christ. The next step is you're *perfected*; you reach a state of *perfection*. And then, according to our little formula over in Moses 8 verse 27, the next step is you *walk and talk with God*. Moroni adds another dimension in there after perfection; *sanctified, holy without spot*. Section 67 says you can't do any of that yet; it's only been a year since the church was organized and nobody is ready to move into this point. So, the Lord says, *"continue in patience until you are perfected."* Isn't that wonderful?

Student 1: It sure is!

Mike: So, not only is it possible for us to be perfect **in** Christ; we are **commanded** to be perfect **in** Christ. The last message of the *Book of Mormon* is to *come unto Christ, be perfected **in** Him, and deny yourselves of all ungodliness.* And verse 32 makes a list of some of the things that are necessary in order to obtain this place.

Now, in closing, let's go over to section 129. Section 129 is talking about various kinds of messengers. And we want to look at verse 3. The first two verses talk about angels with bodies of flesh and bones, and then secondly, the *spirits of just men made perfect*. Did you see that sequence again? *Justification* (being found guiltless, being found blameless before the demands of justice through the grace and Atonement of Christ) leads to perfection. These are men, and I would say, women because *just men* is talking about mankind, who have, while on the earth, become justified through the Atonement and obtained perfection. These are the people we are reading about with Noah, and Enoch, and Seth. And look what it says in verse 3:

> The spirits of just men made perfect, they who are
> not resurrected, but inherit the same glory.

"The same glory" is the celestial glory. The spirits of *just men made perfect* are not destined for a terrestrial world. These are celestial beings. These are gods, with a small **g**, not resurrected

from the dead yet but have obtained the promise of a celestial inheritance, and are functioning as the spirits of *just men made perfect*. Joseph says these are messengers from God. This whole section on 129 is talking about when you receive messengers. Some of these people who have lived on the earth, have become justified and perfected, have died, and now are waiting for the resurrection. And they appear to you as celestial beings, who are awaiting a celestial resurrection. These are spirits of *just men and women made perfect*. See that keyword is not; **become** perfect. Notice it is not "the spirits of *just men* who have **become** perfect." It is *the spirits of just men [who have been] made perfect, which* ties in with what you said, [student 1]. There is no way that perfection can happen by ourselves, or in and of ourselves. We align ourselves with the law. There are formulas and laws in the eternities, and when we align ourselves with those laws and find out the knowledge associated with those laws, they invariably have a set outcome. When you find out what the laws *of becoming perfect in Christ* are then the set outcome is that you will be **made** perfect.

Student 1: Now, I have a question. You said, "gods with a small *g*." I don't understand that concept.

Mike: I mean that gods with a small **g** are people who have obtained the promise that they will be gods in the celestial world, but the reason it is with a small **g** is that they do not have anybody that worships them or looks to them for their salvation and exaltation. They are men and women in progress, but they have obtained promises from God. Go over to section 76 and let me show you a classic example of that. I read these verses for the most of my adult life, and never ever noticed this. In section 76, verses 50 through 70, 20 verses, we are talking about those who inherit a celestial inheritance. Look at verse 54. It talks about those who are members of the Church of the Firstborn, and then in 55:

> *They are they into whose hands the Father has given all things—*

Then skip down to 57:

> *And are priests of the Most High, after the order of Melchizedek,*
> *[58]Wherefore, it is written, they are **gods**, even the sons of **God**—*

271

Notice the small **g** and then the capital **G**. See that? The small **g** means that they have obtained the promise of godhood, are in the process of becoming men and women who are looked to for salvation and exaltation, and are worshiped by their children, as their children strive to become like they are. So, a god with a small **g** is one who has been promised godhood, but who, as of yet, doesn't have a posterity living on an earth, who are now trying to work their way up to become like their Mom and Dad.

Student 1: That's a good explanation. Thank you.

Mike: In summary, tonight, I want to talk to you about this *indwelling*. How we're connected, not physically but according to *Lecture Five*, through the mind, glory, and power of the Father, which resides as a fullness in the Son. And that mind, that power, and that glory of the Son is **in** each one of us to a degree. We're connected. I believe that it is this connection that we have that is one of the ways that God can hear and answer so many prayers at once. We're connected to Him, aside from the fact that He has a lot of messenger helpers, and there is an *indwelling* connection with Them. So, He comes out and says, *"I and my father are one."* On one level, we say They are one in purpose and in desire, and that's true, but there is a deeper level here. They are truly one, in that a part of Them, Their mind, power and glory, which is called the Holy Spirit, dwells inside Them and They are connected to each other, never separated. And that extends to each one of Their children in the telestial world. There has to be this connecting link. Otherwise, Heavenly Father is sending His children into a world where they don't have a chance. There **has** to be this *indwelling*, *"I am in them and they are in Me."* And then what we do through obedience is that we increase that channel and as the channel increases with light and power and glory and intelligence, by law it has an effect on us. You cannot increase light inside this temple and have the temple stay the same. You can't do it. The more light and intelligence that flows into me from Them, through this connection channel, then the more it transforms, purifies, cleanses, sanctifies, and perfects me. It's a natural sequence to the flow of light and truth into my body, which is Their temple.

Student 1: You know, we had no light; we had no power in sacrament meeting today. It came to my mind; just think if there were no light, the Light of Christ in the world, we truly would be devastated. I mean, we had a hard time singing, you know, because there was no light. We had a hard time hearing the speakers because there was no microphone. It made me think how blessed we are that we have the Light of Christ.

Mike: What a wonderful example that was to have that experience today. You know, that Light is pleading with us; it is enticing us all the time. It's a continual flow of, "Let me give you more. Make a choice to receive more." And we either choose that Light, or we choose darkness. The scriptures say that a great Light has come into the world, but men loved darkness more than Light, and their works are in the dark. What a sad commentary. Everything is based upon the agency of man. This voice of *light and truth*, the *mind of Christ*, His power and glory is continually pleading with us to make a decision to open us up to receive more of this Light. And as that Light comes in it has a purifying, perfecting, sanctifying, influence on us until we come perfect in Christ, sanctified in Christ, and holy without spot. When that happens, you walk and talk with God. Joseph said the great challenge for us is to present this body to The Father and The Son pure and clean. And that's no small challenge living in this world, is it? Everything in this world has a tendency to want to take us down into the dark, but thank goodness for that connecting link. Thank goodness They are **in** us and we **in** Them. Otherwise, we wouldn't stand a prayer. I hope that helps us understand a couple of difficult concepts, the *indwelling* of God in His children, and the perfection we're commanded to attain while still in mortality. It is not something to be desired *after* this life. That's a default if we are to get that at all. I think that Satan disguises this, and tricks us every time we hear somebody say, "Well, nobody can become perfect in this life. There's has only been one perfect man." I think that is a subtle, deceptive trap, and hopefully, the doctrine we've talked about tonight resonates with you and distils upon you like the dews of heaven. Hopefully, when you read the scriptures you'll see things in a little different light in terms of justification, sanctification, perfection and the result is to be glorified. That's the other thing, glorification is the end result.

References:

John 17:20 –25
1 Corinthians 3:16 – 17
Sacrament Prayer on the bread
1 Corinthians 2:7 – 9
Fifth Lecture on Faith - the Father, Son and Holy Spirit Matthew 5:48
3 Nephi 12:48
Moses 8:27
D&C 107:43
D&C 67:10 – 13
D&C 88:34 – 35
Moroni 10:32-33
D&C 129:3
D&C 76:50-70

ABOUT THE AUTHOR

 Mike Stroud was born March 1944 to Walt and Eileen Stroud in Salt Lake City, Utah. He attended BYU and received a BA and MA degree.

He is trained in Outdoor Survival and Primitive Living, he has spent a lifetime in the outdoors as a hunter, tracker, and outdoorsman.

Mike enjoys training horses and has spent many years exploring wild places on horseback. He is a western history lover and re-enacts the mountain man era, and the old west.

He served a mission to Bavaria, Germany, and he and Margie have served missions together in Mongolia, Central Philippines, and in New Jersey.

Mike has spent his lifetime as a teacher, working 27 years in The Church of Jesus Christ of Latter-day Saints Church Education System. He retired from CES in 2006.

Mike and Margie reside in Eagar, Arizona. He is the father of 12 children, 29 grandchildren, and 7 great-grandchildren.

Made in the USA
San Bernardino, CA
07 September 2017